CW01510306

Posthumous Editing of a Great Master's Work

Explorations in Indic Traditions: Theological, Ethical, and Philosophical

Series Editor: Jeffery D. Long, Elizabethtown College

Advisory Board: Purushottama Bilimoria, Christopher Key Chapple, Jonathan Gold, Pankaj Jain, Nathan Katz, Kusumita Pedersen, and Rita D. Sherma

The region historically known as the Indian subcontinent (and more recently as South Asia) is rich with ancient and sophisticated traditions of intellectual and contemplative investigation. This includes both indigenous traditions (Hindu, Buddhist, Jain, and Sikh) and traditions that have found a home in this region (Islamic, Christian, Jewish, and Zoroastrian). This series is devoted to studies rooted in critical and constructive methodologies (such as ethics, philosophy, and theology) that show how these traditions can illuminate universal human questions: questions about the meaning of life, the nature of knowledge, good and evil, and the broader metaphysical context of human existence. A particular focus of this series is the relevance of these traditions to urgent issues that face humanity today—such as the ecological crisis, gender relations, poverty and social inequality, and religiously motivated violence—on the assumption that these traditions, far from being of merely historical interest, have the potential to enrich contemporary conversations and advance human understanding.

Recent Titles in Series

Posthumous Editing of a Great Master's Work: Special Focus on the Writings of A. C. Bhaktivedanta Swami Prabhupāda, edited by Graham M. Schweig

A Śākta Method for Comparative Theology: Upside-Down, Inside-Out, by Pravina Rodrigues

Forms of Krishna: Collected Essays on Vaishnava Murtis, by Steven Rosen

The Politics and Promise of Yoga: Contemporary Relevance of an Ancient Practice, by Anjali H. Kanojia

The Hindu Self and its Muslim Neighbors Borders of Belonging in Bengal, by Ankur Barua

The Philosophy of Sri Chinmoy: Love and Transformation, by Kusumita Pedersen

Gandhi and Rajchandra: The Making of the Mahatma, by Uma Majmudar

Swami Vivekananda: His Life, Legacy, and Liberative Ethics, edited by Rita D. Sherma

Beacons of Dharma, edited by Jeffery D. Long, Michael Reading, Christopher Miller

Posthumous Editing of a Great Master's Work

Special Focus on the Writings of A. C. Bhaktivedanta Swami Prabhupāda

Edited by
Graham M. Schweig

LEXINGTON BOOKS
Lanham • Boulder • New York • London

Published by Lexington Books
An imprint of The Rowman & Littlefield Publishing Group, Inc.
4501 Forbes Boulevard, Suite 200, Lanham, Maryland 20706
www.rowman.com

86-90 Paul Street, London EC2A 4NE

Copyright © 2024 by The Rowman & Littlefield Publishing Group, Inc.

All rights reserved. No part of this book may be reproduced in any form or by any electronic or mechanical means, including information storage and retrieval systems, without written permission from the publisher, except by a reviewer who may quote passages in a review.

British Library Cataloguing in Publication Information Available

Library of Congress Cataloging-in-Publication Data

Names: Schweig, Graham M., 1953- editor.
Title: Posthumous editing of a great master's work : special focus on the writings of A. C. Bhaktivedanta Swami Prabhupāda / edited by Graham M. Schweig.
Description: Lanham : Lexington Books, 2024. | Series: Explorations in Indic traditions: theological, ethical, and philosophical | Includes bibliographical references and index.
Identifiers: LCCN 2023057297 (print) | LCCN 2023057298 (ebook) | ISBN 9781666939477 (cloth) | ISBN 9781666939484 (ebook)
Subjects: LCSH: A. C. Bhaktivedanta Swami Prabhupāda, 1896-1977—Criticism, Textual. | International Society for Krishna Consciousness. | Hare Krishnas. | Krishna (Hindu deity)—Cult. | Bhakti.
Classification: LCC BL1285.892.A28 P675 2024 (print) | LCC BL1285.892.A28 (ebook) | DDC 294.5/512—dc23/eng/20231220
LC record available at https://lccn.loc.gov/2023057297
LC ebook record available at https://lccn.loc.gov/2023057298

In Memoriam
Śravanānanda Dāsa

February 21, 1953–August 14, 2019

Śravanānanda Dāsa was a loyal disciple of Prabhupāda
for fifty years and was singularly responsible
for raising most of the funds that supported the symposium
on Posthumous Editing of a Great Master's Work
at the Graduate Theological Union,
which made this book possible.

A NOTE ON THE COVER IMAGE

This is an ancient symbolic composition, or Yantra. The Yantra consists of the six-pointed star within the green bhupur enclosure, or four-gated square. It represents the energy pattern reverberated by the Goddess of learning, books and knowledge, known as Sarasvati Devi. It is surrounded with a Jupiter Mandala, the circular geometric representation of the Guru, or master, depicted in shades of yellow and orange, otherwise known as Brihaspati. The Yantra and Mandala were constructed using the mathematics of the Vedic square according to the tradition's specifications pertaining to their respective numerical perimeters, patterns, and symmetries. They were then painted in colors consistent with the light frequencies that correspond to the energies of Sarasvati Devi and Brihaspati, while sounding their respective mantras. This Yantra and Mandala combination is said to bestow sacred knowledge. In the Vaishnava Bhakti tradition coming from India, it is understood that books produced by great masters overflow with such sacred knowledge.

The cover image with the above explanation was created by Catherine L. Schweig for this book. Materials used are Gouache paints on recycled, acid-free drawing paper; size 12 x 12 inches.

Contents

Acknowledgments

First, I would like to recognize the financial support from many key followers of Prabhupāda that made the conference out of which the chapters of this book were possible. Their donations, small and large, poignantly and powerfully express the love they have for their spiritual teacher and the value they see in his original, untampered works. Without their extraordinary support, this book would never have come about. My gratitude goes to all these donors.

I am especially grateful to Sravanananda Das, a direct disciple of Prabhupāda, the person to whom this book is dedicated, who did the most to raise funds to see the symposium out of which this book emerges. And his dear wife, Ananda Gopi Dasi, has carried forth the same spirit of her husband on this issue and also very generously made contributions to support this effort.

Additionally, Austin Gordon, pictured in the top left of the photograph of the symposium participants below (see figure 1.1, page 4), departed this world on October 31, 2020, following the submission of his important chapter included herein. We are grateful to have known him and to have received his deeply insightful contribution. I would especially like to acknowledge his good friend and mine as well, Patrick Hogan, whose deep insights into the issues surrounding the editing of Prabhupāda's books have been indispensable, and his own analyses of Prabhupāda's instructions for his work have been a great source from which I have drawn in building my own knowledge of this book's theme.

I would like to express my gratitude to Rita D. Sherma, director of the Center of Dharma Studies at the Graduate Theological Union (GTU) in Berkeley, California, for hosting the symposium at GTU's beautiful conference room in the Flora Lamson Hewlett Library. I am grateful to two persons who were key assistants in the practical matters of the symposium: Pravina Rodrigues and Maria Shaheen. I would also like to recognize here the many person who have dedicated years of painstaking work for understanding and analyzing the BBT's editorial processes.

Also, I would like to acknowledge Jeffery D. Long, series editor of "Explorations in Indic Traditions" at Lexington Books, and Megan White, editor, and her production staff at Lexington Books. Any publisher who agrees to work with me as an author or editor of a volume must exercise much patience, and they certainly have done so with me.

Finally, I desire to acknowledge my partner in life, my dear wife, Catherine. I especially thank her for the beautiful Sarasvatī Yantra that she painted specifically for the cover of this book. Catherine always supports me in all my scholarly endeavors, and as she will do often, as she has done with this volume, she would often offer me invaluable editing and feedback for specific portions of the text. It is her amazing love and support that energize everything I do.

Introduction

How is the completed written or published work of a deceased author to be editorially treated? The answer to this question seems apparent. Most persons confronted with this question immediately draw from the gut by saying, "Leave the work alone! Leave it as the author left it," or "Treat the work in whatever ways the author instructs. Not more, not less." A natural response from an ethical intuitionist stance is that the work belongs to the author, and no one has the moral right (or arguably the legal right) to alter such a work. It should remain as it was when it was finalized and published prior to the time the author departed this world. Simple enough.

Yet, for some, apparently it is not so simple. Audacious editors have attempted to edit, alter, and even improve the works of great authors. Indeed, the highly trained textual scholars of English literature in the MLA (Modern Language Association) have drawn from a wise review of the problem in an article whose title is quite telling: "Posthumous Publication Is a Wicked Literary Problem." In this article, Francesca Peacock, a literary journalist, critiques an editor by the name of Jenks, who dares to edit the work of Ernest Hemingway in the following colorful words:

> No matter how good an editor is or, as Jenks puts it, how much they try to make the "same sorts of decisions" as the (dead) author would, there is still the unavoidable—and disconcerting—fact that these edits *were* made without Hemingway's knowledge. If you're feeling kind, the book is a brilliant, hard-fought work of literary necromancy: bringing an author back to life by ruthlessly editing their dead prose. If you're feeling cruel, the book is little more than an editorial version of Frankenstein's monster: something sewn together using patches of manuscript, without the hand of the author to make it truly whole.[1]

It is interesting to note that Hemingway was an author who gave explicit instructions to not change any of his writings after his death or publish any unpublished writings, unless he had agreed to it. In any case, Peacock, utilizing the example of an editor of Hemingway, implies how editing the work of a deceased author can be seen as unethical, while outrightly claiming that such an editorial task is downright impossible, a task she characterizes as "literary necromancy."

All this said, the reality of the situation is that creating literature is complicated. The process of how an author's voice moves from his or her mind and heart to the page, the computer screen, the dictation machine, and so on, how an author moves through a critical process of reviewing his or her own work, miscommunications or misunderstandings between an author and his or her writing or editing assistants, and from there how the work moves into a final manuscript, then on to a publisher who undoubtedly will suggest editorial corrections and improvements to be approved by the author, and then the penultimate stage of a work taking the form of proofs, yet another stage of review, and then finally into the physical manifestation of the printed page, all this is just plain complicated. Thus, there are always some slips between the completed manuscript that is submitted for publication and what ends up resulting in the final published work itself, such as misspellings, typos, formatting issues, and so on. Human error is inevitable. And the human drive to perfect or to better something strongly persists.

How to treat a deceased author's work deemed to be great literature is a difficult enough question. But greatly complicating the issue even more is when a great piece of literature is seen to be or is related to as sacred or religious. There is even more at stake when the power of sacred art or literature reveals how the world of the divine or the spiritual pierces through this world to humans, who live and breathe these works throughout their lives. Sacred works are both scripture and literature at the same time, and, as such, considerations of traditional alignment and spiritual authority are critical when treating a work of a great spiritual teacher. And this is precisely what is at hand in the present work.

THE NATURE AND FOCUS OF THIS WORK

This volume brings together the thinking of twelve scholars to examine how a leading figure's authored hallowed works within religious communities should be editorially treated following the leader's departure from this world. Specifically, the theological, ethical, social, and legal implications of posthumous editing, and even improving, a great master's works are addressed herein. It is on the extensive posthumous editing of the work of

A. C. Bhaktivedanta Swami Prabhupāda (herein referred to as Prabhupāda), the original world-teacher of Krishna *bhakti,* that is the major focus of this volume.

This book is a result of the completed paper presentations at a closed conference that I arranged and led at the Graduate Theological Union (GTU) in Berkeley, California, on February 21st through the 23rd, 2020. This conference was sponsored by GTU's Center for Dharma Studies, directed by Rita D. Sherma. And the wording of the conference theme is also retained here as the title of this book.

Fourteen scholars from England and from around the United States came together for a very lively and vibrant discussion on a specific theme for which there is virtually no scholarship. Prior to arranging this conference, I had identified over sixty professional articles and chapters that address related issues to our theme and even about twenty articles that more directly address our theme. However, the result is that this specific theme has gone unaddressed in the academy and therefore this conference and the papers produced for it represents a way into uncharted territory.

While it is hoped that this volume can make some important contributions to scholarship, it is also intended to assist in better understanding the struggles surrounding the posthumous editing of a great master's work that can easily arise in any religious community. Indeed, the challenges of posthumous editing have arisen in the institution that Prabhupāda himself established in 1966, the International Society for Krishna Consciousness (ISKCON), or the worldwide Krishna movement.

My interest in the theme of this volume began when mature and deeply concerned members of the International Society for Krishna Consciousness (ISKCON) approached me to shed light on the issues and challenges in the posthumous editing of the published works of ISKCON's founder, Prabhupāda. I learned that this issue had been plaguing the Society for well over three decades and had reached a crisis level, and thus I was brought in to be consulted on the matter several years ago, in the summer of 2017. After becoming acquainted with the various aspects of the society's editing crisis, I agreed to look into the matter in great depth. All this led to the conference, which formed the foundation of this volume and a culmination of my own thinking on the matter. What was spoken was transcribed and subsequently committed to published pages.

SUMMARY OF THE PROBLEM

The problem of the Bhaktivedanta Book Trust (BBT) editing can be summarized fairly well with four concise points: (1) *False Assumption of Authority*:

Figure I.1 The Presenters at the Symposium on the "Posthumous Editing of a Great Master's Work," Held at the Graduate Theological Union, in Berkeley, California, on February 21st–23rd, 2019: Top from left: Austin Gordon, Alan Keisler, Julius Lipner, Jonathan Edelmann, David Buchta, Kenneth Rose; bottom from left: Ramdas Lamb, Rita D. Sherma, Michael Gressett, Edith Best, Anna King, Barbara Holdrege, and Graham M. Schweig. *Source*: Image courtesy of Author.

where Prabhupāda only granted conservative, provisional authority, the BBT editors assumed unrestricted, open-ended authority. (2) *Editorial Overreach*: where Prabhupāda requested only simple copyediting and correction of obvious mistakes, the BBT editors took great liberties in revising, omitting, and even attempting to correct the author's content. (3) *Noncompliance with Scholarly Standards*: where Prabhupāda requested scholarly editorial standards, the BBT editors misapplied scholarly textual methods and employed arbitrary and inconsistent editing practices. (4) *Editorial Changes without Transparency*: where devotional and scholarly editorial standards compelled full transparency, the extent of editorial changes by the BBT editors are undisclosed in the author's works.[2]

Prabhupāda regarded his writing as the most important among all his many achievements. He scrupulously supervised the production of his books, whether it was his early books, published by variously named in-house presses, or his shorter edition (1968) and his later complete edition (1972) of the *Bhagavad-gītā As It Is*, both published by Macmillan. He guided the editors, who were working under his supervision, with cautionary words, such as these, which he wrote in 1970: "Our editing is to correct grammatical and spelling errors only, without interpolation of style or philosophy."[3] This directive also applied to any editing by the BBT, the in-house publisher that Śrīla Prabhupāda founded and directed to preserve and publish his books. The question here is this: Do these instructions from Prabhupāda for the editors working under his live supervision apply to the editing after he has left this world? And if so, how?

It is important to appreciate that what Prabhupāda "wrote" is technically mostly what Prabhupāda actually "spoke." Prabhupāda's writings are his spoken words, which are then transcribed. In many ways, this process of speaking and then transcribing makes Prabhupāda's literary and publishing achievements all the more remarkable. Indeed, Prabhupāda spoke into a dictaphone to translate from Sanskrit in order to create extensive commentaries, which he titled "purports." Thus, what became Prabhupada's writings are mostly what his disciples transcribed from his dictations.

Several years following Prabhupāda's departure from this world, the BBT publisher publishes a heavily "revised" and "expanded" second edition of *Bhagavad-gītā As It Is.* Very far in the back of this book is found the editor's "A Note About the Second Edition," in which he justifies his heavily edited second edition:

> The new American disciples who helped Śrīla Prabhupāda ready the manuscript for publication struggled with several difficulties. Those who transcribed his taped dictation sometimes found his heavily accented English hard to follow and his Sanskrit quotations strange to their ears. The Sanskrit editors had to do their best with a manuscript spotted with gaps and phonetic approximations.[4]

Clearly, the intention seemingly declared here in these words by the editor, representing the publisher, was to make Prabhupāda's flagship work intelligible and free of blatant mistakes and errors.

However, eleven years after the original Macmillan edition had been in print and widely distributed around the world in the millians, many sincere and dedicated followers of Prabhupāda became aware that the leading BBT editor, with the approval of the BBT board and the leading ecclesiastical body of ISKCON (known as the Governing Body Commissioners, or "the GBC"), created a significantly different, heavily edited version of Prabhupāda's flagship work, *Bhagavad-gītā As It Is.* And as this disparity between Prabhupāda's original author-authorized edition and BBT's unauthorized second edition became more and more known to many, certain followers of Prabhupāda went to great pains to compare Prabhupāda's original work with the heavily edited second edition, bringing out what they considered excessive, intrusive, and even disrespectful changes of the original work.

The BBT editor and leaders boldly claimed that they had achieved "a work of even greater richness and authenticity." Yet, it was well known that the author never expressed any dissatisfaction with his original work, nor did he ever express any desire whatsoever for a second edition of his work. While the BBT felt that they came out with a new and improved version of the author's work, nevertheless, many intensely disapproved of the second edition that was to replace Prabhupāda's original book.

In response to the widespread objections to the posthumously produced heavily revised second edition, the BBT's editor and his protegé, waged a major campaign for years, beginning in 1986, which is still going on nearly forty years later, attempting to convince the greater world of ISKCON communities of their new and improved *Bhagavad-gītā As It Is.*[5] The two editors of BBT traveled for years, soliciting support for his second edition, offering lectures and talks on the subject, writing extensive papers explaining their editing and responding to many letters of objection, and in the twenty-first century, constructed an elaborate website, www.bbtedit.com (beta), containing videoed testimonials from institutionally authoritative voices from within ISKCON and the BBT, responses to known and anticipated challenges to their work, and so on.

SOME IMPORTANT QUESTIONS ASKED

Following Prabhupāda's departure from this world, the principal editors of Prabhupāda's private publishing house, Bhaktivedanta Book Trust (BBT), claim that his works need extensive editing, both for style and philosophical clarity and consistency, while there are other senior disciples who object to anything more than the absolute minimal editing, if any at all. How can both needs find a solution?

Generally speaking, how much or how little editing should any published author expect of his or her work after they have departed this world? In the case of Prabhupāda's works specifically, what compelling theological and devotional implications are there with each side of the issue? What were the various general and also personal instructions given by the author to his followers? What were the challenges for the editors who sought to present his works appropriately to the greater readership? What can we learn from the experience of editing of a great master's work in other traditions? What exactly are the criteria for doing any editing of Prabhupāda's books after he has departed this world? And is such editing being executed according to the clear instructions that Prabhupāda himself gave his disciples? Perhaps it can be asked whether such posthumous editing violates the moral rights of any departed author. These and other questions are addressed by the scholars' contributions that focus on the textual and historical scholarship on the worldwide Krishna movement and on other areas relevant to this volume's theme.

Beginning in the spring of 2017, sincere and very concerned senior disciples and devoted followers of Prabhupāda asked me to examine and evaluate the quality and validity of the editing of their master's books, beginning with and especially the editing of Prabhupāda's *Bhagavad-gītā As It Is*. At the urging of so many sincere and concerned followers, who knew of my academic background and experience with my own editing of works by deceased authors and my extensive publishing experience, it is my hope that my efforts in my own research on the matter as well as the arranging for a conference on this theme would bring clarity and resolution to those who have agonized over both sides of this issue for well over three decades.

Many persons have expressed to me that they felt that I would be best able to understand and evaluate this divisive issue given my knowledge and many years of study and experience of ISKCON. After combing my knowledge in the field of textual scholarship and textual criticism, consulting with dozens of colleagues who are associated with the issue in the Modern Language Association, as well as editors of publishing houses with whom I have worked for my own publications, and finally reviewing everything that Prabhupāda had written regarding the editorial treatment of his own work, I had come up with some resolution on the matter that I will present in the last chapter of this volume. However, I felt the need to bring together some of the most knowledgeable colleagues in my field to shed light on the theme of posthumous editing of a great master's work to critique, fortify, and refine my understanding and conclusions. My sincere hope is that I can bring forth some genuine conclusion and thoughtful resolution to the minds and hearts of the practitioners within the Krishna *bhakti* tradition, and perhaps even other religious traditions that may struggle with the same theo-literary challenges of posthumous editing and preservation.

NOTES

1. See "Posthumous publication is a wicked literary problem" by Francesca Peacock (September 22, 2022) on the website Engelsberg Ideas: https://engelsbergideas.com/notebook/posthumous-publication-is-a-wicked-literary-problem/

2. The idea of these four concise points come from Patrick Hogan, from whose I derived, with his permission, the slightly modified version of the information he presented.

3. Letter to Rupanuga Das Adhikary from Śrīla Prabhupāda (Written and sent from Los Angeles, February 17, 1970, page 1).

4. Second printing, 1985, third printing, 1986, eighth printing, 2001, all on page 866; first printing, 1989, page 868;

5. "Jayadvaita Swami [the leading BBT editor] will directly challenge and defeat the attacks from certain quarters of the movement that the new edition of the Bhagavad-gita put out by the RBT [sic] is not bonafide. He shall show fron [*sic*] the original manuscripts how the editor of the book in the early 1970's distorted* [*sic*] and changed Prabhupada's ori'ginal [*sic*] .words" (International BBT Meeting minutes, No. 11, Dallas, Texas, November 30–December 1, 1986).

Chapter 1

On Revealing the Face of Truth

Julius Lipner

Though[1] I have had some experience of collating and editing (and where relevant, translating) work by thinkers who have passed away—for example, with George Gispert-Sauch s.j., of the published but dispersed writings in Bengali and English of the well-known "Hindu Catholic" Indian nationalist, Brahmabandhab Upadhyay (1861–1907),[2] and, in the role of editorial precursor to Graham Schweig himself, of the doctoral dissertation at the University of Cambridge of my late-lamented ISKCON student, Tamal Krishna Goswami (who died tragically when his thesis was close to completion)[3]—I must admit that my own thinking as potential editor of posthumous works has evolved considerably from those times to the present day. I had not fully appreciated how theory-laden such editing can be. In other words, I have become editorially more "woke." In this essay, therefore, I propose to raise some of the major questions that arise out of this wokeness on the subject at hand.

But first, some clarifications and caveats. My wider scenario comprises the process and objectives of editing in general, sharpened by the lens of editing work by authors who have passed away. Unless one has this filter as a starting point, one cannot proceed to our specific focus: the editing of Swami Prabhupāda's (1896–1977) *oeuvre*. Thus, I see my job as providing the philosophical and theological underpinning—the theory behind the scenes, if you will—of the editorial process, though throughout I make reference to how such theory might pertain to Swami Prabhupāda. Second, I am not an ISKCONite, nor am I—and followers of Prabhupāda must forgive me for shortcomings in this respect—a Prabhupāda scholar. But this is another reason for approaching our topic through the wider gate: it raises issues that govern the task of *all* editing, not least that done after the death of the author concerned. This leads me to my third caveat. In this essay, I propose to read the "Master" of the title given to me as a gender-neutral rather than gender-inclusive term (as I do for "*guru*"—see later), analogous to the way "actor" is often used now. The (literary) political implications of "gender-neutral" differ from those of "gender-inclusive,"[4] and I am more comfortable working with the former than with the latter.

In his invitation to attend the symposium, Professor Schweig sets the scene as follows:

> In the Hare Krishna movement, a controversy has been building for at least two decades regarding the editing of Śrīla Prabhupāda's books: after Śrīla Prabhupāda's departure from this world, the principal editors claim that his works need fairly extensive editing, both for style and philosophical clarity and consistency, while there are other senior disciples who object to anything more than the absolute minimal editing.
>
> Generally speaking, how much or how little editing should any published author expect of his or her works after they have departed this world?[5] In the case of Śrīla Prabhupāda's works specifically, what compelling theological and devotional underpinnings are involved with each side of the issue? What were the various general and also personal instructions given by the author to his followers? What were the challenges for the editors who sought to present his works appropriately to the greater readership?[6]

I regard the fact that I had not been privy to these debates as a methodological advantage for writing this essay, for this means that I can claim personal neutrality in the matter. Similarly, since I am not a member of any Hare Krishna group—I am aware that there has been some factionalism in this movement—I feel free of any obligation to bow to one faction or another. In fact, I had thought it wise not to read the arguments *pro* and *con* within the ISKCON fold with regard to the editing of Swami Prabhupāda's works before writing this essay (though I have been apprised of some of the arguments during the course of the symposium). The way was clear for me, therefore, at the start to proceed with studied neutrality, from the viewpoint of an outsider. This is the basic stance of this essay.

Editing has a very broad remit. One can edit written work (prose or poetry); oral records of lectures and talks given but not hitherto committed to writing (I seem to recall Tamal Krishna Goswami, who was Swami Prabhupāda's secretary for a number of years, mentioning many tapes of teachings given by his *guru* via Dictaphone); musical compositions, including songs and instrumental notation (not least by extemporization and improvisation); and, of course, film. And now we have the technology to edit the genetic makeup of humans and other forms of life. Further, authors themselves can be great auto-editors; this raises important questions to which we shall return later. In Professor Schweig's invitation to attend the symposium, he speaks of

Prabhupāda's "books." However, our scope will take in all of Swami's output, not least because some of his books arise from transcriptions and editions of various spoken addresses and lectures. Here we must remember an important fact: Prabhupāda is regarded as a *guru* by his followers, and presumably by his in-house editors too, with all the authoritative weight—after all, "*guru*" literally means "heavy"—that this term in its religious context implies. This too carries important methodological implications for us, as we shall see.

In her fine book *The Work of Revision,* Hannah Sullivan points out that there are three modes of editorial revision: (a) addition, (b) excision, deletion, or subtraction, and (c) substitution.[7] Let us look at each in turn.

(a) By addition, of course, the work grows in size. Such growth can be "horizontal" or "vertical." Horizontal growth is alteration in degree, by way of "incidentals" or "accidentals," rather than in kind; it is largely stylistic or simply parataxic. Incidental stylistic changes include such alterations as "some" for "a number of," the inclusion of adjectives or qualifying descriptions that are not decisive (Sullivan gives the example of Joyce changing "Then he went to the dresser, poured milk on a saucer and set it slowly on the floor," in the first set of proofs of *Ulysses*, to "Then he went to the dresser, poured *warm-bubbled* milk on a saucer *from the jug Hanlon's milkman had just filled for him*, and set it slowly on the floor" for the published version in *The Little Review* in 1918[8]) and so on. An example of parataxic change would be the piling on of adjectives for effect, as in "He was tall and sturdy" to "He was tall, muscular, and sturdy", or extending a point by means of a number of not particularly informative descriptive terms, as, for instance, in "There were some bathers on the beach, as well as a few energetic dogs and their owners" to "There were some bathers on the beach, as well as a few energetic dogs and their owners, not to mention an assortment of stalls selling hotdogs, jellied eels, and seashells." The list could go on and be picked-at indefinitely.

Similarly, for b) excision or deletion, and c) substitution. These can be done either contingently or substantially. As to the former, coming back to our beach, I could start with a description of the scene with its bathers, dogs and their owners, and stalls, and then pare this down to the bathers only and leave the essence of the story intact. I could also substitute "a few wheeling and raucous seagulls" for the dogs and their owners without affecting the gist of what I want to say.

Such incidental addition, subtraction, or substitution does not alter the plot, the characters or the structure of a text, as in vertical or substantial editing. With the latter, we have a properly *new* product. After T.S. Eliot gave Ezra Pound a free hand to edit *The Waste Land,* the 434-line poem that emerged in 1922 was the result of a cut of *hundreds of lines* from the original manuscript handed over to Pound. "Slasher" Pound, with Eliot's approval, immortalized the poet by, it was half-jokingly said, removing the waste from *The Waste*

Land, or, we may add, excising rather more than a "pound" of textual flab, and in consequence helped create what some literary critics say is the greatest piece of poetry of the western world in the twentieth century.[9] This was the result of substantial deletion, not to mention a generous measure of skeletal substitution. So, on occasion, vertical editing can be adjudged to substantially improve the quality of the work.

Here is another example involving mainly consequential substitution (with some addition thrown in) in an amazingly anomalous act of translation (though one would hesitate to call it this). I am referring to a passage from Basanta Koomar Roy's well-known rendering into English of *Ānandamaṭh,*[10] Bankim Chatterji's famous Bengali religio-political novel of the late nineteenth century, which gave India its National Song[11] and which played an important part, especially among Hindus, in stimulating a nationalist agenda.[12] One must remember that the novel was written at a time when Muslim rule of the Bengal area (and other parts of the subcontinent) still rankled largely in the Hindu mind, even as this rule was being supplanted by British political paramountcy. The passage I have in mind is taken from Part 1, Chapter 10 of the novel. However, first let me quote my own translation of the extract (here, two leading characters in the story are in conversation):[13]

> "[Mahendra asked] "You're comparing the Bengalis to the English!"
>
> "Why not?" answered Bhabananda. "There's a limit to physical strength. Do you think a stronger person can make a bullet fly faster?"
>
> "Then why is there such a difference between the English and the Muslims?" asked Mahendra.
>
> "Listen," said Bhabananda, "an Englishman won't flee even to save his life, whereas the Muslim will run off when he begins to sweat; he'll slope off in search of a cool drink! Again, the English hang on, they'll finish what they've begun. But the Muslim plays fast and loose. The sepoys[14] risk their lives for money, and even then, they don't get paid. And finally, it's a question of courage. The cannonball can fall only in one place not in ten, so there's no need for two hundred to run when they see a single cannonball. Yet when they see a single cannonball a whole tribe of Muslims will flee, whereas a tribe of cannonballs can't make a single Englishman run!"[15]

Now here is Roy's version:

> [Mahendra said] "When it comes to warfare, there is a world of difference between the British and the people of India."
>
> [Bhabananda replied:] "You do not fight these days with mere physical strength. The bullet does not travel faster nor further because a stronger man fires a rifle."
>
> "Then what makes this difference between the British and the Indian soldier?"

> "Because the British soldier would never run away even to save his life. The Indian soldier runs away when he begins to perspire; he seeks cold drinks. The Englishman surpasses the Indian in tenacity. He never abandons his duty before he finishes it. Then consider the question of courage: A cannon ball falls only on one spot. But a whole company of Indian soldiers would run away if one single cannon ball fell among them. On the other hand, British soldiers would not run away even if dozens of cannon balls should fall in their midst."[16]

Even a cursory comparison between the two renderings will reveal that they differ in important respects. Roy's version includes paraphrase ("When it comes to warfare"), addition ("The Englishman surpasses the Indian. . . . He never abandons his duty"), and gross substitution with reference to the question, "Where have all the Muslims gone in his translation?" to which the answer is: "They have been edited out of the novel entirely!" They have no role to play in his rendition. Here, the Muslim becomes the "Indian" or "Indian soldier." Roy has the grace to say on the cover page of his book: "Translated and Adapted from Bengali." But this is some adaptation! Clearly, Roy (who was himself a Hindu) has an agenda to serve, viz. introducing a form of political correctness to save Muslim blushes at what may be regarded as a sensitive period of Indian history (1941). Nevertheless, his adaptation, to quote again from my book, "is like adapting Shakespeare's *The Merchant of Venice* to get rid of Shylock" for similar reasons. "The Muslims play a key role in *Ānandamaṭh*", I observe in my book, "for a variety of political and narratival reasons, including the "political rage" Bankim felt at Muslim self-indulgence in ruling Indian territories (it is this that lies behind the unfavorable comparison described in the passage [quoted]). To banish all trace of Muslims in one's translation [of the novel] is not to solve a problem but to defer it, if not to exacerbate it,"[17] not least because *Ānandamaṭh,* both in Bengali and in translation, became a highly influential novel among the general public in India. Roy's editorial changes only served to highlight the incongruity of the original contrast between the British and the Muslims; they did not do it any favors.

This raises the issue of editing for political purposes, both for reasons of political correctness and the social and political reconstruction of history. As to the latter, one only has to study the role of history books in the school-curricula of various nation-states to appreciate how consequential this subject can be, in particular with regard to factionalism within and between countries. We shall return to editing and political correctness in due course, but here we can raise the following questions: Would issues of historical import and also of political correctness come into play in the editing of a spiritual master's works (with special reference to Prabhupāda)? After all, the *guru* is a human being of a particular culture of a particular period of time, with the range of consequences that follow from this. In short, the *guru*'s backstory would have left its mark on the teaching and behavior left behind. On the other hand, one presumes that in general, this teaching was not intended to be gender- or race-restrictive but rather of universal import. But times move on, and political correctness will have its say. How woke must posthumous editing be? We shall take this issue up in due course.

But to return to our earlier distinctions: no doubt, the distinction between incidental and substantial editorial change, as outlined earlier, is not watertight. If the addition of "from the jug Hanlon's milkman had just filled for him" in the example cited from *Ulysses* had been inserted as an important material clue in some intricate whodunit, it would not be an accidental addition but a substantial one. Context in editorial matters can be decisive, and we need to keep this in mind as we move on to our next point.

Consider the theme underlying a book like Paula Richman's (edited) *Many Rāmāyaṇas*. The noted historian Romila Thapar is quoted here as follows:

> The appropriation of the [*Rāmāyaṇa*] story by a multiplicity of groups meant a multiplicity of versions through which the social aspirations and ideological concerns of each group were articulated. The story in these versions included significant variations which changed the conceptualization of character, event and meaning.[18]

The edited retellings of a text can alter it substantially, especially when such retellings are part of an ongoing tradition of multiple versions, as in the case of the *Rāmāyaṇa* and that other great epic, of course, the *Mahābhārata*. True, there may be a familiar and discernible storyline and/or core of characters in most, if not all of these versions, but these reappear in different contexts and mean and do different things. It is no accident that such multiple editing tends to take place in texts most at home in the much more fluid (and fallible) medium of *oral* promulgation, as in the case of the *Mahābhārata* and *Rāmāyaṇa*. In the case of oral texts, that is, texts that derive from oral composition and its dissemination—and in one way or another, the Hindu traditions are reliant on these—there is often the expectation that there *will* be multiple retellings according to circumstance and need. This is supposed to give vitality and continuing relevance to the promulgated text, just as seed sown in different kinds of soil yields crops that take on the variable characteristics of the particular earth in which it is grown. Here, the Lévi-Straussian idea of *bricolage,* of seeking coherence by managing the instability of textual meaning and its dissemination through various ensembles, crops up with special force (more about this later). How is the editor able to control, or direct, this inherent play of words, not least when originally presented orally? And we may ask: How does this apply to Swami Prabhupāda? As a "Hindu" rooted in tradition, did the Swami recognize and exploit the semantic instability of language and, in particular, the distinction between written and oral presentation? Oral presentation is usually informal, ad-libs a lot, contains mistakes and deviations from former pronouncements that are often not spotted or rectified on the spot, and does not always adhere to a clear structure. Did Swami Prabhupāda express a view on these matters? Even if he did not, does it fall to his editorial disciples to attempt to "tidy up," regularize, or stabilize deviations or inconsistencies in his recorded spoken words, not least if these were meant to be transcribed and published? I am not speaking only of stylistic infelicities here. We shall return to the idea of bricolage at the end of this essay. But to continue our argument, oral proliferation gives rise to several further considerations that do not necessarily exclude non-oral promulgation, and it is to these that we now turn.

First, there is the question of intention, which, of course, applies to both oral and written output. There has been a debate about the role—or lack of it—of intention in reviewing or assessing an author's work, particularly with a view to its editing. Hannah Sullivan summarizes this debate in terms of the various dominant approaches. First, we have the New Criticism. This approach is strongly anti-intentionalist, incorporating "a critical practice that disavow[s] inquiries into intention."[19] When the Nobel laureate, William Golding, said in an interview, "The writer probably knows what he meant when he wrote a book, but he should immediately forget what he meant when he's written it,"[20] he seemed to be making light of intention as a key to understanding. The school of New Criticism maintains that once a work is in the public forum, the critic, and we may add, an editor, must abandon any purported intentionality underlying its composition for a range of reasons: the author may not be clear about the intention motivating the work, or may change intention as the work continues, or perhaps is disingenuous or dishonest in stating intention, or indeed may not regard intention as important, or may not be able to identify deeper forces as part of a complex interplay driving the work—and withal, is powerless to determine the intentionality of others in interpreting what has been presented. Of course, to complicate matters even further, these factors could exert their influence in various permutations and combinations. Golding, in the same interview, seems to testify to the opacity of discerning intention when he was prompted about features of his writing compared with those of others: "Time and time again", he responded, "people bring to my notice parallels, oppositions, appositions, levels, of which I was unaware".[21] No doubt such unawareness also applies to Swami Prabhupāda. How does "intention" figure in the editing of his work? How may we discern any intention he may have expressed—perhaps inconsistently or hesitatingly on several occasions and over a considerable period of time—with regard to editing some or all of his works? We shall come to this question in due course.

In fact, the French *Critique Génétique* school "understands intention as a less conscious and controlled process"[22] than many intentionalists, by contrast, claim is the case. The latter regard discerning or incorporating authorial intention as a key factor for understanding, interpreting, or editing, though it is not easy to see how they can be so confident of ascertaining what appears to be so elusive a goal. Nevertheless, I believe that expressed intention by the author, both about the work and then its editing, is an important factor for the redacting process, for we can take it on trust, I suppose, that both aspects have played some significant role in directing and consolidating the original work. Further, this intention can assume increasing importance as and when authors edit their own work, oftentimes continuously, before they pronounce themselves satisfied with it or feel forced to call a halt (perhaps because of publication or other deadlines).[23]

But the matter does not end there, for with intention comes agency, and the explicit combination of these two factors evokes yet another approach about the role of intention in editorial work, that of those who argue that intentionality is a shared enterprise. This is the approach of "social-text editing."[24] Even though I have written this paper, you could say that I am not its sole author. Through my research for it, others have contributed to its composition, either explicitly (e.g., by way of quotation) or implicitly (through influence). Further, as I release it, you—its audience—are shaping, determining, interpreting, and prioritizing—that is, editing—aspects of its reception, for your own purposes—something I cannot control. You participate in its authorial embrace. What I can control is awareness of *responsibility*—to the object of my study, and to its recipients—in formulating what I produce and in seeking to determine how it is received. These obligations also apply to the editorial process. Swami Prabhupāda has passed away. What are the responsibilities of his editors as potential co-participants in the new authorial process? As deceased, the Swami can no longer express authoritatively a change of view. In this respect, does it help or hinder the outcome if some of these editors knew him personally and affirmed that they could pronounce on his views? Can his editors speak of a *devolved responsibility* in arriving at decisions, not only on his behalf but as co(-editorial) authors in their own right?

We come now to a major complicating factor in the discussion: the fact that Swami Prabhupāda is recognized as a or *the* defining *guru*, or guiding figure in spiritual matters, in his movement. For their disciples, *gurus* speak inspired words, words laden with authority and salvific efficacy. We recall the words of the famous *stotra* or hymn dedicated to the *guru*, the *Śrī Guru Aṣṭakam*:

śarīraṃ surūpaṃ tathā vā kalatram, yaśaś cārū citraṃ dhanaṃ merutulyam,
manas cen na lagnaṃ guror anghripadme, tataḥ kiṃ, tataḥ kiṃ, tataḥ kim.

> *You may have a beautiful body and a beautiful wife too, and your renown may be glorious and far-reaching, and your wealth as great as Mount Meru, but if your mind is not fixed on the guru's lotus feet, what is the point of it all?* (see verse 1, and refrain to the following verses).

And Vaiśaṃpāyana teaches in the *Mahābhārata:* "Those who do not venerate the revered *guru*, sink into evil, abysmal worlds."[25] If Swami Prabhupāda is regarded as such a weighty authority-figure, how, in the light of what we have said so far about editorial responsibility, is the *disciple* to edit his *oeuvre*? We shall offer guidelines later in this essay.

Guru he may have been, but Swami Prabhupāda was also human, born and bred in specific circumstances, and conditioned by a particular life history. His mother tongue was Bengali, yet because of the force of circumstances of his chosen mission, he wrote and taught largely in English. Guruship does not safeguard one from stylistic idiosyncrasies and errors, lapses of memory, and inadvertent inconsistency of content. This is what it means to be human. Further, there can be no doubt that Swami Prabhupāda's English did not have the assurance or clarity of a native speaker of the language. The editor, as in the case of other *guru*s, may understandably feel called upon to rectify this fallibility. This means that the editor must be knowledgeable about the subject matter and the professed "intention," if discernible, of the author. I have been informed that some of the early transcribers of Swami's addresses were not familiar with many of the ideas of his teaching and the Sanskrit he quoted to back it up, and not infrequently garbled what he said. This is understandable, and the same would apply, no doubt, to recording what other *guru*s in similar circumstances would have said. But the question remains: How does one go about (re?-)editing such material? This question too will be addressed in due course.

But first we must discuss the concept of the "ideal" or "complete" text to which the editor may aspire.[26] To aid our considerations, let me recall this aspiration from the *Īśa Upaniṣad:*

> *Hiraṇmayena pātreṇa satyasyāpihitam mukham,*
> *tat tvaṃ pūṣan apāvṛṇu satyadharmāya dṛṣṭaye* (vr.15).[27]
>
> "The face of truth is covered by a golden vessel. Reveal it, O Pushan, so that I may behold it for the sake of truth's law."

Though this text is translated in various ways, no one disputes the directive to the Vedic deity Pushan (associated with taking the traveler to a designated goal) to uncover the face of truth for the truth-lover. But the question arises: what might be expected of Pushan in this regard? Two contrasting paradigms of Pushan's task come to mind. First, he is to reveal the truth that *is already there*: in our terms, the truth of the "ideal text" that has already been achieved (even though for one reason or another it may be lost to view), or which, in fact, awaits our gaze in the future. Either way, the text is supposed to be achievable; the task of the editor is to attain it. But second, rather than unveiling what is already there, Pushan, the inspirer, might be expected to take us on a journey toward a goal that is, in fact, an endlessly receding target—the ideal text in this reading—which the editor can never achieve. Here, it is the journey that matters—the striving along the way—which becomes the goal, not some fixed outcome. Let us consider each option in turn in the context of our discussion.

There was a tendency in the nineteenth century, especially among the Romantic poets, to regard the original composition as ideal, for it was supposed to emerge spontaneously, freshly and organically minted. As such, in essence, it could not be bettered. To seek to improve it by editorial, especially auto-editorial revision (except for minimal correction of grammatical and other infelicities as a nod to human fallibility), was a mistake, for this invariably diminished the quality of the original. Such revision was an act of dismemberment, of mutilation—a slap in the face of the muse of inspiration. It was with this in mind that the well-known Romantic poet, Lord Byron (1788–1824), protested against the prospect of revising by comparing his initial effort to the spring of a tiger: "I am like the tyger (in poesy) if I miss my first Spring—I go growling back to my Jungle.—There is no second.—I can't correct—I can't—and I won't."[28] The first spring of inspiration produces the goods, and the project diminishes through subsequent revisionary effort. It is as if the text "writes itself" with this successful, original surge of insight. Do not writers and poets often use this expression—of the text "writing itself"—with a sense of wonder and completion? How then could one revise such "complete" work? According to this understanding, the ideal text is a datum, a given, and a work is at its best when it first emerges from its gestation in the creative mind. If it is to be edited, all the editor has to do is to recover it in its pristine glory, perhaps by a bit of verbal dusting here or textual polishing there—in effect, by simply uncovering the face of truth. And is not the work of the *guru,* Swami Prabhupāda in this instance, a work of inspiration? Which editor would dare seek to "revise" such a precious bequest? That is the argument.

This reverence for the integrity of the original inspired work can lead to one's experiencing its immediate present, often subsuming the presence of its author, with a *Dasein*—a "being there"—of Heideggerian intensity that provides the best chance of awakening one to the empowering effect of the original. The sense of the immediate, gracious present is evoked beautifully in the following extract taken from Annie Dillard's *Pilgrim at Tinker Creek*:

> It is early March. I am dazed from a long day of interstate driving homeward; I pull in at a gas station in Nowhere, Virginia, north of Lexington. The young boy in charge . . . is offering a free cup of coffee with every gas purchase. . . . The cheerful human conversation wakes me, recalls me, not to a normal consciousness, but to a kind of energetic readiness. I step outside. . . . I am absolutely alone. There are no other customers. . . . Before me extends a low hill trembling in yellow brome, and behind the hill, filling the sky, rises an enormous mountain ridge, forested, alive and awesome with brilliant blown lights. I have never seen anything so tremulous and live. . . . I watch the mountain. . . . Shadows lope along the mountain's rumpled flanks; they elongate like root tips, like lobes of spilling water, faster and faster. . . . The whole mountain looms miles closer; the light warms and reddens. . . . I am more alive than all the world. This is it, I think, this is it, right now, the present. . . . And the second I verbalize the awareness in my brain. . . . I am opaque, so much black asphalt. . . . Catch it if you can. The present is an invisible electron . . . fleeing and gone. . . . Experiencing the present purely is being emptied and hollow; you catch grace as a man fills his cup under a waterfall. . . . These are our few live seasons. Let us live them as purely as we can, in the present.[29]

By editorial excision and compression—this relatively short extract has been cut and pasted from out of five pages of the original, gloriously evocative writing—I think I have more or less made the point I want to make, viz. to evoke the immediacy and transformative power of the present, more or less to my satisfaction. But I have also substantially condensed the original (as the interjecting dots indicate)! So, have I edited successfully and seamlessly enough? Or have I deformed the original by an act of editorial vandalism? Have I induced you to go back for more? If the latter, then, in one respect, I have not failed. For Dillard, the present is an occasion for receiving grace. This accords well with another feature of evoking the grace-bestowing present from our point of view: the presence also of the source of grace—the *guru*—through the immediacy of the *guru*'s teaching. Is capturing the preceptor's presence in this way (including the preceptor who has passed away) more susceptible to harder or softer editing? How much of the *guru*'s words is alterable before the *guru*'s presence fades away from the text? What kind of editing will uncover the face of truth here? Does not "cleaning up" the *guru*'s words by editing out stylistic infelicities and idiosyncrasies, inconsistency of content, and so on, not to mention even characteristic terms of abuse,[30] work toward masking the individuality, and so the immediate presence, of the *guru* for the recipient, and indeed of imposing another individuality—that of the editor—on the work? The relationship between the *guru* and disciple is unique and sacrosanct. Who has the authority to tamper with this? I shall venture an answer later in this essay.

But there is another reason why, in the minds of some, the author's work, especially that of the *guru*, should not be revised. This is because revision points to imperfection in the author, perhaps even moral imperfection, the suggestion being that the author may have been inadequate in important respects or too lazy or too slipshod to have done a better job, so that it is for the editor to take remedial action. Perhaps this is the main reason why, to hark back to Professor Schweig's statement of invitation, "some senior disciples object to anything more than the absolute minimal editing" of Swami Prabhupāda's *oeuvre*. Further, in line with the point made earlier, it could be thought that more than minimal editing undermines the freshness and integrity of the original—with respect to both the work and its promulgator—and so their immediate and transformative presence.

But now we must consider the second paradigm underlying Pushan's task, that of the "ideal text," which, by definition, can never be achieved—of a "completion" that is forever in the making. This is the state of affairs, so the argument goes, because effort by humans, even inspired humans, continually calls for revision, for such effort is inevitably time- and circumstance- sensitive, both from the authorial side and that of the receiver. And time and circumstance are inherently changeable. "Words strain, / Crack and sometimes break, under the burden," says Eliot in *Burnt Norton.*

Words need constant revision, replenishing, and editing to convey their force and meaning. Even sacred words. The King James Bible is an exercise in translation, which, of course, is another form of editing. But translation requires attention not only to meaning—to the semantics of the original language(s) as well as of the target language—but also to their context and the circumstances of their production and reception. Some of these effects can be long-lasting. Even though the King James Bible is four hundred years old, it has bequeathed to English a host of words and phrases that are still in use. The fact that this is an authoritative translation of a sacred text authoritatively disseminated has played a big part in its longevity. But this does not mean that the Bible, as a sacred text, cannot or should not be re-translated, that is, re-edited, into English (and other languages) again and again to meet the continually changing demands of semantic and compositional intelligibility. Joseph Ratzinger, the former Pope Benedict XVI, hints at this requirement when speaking of "canonical exegesis" with regard to the Bible. In the Foreword of his book *Jesus of Nazareth,* he refers to

> the process of constant rereading that forged the words transmitted in the Bible, into Scripture. Older texts [of the Biblical corpus] are reappropriated, reinterpreted, and read with new eyes in new contexts. They become Scripture by being read anew, evolving in continuity with their original sense, tacitly corrected and given added depth and breadth of meaning. This is a process in which

> the word gradually unfolds its inner potentialities, already somehow present like seeds, but needing the challenge of new situations, new experiences and new sufferings, in order to open up.[31]

And why this semantic fluidity, this flux of meaning? Because, he continues, harking back to a point we made earlier, "It is necessary to keep in mind that any human utterance of a certain weight contains more than the author may have been immediately aware of at the time."[32] To transpose these ideas into our Hindu context, the "potentialities," the "seeds" of which Ratzinger speaks, recall the role of the *sūtra* in undergirding so much of pioneering Sanskrit thought. The *sūtra* is meant to pack a semantic punch; its shotgun style is meant to have the capacity to release a spectrum of possible meanings when unlocked by the attuned mind seeking to grasp its purpose. Consider the *Brahmasūtra*s of Bādarāyaṇa; every student of Vedānta knows that they have generated commentaries ranging from *Advaitic* through *Viśiṣṭādvaitic* to *Dvaitic* points of view. One supposes that the *guru*'s words are similarly pregnant with meaning for the attentive follower. As seeds waiting to germinate and bear fruit in the mind and heart of the disciple, the *guru*'s utterances carry, to recall Ratzinger's words, "a certain weight [that] contains more than the author [and hearer] may have been immediately aware of at the time." If so, do they not need regular revisionary weeding of obsolete or inappropriate terms or ideas—inevitable with the passage of time (especially with regard to such things as outdated scientific pronouncements)—to release, unobstructed, the germinating potential of their semantic content?

This leads us to consider at some length another issue in the editing of sacred (or sacrosanct) text, whether written or oral: the matter of its translatability. Muslim theologians are uncomfortable with the idea of the Qur'ān being "translated" in any strict sense of this term. The original Arabic of the Qur'ān is thought to have become so ennobled by the reception of the word of the Almighty, revealed to the Prophet Muhammad, through its linguistic cadences and rhythms, vocabulary, and compositional style, that seeming to challenge its *appropriateness* as the receptor text for divine communication by setting up a target language for translation, apparently on a par with the Qur'ān itself, comes across as nothing short of sacrilegious. It is the Almighty who has promulgated the "complete" and final version of the Qur'ānic text, through the instrumentality of the Prophet and the Arabic of the time. All that humans can do is recognize this fact, check that the original is intact, and receive it with humility. The Qur'ān cannot properly be edited, either by way of reconstitution into a more perfect "critical edition," or the construal of translation.[33] One can, of course—indeed, if Islam is to consolidate or enhance its future as a major religion of the world, one must—attempt to render its meaning into other tongues for the sake of comprehension (*tafsīr*), and this has continued apace throughout history. But this is not meant to challenge the sacrosanct status of the original from a linguistic, semantic, or literary point of view.[34] Such strictures do not apply to the Hebrew and Greek of the Bible as received by Jews or Christians, for example, as Joseph Ratzinger's words, quoted earlier, imply. In fact, the first major task Christian missionaries attempt in the field is a *translation* of the Bible into the language(s) of their mission. The Christian Bible, composed over centuries (in contrast to the Qur'ān, promulgated in a single lifetime), has assumed shape and meaning through a process of painstaking and judicious reconstitution.[35] The word of God for Christians is editable in human terms, by way of what we may call joint participation with divine inspiration. Sanskrit, as the elite language of Hindu scripture, in particular in its Vedic form, seems to occupy an anomalous position in this regard. The content of the Vedic *saṃhitā*s, in particular the *mantra*s or hymns, is not editable in any significant sense; their effective power resides in proper, ritualistic, and literal recitation, in contrast to the Upanishads, dubbed the *Vedānta* (the "end of the Veda"), which are largely a repository for meditative understanding. The number of authoritative Upanishads varies among Hindu theologians in accordance with the *sampradāya* or interpretive tradition to which each belongs—and this presupposes a kind of sifting or editing.

Where is the *guru*'s place in all this? Should the *guru*'s works, the product of but one lifetime, be regarded as non-editable in line with the paradigm of the Vedic *mantra*s? To revert to Swami Prabhupāda: as teacher, translator, commentator, and definer of scriptural content (consider, for instance, his prioritizing of the *Bhāgavata Purāṇa,* among scriptural texts), he had a robust view of communicating his understanding of scripture. This makes him an editor *par excellence.* In this light, he must have appreciated the fluid nature of the text. Could he, then, object ineluctably to the suitable editing—indeed, even the post-mortem re-birthing in a linguistically variegated world—of his own *oeuvre*? There is further consideration here. Is not Swami's straightforward and homely communicative style, intended for dissemination to all and sundry, more in keeping with the language and constitution of the Bible, which some have contended seems to call for editing and translation, than with the more ritually purposeful language of the Vedic *mantra*s and Qur'ān, which are seen as resisting redaction for this very reason?[36]

Let us deal now with those two cantankerous auxiliaries of the editor: the footnote and the commentary.[37] Academics tend to exult in a forest of footnotes. They are never happier than when swinging rapidly, like that well-known exponent of arboreal dexterity, Tarzan of the Apes, from one footnote to the next in a text studded with notifications of one kind or another. And I must admit that I am a compulsive reader and writer of footnotes. But not everyone is an academic, and the *guru*'s teachings are generally not aimed at academics. As we have seen in the case of Swami Prabhupāda, his style was direct and homely; such a style is not enhanced by a text spiked with footnotes, and the chances are that many of his readers would not bother to read or follow such editorial notifications. They seek the words of the Master himself. Nevertheless, there may well be a place for a few judicious footnotes in the edited text of the *guru*'s work. In his book mentioned earlier, Anthony Grafton writes as follows about the function of [in particular] the [historical] footnote:

> Both experience and logic . . . suggest that . . . no accumulation of footnotes can prove that every statement in the text rests on an unassailable mountain of attested facts. Footnotes exist, rather, to perform two other functions. First, they persuade: they convince the reader that the historian has done an acceptable amount of work, enough to lie within the tolerances of the field. . . . Second, they indicate the chief sources that the historian has actually used.[38]

According to Grafton, footnotes function to certify, convince, and consolidate, and we can add: to clarify too. Footnotes can clarify obscure, convoluted, or bemusing text. It would seem that this last, clarifying function would have a significant role to play in editing the spiritual preceptor's work. When was this recorded, who was the interlocutor, what was its context, where does it come from, and so on: sufficient to clarify the text, with minimal intervention—no more. In other words, in the case of footnotes to text disseminated to the general public in our context, less indeed is more.[39]

And now to the commentary or gloss—the *bhāṣya,* or *vṛtti,* or *ṭīkā,* in the Sanskrit tradition.[40] This tradition has been heavily reliant on the commentary to clarify the terminology and ideas of authoritative texts in almost every branch of human endeavor, to debate, justify, and denounce in the process of argument, and, last but not least, to introduce new thinking under the guise of unassuming exposition or ratification. Swami Prabhupāda resorted to commentary under the rubric of "Purpose" in his exegesis of Sanskrit texts. So, commentary has a place in the exposition (and editing) of text. But even here, unless it is an auto-commentary made by the author—in which case the commentary becomes a new text (perhaps awaiting further commentary)—it should not be allowed to usurp, displace, or dilute the efficacy of the original work, especially when this emanates from the spiritual preceptor. There are a number of reasons for this: the freshness and impact of the original, its status as the source of a particular train or distinctiveness of thought, and its function as the locus of the felt presence of the *guru.*

And now for a comment or two on the topic the reader has been waiting for—the editing of digital-born text, so pervasive a feature of our contemporary world. In her book, *The Work of Revision,* Hannah Sullivan contends that the association of endless revision and literary value,

> is the legacy of high modernism and the print culture that nourished it. Modernist writers revised overtly, passionately, and at many points in the lifespan of their texts. They used revision, an action that implies retrospection, not for stylistic tidying up but to *make it new* through large-scale transformations of length, structure, perspective, and genre.[41]

In our times, print has had to, if not give way, then at least live to some extent in uneasy competition with text created, reared, and disseminated solely by electronic means, viz. text that has not "descended"[42] to any state outside of what we now call virtual reality. Whether we realize it or not, and whether we like it or not, as children of the modernist revolution (as described by Sullivan above), educated in the aftermath of a culture constantly demanding the discernment of fresh revision, we have all been touched by the urge not only to normalize but also to *normaTize* alteration, by way of textual revision, new editions, and changes in terminology, literary styles, and genres. This has been facilitated first by increasingly cheaper and rapidly improving print technology, and now by the even greater economies of digital know-how. But this has also generated a culture worldwide of rampant fake news. Rather like the swan in the Tamil image, which is able to extract with its beak only the milk when presented with a mixture of milk and water, we are now increasingly faced with the prospect of having to separate truth from falsity and authentic news from fake. In other words, we have learned to appreciate even more the role of *editing* for arriving at properly-sourced information.

I have long abandoned my early discipline of composing first in longhand, and then on the typewriter, before submitting my work for publication. For years now, I have been composing directly on my computer, translating thought into its digital home, secure in the knowledge that I can do and undo, that is, auto-edit, at least incidentally, as I go along, till the last possible minute, even after I have received the final proofs by email.

We now live in a time when text published one or more generations ago can be uploaded and promulgated in digital format. This applies to Swami Prabhupāda's *oeuvre* too. In light of what we have just been saying, the temptation will arise to revise and "improve" this work in quest of that ideal text that will throw the Master into the best relief. But this is a highly sensitive matter for a number of reasons already given pertaining to the privileged nature of the *guru*'s original words, in which the presence and authenticity of the *guru*'s voice can be discerned.

Readers will no doubt have noticed that in formulating my ideas I have adopted what may be called a "radial" approach, that is, I have sought to raise the *pro*s and *con*s of the topic at hand from a number of angles as equitably as possible, without taking sides in what seems to have become an acute (*tīkṣṇa*) subject of dispute within the ISKCON movement.

Nevertheless, perhaps it is incumbent on me now to be more forthcoming and to suggest some guidelines as to how one might go about the posthumous editing of a spiritual preceptor's works, with special reference to Swami Prabhupāda.

The key point, in my estimation, is how one deals with the post-mortem editing of works by someone who is deferred to *as a guru* within the so-called "Hindu" tradition. I have already made some observations about the exalted or inspired status of a *guru* in this tradition.[43] Is it right to seek to edit the published (or unpublished) works of the spiritual preceptor? Further, if the *guru* has left pre-published or pre-publicized work, in whatever form, what role should such work play in the post-mortem assessment of the *guru*'s teaching? These queries fall under the broader scope of the following question: has the preceptor expressed a view on the matter? If so, can we recover the exact words and their context in which this intention was revealed? This is not a simple question. The intention may have been expressed more than once over a period of time and in a manner that may not have been clear, comprehensive or wholly consistent. If there is room for doubt here, then, considering that we are speaking of a Hindu *guru*'s *oeuvre* and its sacrosanct nature, one's advice would be to edit or alter posthumously as little as possible so as to preserve the presence of the guru and the authenticity of the teaching through the text. If the *guru*'s work had been subject to editing in some way while the *guru* was still alive, for example, under the *guru*'s supervision or by the *guru*'s subsequent pronouncements on text edited earlier, then the extent and kind of editing achieved while the *guru was still alive* should be the template for the editing attempted after the *guru*'s demise.[44] We may raise the question here of editing factual errors and what may be regarded as material perceived as offensive in some way (perhaps appearing more so with the passage of time) relating to gender, age, ethnicity, and so on. Factual errors pertaining to scientific data, dates, names, and so on may, in my opinion, be signaled by a straightforward footnote. Offensive material perceived as such from the viewpoint of gender, ethnicity, and so on should also be signaled in the same way, on the grounds that *guru*s hardly wish to alienate, gratuitously, either their prospective followers or their potential critics. Nevertheless, to preserve the integrity of the *guru*'s work, the editing of so-called offensive material should be judicious and restrained; there is a limit to the wokeness that can be applied here. In other words, all editing of the *guru*'s works should be done *in good faith* and *with due competence.* Let me comment further on the two phrases highlighted in the previous sentence.

(a) "in good faith": in her book, *Roman Faith and Christian Faith,* Teresa Morgan points out that *trust* is a virtue "foundational to every society."[45] "Throughout Graeco-Roman literature," she writes, "tyranny is the opposite of a relationship of love or friendship and trust, and it is a topos of Greek and

Latin literature that tyrants neither love nor trust anyone, nor does anyone love or trust them."[46]

I suppose the Sanskrit term I have in mind for "trust" and its cohort of connotations here (to include the semantic scope of such *guṇa*s or qualities as fidelity, confidence, and steadfastness) is *śraddhā. Śraddhā,* in Hindu tradition, is a virtue acquired as a result of a certain discipline of attentiveness, ultimately to the voice of scripture and its authoritative interpreter, the *guru,* and then to the application of such attentiveness in a certain way of life. *Śraddhā* is always relational and, implicitly a social event. It is expressed as *manovākyakāyena,* that is, through thought, speech, and action, functioning as a single unit. For reasons already given, the editor cannot seek to improve substantively or radically on the teachings of the *guru.* To seek to do so would be a breach of trust—of *śraddhā* in the *guru* and of the *guru*'s trust, even posthumously, in the editor—for, post-mortem, the *guru* is in a way trustfully dependent on the editing disciple to respect the authenticity of the *guru*'s teachings. It is with a sense of humility and of being "entrusted" for the task, then, that the editor must hope to serve the *guru*—by assisting the *guru* to unveil, post-mortem, the face of truth. This is what I mean when I say that the editor must act "in good faith" in revising, according to the template mentioned earlier, the *guru*'s work.

But (ii) such faith must be accompanied by "due competence." "Due competence" embraces a number of considerations: familiarity with the *guru*'s *oeuvre,* familiarity with the various sources and relevant intellectual tools and aids the *guru* has had recourse to, awareness of any intentionality expressed by the *guru,* the linguistic and other apparatus of translation with regard to both host and target languages used, and, finally, perhaps most important, recourse to editorial collegiality. By the last, I mean that one cannot "go it alone" in the editing of the *guru*'s work. The entrustment of which I speak in the previous paragraph requires an editorship that is conscious of acting on behalf of the whole community of believers, to whom the fruit of the editorial labor will be released. Through the work of editing, the *guru* continues to speak to discipleship, actual and potential, and to both the individual and the community. Thus, such editing is a solemn responsibility that cannot be discharged lightly; it is best accomplished by *the scholarly collegiality of a team of editors,* acting in concert. How many in this team? In analogous circumstances, to ascertain an important point of *dharma* (we could say in our case that this applies to the *dharma* of the *guru*'s teaching and the *dharma* of its editing), the lawgiver Manu recommends, ideally, what appears to be a fairly large number—each with varying editorial skills—acting as a team. I quote Bimal Matilal here:

> In the case of dispute over *dharma,* where it is not easy to decide which course of action should be followed. . . . Manu suggested [in Chapter 12, verse 110 of

> the *Manu Smṛti*] . . . "An assembly of not less than ten persons, or (if ten are not available) not less than three persons, should deliberate and reach a decision on *dharma,* and that *dharma* (thus arrived at) should not be transgressed."[47]

However, as the quotation shows, the maximum number suggested can be whittled down, depending on circumstance and availability. I would recommend a team, optimally of four or five suitably qualified experts.[48] This would give authority to their joint decisions. "In good faith" combined with "due competence," would imply exercising the *devolved responsibility* of editorship, in participation with the authority of the *guru,* discussed earlier in this essay.

Shaping the intentionality of such editing should take into account the *guru*'s spiritual lineage (*paramparā*) and denominational allegiance (*sampradāya*). It is not enough to focus on the spiritual preceptor alone, which, in fact, is often done. In Swami Prabhupāda's case, his *sampradāya* was of Vaishnava derivation, while in the case of his *paramparā,* his two previous predecessors were Bhaktisiddhānta Sarasvatī Gosvāmī Mahārāja Prabhupāda and Gaurakiśora dāsa Bābājī Mahārāja, respectively.[49] Both these sages would have contributed directly to shaping his religious terminology and vision.

At this point, the question of "bricolage"—the coherent, if improvised, assemblage of the spiritual preceptor's *oeuvre*—comes into play. The *guru*'s legacy may derive from various types of output: written, spoken, sung, published, unpublished, and so on. How is all this to be presented and transmitted, not least after the *guru*'s demise, to the world? Is this to be done piecemeal, or, with bricolage in mind, in some ordered manner? If the latter, what kind of coherence should be sought in collating the *guru*'s work? The ordered coherence that the editor strives to achieve may well be deliberately unstable, viz. alterable to accommodate new forms of ensemble-coherence if/when new items for inclusion are discovered or fresh visions of the ensemble itself are adopted.[50] Bricolage properly effected can minimize inconsistency and can give an overall intelligibility or direction to the *oeuvre* as a whole. For this, the editors need approved guidelines, one for editing the various kinds of works involved and one for editing the *collection* of works available. These guidelines may be encapsulated, respectively, in two *Memoranda of Understanding* formulated by the editorial team in consultation with the leadership of the *guru*'s followers. In this way, the *Memoranda* becomes the property of the whole community of discipleship.

Finally, is the ensemble of works to be available by way of a combination of different media: print, discs of various kinds, film in one form or another, digitally?—in which case, other considerations come into play: the availability of funds, the ongoing availability of suitably qualified editors, and centralized—or otherwise—methods of production and dissemination. But I cannot expatiate on this here. This would take us too far afield. Nevertheless, it should have become clear by now that editing the spiritual preceptor's works posthumously is no light or easy task. It is a responsibility fraught with caveats and admonition, but a task that is often necessary, and so, worth the accomplishment.

NOTES

1. The diacritical on the penultimate "a" only of "Prabhupāda" has become the conventional way of writing A.C. Bhaktivedanta Swami Prabhupāda's name within the ISKCON movement. This essay is a revised version of the keynote address given at the symposium convened by Professor Graham Schweig on the subject of this essay, and hosted by the Mira and Ajay Singhal Center for Dharma Studies and its Director, Professor Rita Sherma, under the auspices of the Graduate Theological Union, at Berkeley, CA. I am grateful to our hosts and to the other participants of the symposium for their helpful comments and discussions.

2. This resulted in the publication of my *The Writings of Brahmabandhab Upadhyay,* Vols. I & II, The United Theological College, Bangalore, 1991, 2002; and *Brahmabandhab Upadhyay: The Life and Thought of a Revolutionary,* Oxford University Press, Delhi, 1999.

3. Eventually published as *A Living Theology of Krishna Bhakti: Essential Teachings of A.C. Bhaktivedanta Swami Prabhupāda,* edited with Introduction and Conclusion by Graham M. Schweig, Oxford University Press, New York, 2012. Schweig's work was invaluable in bringing Goswami's thesis to completion, and in publishing it as a book. For my part in this process, see Schweig's description on pp. 16–17.

4. "Gender-inclusive" tends to carry the implication of privileging a particular gender, viz. the gender that is deemed to "include" other genders, whereas "gender-neutral" does not.

5. Note the general nature of this question.

6. Email of March 6, 2019.

7. "At the simplest level, we can say that a revising writer has three choices: a) to add material, so the final version is longer than the first draft, b) to delete, so it is shorter, and c) to substitute, producing a first and final draft of similar length." Sullivan, Hannah. *The Work of Revision,* Harvard University Press, Cambridge, MA and London, 2013, p. 15.

8. Ibid., p. 15.

9. See Sullivan's account in Chapter 3 of her work mentioned. Eliot, T.S. *Burnt Norton.* See *T. S. Eliot: The Complete Poems and Plays*, Faber and Faber, London and Boston, 1969.

10. Roy, Basanta Koomar. *Bankim Chandra Chatterji: Anandamath, Translated and Adapted from Original Bengali,* Vision Books, New Delhi and Bombay, 1992.

11. As distinguished from India's National Anthem.

12. Roy's work was initially published in 1941 by The Devin-Adair Company (New York) as *Dawn over India by Bankim Chandra Chatterji,* under which we have, "Translated and Adapted from Bengali by Basanta Koomar Roy, Author of 'Rabindranath Tagore'". In 1992, it was published by Vision Books, New Delhi and Bombay, under the title, *Bankim Chandra Chatterji.*

13. Taken from my translation of *Ānandamaṭh,* with an extensive Introduction and Critical Apparatus; cf. 2005: 120–22, where I add Aurobindo Ghose's translation into English of the same passage, for greater comparative effect.

14. Indian soldiers in the British army in colonial times.

15. Reference to Muslim sepoys reflects the fact that the rulers of the Bengal area during the time in which the novel is set (the late eighteenth century) were Muslims. These rulers naturally tended to employ a large proportion of Muslim soldiers in their armies. Chatterji, Bankimcandra. *Ānandamaṭh,* or *The Sacred Brotherhood,* translated with an Introduction and Critical Apparatus by Julius Lipner, Oxford University Press, New York, 2005, pp. 147–48.

16. Roy, *Bankim Chandra Chatterji,* p. 41.

17. Chatterji, *Ānandamaṭh,* p. 122.

18. Richman, Paula (ed.). *Many Rāmāyaṇas: The Diversity of a Narrative Tradition in South India,* University of California Press, Berkeley, Los Angeles, and Oxford, 1991, p. 4.

19. Sullivan, Hannah. *The Work of Revision,* Harvard University Press, Cambridge, MA and London, 2013, p. 46.

20. Haffenden, John (ed.). *Novelists in Interview,* Methuen, London and New York, 1985, p. 109.

21. Haffenden (ed.) 1985: 102.

22. Sullivan, *The Work of Revision,* p. 50.

23. The concept of the "completion" of a work is itself contentious, and will be taken up later.

24. See Sullivan, *The Work of Revision,* p. 50.

25. *Ye nādriyante gurum arcanīyaṃ, pāpāl lokāṃs te vrajanty apratiṣṭhān.* Poona edition, 1.71.51b. Unless stated to the contrary, all translations from the Sanskrit in this essay are by the author.

26. One could include the "critical edition" in this company.

27. See also *Bṛhadāraṇyaka Upaniṣad* 5.15.1.

28. Quoted in Sullivan, *The Work of Revision,* p. 29.

29. Dillard, Annie. *Pilgrim at Tinker Creek,* Picador edition, London, 1976, pp. 77–81.

30. Swami Prabhupāda was partial to a liberal use of the term "rascal" to describe those with whom he did not agree.

31. Ratzinger, Joseph. *Jesus of Nazareth,* Bloomsbury, London, New York, and Berlin, 2007, pp. xviii–xix.

32. Ibid., p. xix.

33. For an account of what "critical text" (or edition) might mean, see Frazier, Jessica. *The Continuum Companion to Hindu Studies,* Continuum, London and New York, 2011, pp. 203–5.

34. See Professor Stefan Wild's lecture, "The Qur'an Today: Why Translate the Untranslatable?" in https://bible-quran.com/stefan-wild-why-translate-the-untranslatable, (2018?).

35. In his book *The Footnote: A Curious History,* Anthony Grafton notes, "Michael Fishbane has shown . . . how scribes and authors alike worked veins of commentary directly into the text of the Hebrew Bible. Brief glosses on unusual words and phrases became organic parts of the texts they clarified." Cf. Fishbane, Michael. *Biblical Interpretation in Ancient Israel,* The Clarendon Press, Oxford, 1985.

36. Professor Wild in his lecture mentioned earlier, makes the point that in contrast to the unique linguistic elegance of the Qur'ān, recitation of which is an important reason for resisting its translation, the language of the Christian Bible is on the whole rather pedestrian, as if this feature functioned to invite translation into other tongues.

37. Both are often found in the company of such fellow-travelers as the Preface, Foreword, Appendix, Postscript, and so on.

38. Grafton, Anthony. *The Footnote: A Curious History,* Faber and Faber, London, 1997, pp. 22–23.

39. Much of this work can be done with an appropriate Introduction.

40. For an account of how commentary can illuminate the understanding of text, see David Buchta's contribution in this book.

41. Sullivan, *The Work of Revision*, p. 2. Continuous revision is not confined to "high modernism." Leonardo da Vinci (1452–1519) continually re-touched the Mona Lisa, so much so that the painting was never handed over to the nobleman who commissioned it.

42. I use "descended" here to contrast with "uploaded" with respect to recording digital text.

43. "*Guru*" is now a familiar term in English. As noted earlier, I am not using "*guru*" (the feminine of which is *gurvī*) pedantically, to refer only to a male individual, but in a gender-neutral sense.

44. In Swami Prabhupāda's case, there has been debate over his intention in this respect. See Urmila Devi dasi's essay in this book. In an email to me dated March 28, 2020, she says, "Srila Prabhupāda never explicitly expressed anything about posthumous editing of his books. Anything we infer is from extrapolation."

45. Morgan, Teresa. *Roman Faith and Christian Faith: Pistis and Fides in the Early Roman Empire and Early Churches,* Oxford University Press, Oxford, 2015, p. 502.

46. Ibid., p. 452.

47. Matilal, Bimal K. "*Dharma* and Rationality," in Jonardon Ganeri, ed., *The Collected Essays of Bimal Krishna Matilal: Ethics and Epics*, Oxford University Press, New Delhi, 2002, 2: 49–71.

48. In ISKCON, I understand that the responsibility of editing Swami Prabhupāda's works rests on members of the Bhaktivedanta Book Trust, who seem to have a semi-autonomous status in these matters. Obviously, it is incumbent on all segments of ISKCON concerned to act as one in editing the *guru*'s work posthumously.

49. Cf. Prabhupāda, A.C. Bhaktivedanta Swami. *Bhagavad-Gītā As It Is,* Abridged edition, Bhaktivedanta Book Trust, New York, Los Angeles, London, and Bombay, 1972, p. xxxvii.

50. "In the case of bricolage . . . there are several solutions to the same problem. The choice of one solution involves a modification of the result to which another solution would have led, and the observer is in effect presented with the general picture of these permutations at the same time as the particular solution offered. He is thereby transformed into an active participant without even being aware of it. Merely by contemplating it, he is, as it were, put in possession of other possible forms of the same work." Lévi-Strauss, Claude. *The Savage Mind,* Weidenfeld and Nicholson, London, 1966, p. 24.

REFERENCES

Chatterji, Bankimcandra. 2005. *Ānandamaṭh,* or *The Sacred Brotherhood.* Translated with an Introduction and Critical Apparatus by Julius Lipner, Oxford University Press, New York.

Dillard, Annie. 1976. *Pilgrim at Tinker Creek,* Picador edition, London.

Eliot, T.S. 1969. *Burnt Norton.* See *T. S. Eliot: The Complete Poems and Plays,* Faber and Faber, London and Boston.

Fishbane, Michael. 1985. *Biblical Interpretation in Ancient Israel,* The Clarendon Press, Oxford.

Frazier, Jessica. 2011. *The Continuum Companion to Hindu Studies,* Continuum, London and New York.

Grafton, Anthony. 1997. *The Footnote: A Curious History,* Faber and Faber, London.

Haffenden, John (ed.). 1985. *Novelists in Interview,* Methuen, London and New York.

Lévi-Strauss, Claude. 1966. *The Savage Mind,* Weidenfeld and Nicholson, London.

Lipner, Julius. 1991. 2002. *The Writings of Brahmabandhab Upadhyay,* Vols. I & II, The United Theological College, Bangalore.

Lipner, Julius. 1999. *Brahmabandhab Upadhyay: The Life and Thought of a Revolutionary,* Oxford University Press, Delhi.

Lipner, Julius. 2005. *see under* Chatterji, Bankimcandra.

Mahābhārata, Ādiparvan, critically edited by V.S. Sukthankar et al., Bhandarkar Oriental Research Institute, Poona, 1933.

Matilal, Bimal K. 2002. "*Dharma* and Rationality," in Jonardon Ganeri, ed., *The Collected Essays of Bimal Krishna Matilal: Ethics and Epics,* 2: 49–71, Oxford University Press, New Delhi.

Morgan, Teresa. 2015. *Roman Faith and Christian Faith: Pistis and Fides in the Early Roman Empire and Early Churches,* Oxford University Press, Oxford.

Prabhupāda, A.C. Bhaktivedanta Swami. 1972. *Bhagavad-Gītā As It Is,* Abridged edition, Bhaktivedanta Book Trust, New York, Los Angeles, London, and Bombay.

Ratzinger, Joseph. 2007. *Jesus of Nazareth,* Bloomsbury, London, New York, and Berlin.

Richman, Paula (ed.). 1991. *Many Rāmāyaṇas: The Diversity of a Narrative Tradition in South India,* University of California Press, Berkeley, Los Angeles, and Oxford.

Roy, Basanta Koomar. 1992. *Bankim Chandra Chatterji: Anandamath, Translated and Adapted from Original Bengali,* Vision Books, New Delhi and Bombay.

Schweig, Graham M. 2012. *A Living Theology of Krishna Bhakti: Essential Teachings of A.C. Bhaktivedanta Swami Prabhupāda,* Oxford University Press, New York.

Sullivan, Hannah. 2013. *The Work of Revision,* Harvard University Press, Cambridge, MA and London.

Wild, Stefan. 2018. "The Qur'an Today: Why Translate the Untranslatable?," Lecture, cf. https://bible-quran.com/stefan-wild-why-translate-the-untranslatable.

Chapter 2

The Posthumous Editing of the Books of A. C. Bhaktivedanta Swami Prabhupāda

Edith Best (Urmilā-Devī Dāsī)

INSTRUCTIONS OF THE AUTHOR

When an author self-publishes, or publishes books with his own publishing house, that author has the final say over editing, proofreading, layout, binding, illustrations, and so on. It seems obvious that what is done with an author's published books after the passing away of that author should also follow the author's direct instructions.[1]

However, we find the following in "Responsible Publishing" of the Bhaktivedanta Book Trust (Śrīla Prabhupāda's own publishing house, henceforth called the BBT), written specifically to address posthumous editing concerns:

> Did Śrīla Prabhupāda want his books edited? Yes, he did. And are the BBT editors who continue to correct errors in Śrīla Prabhupāda's books acting under Śrīla Prabhupāda's instructions? Yes, they are.[2]

However, they only provide evidence for Śrīla Prabhupāda's desire for editing done in his personal presence. They provide not one piece of evidence that those who "continue" to edit are acting under instructions to do so. There is simply an unstated assumption that there is no difference between editing in the author's presence and editing after that author passes away.

This lack of evidence is due in part to the fact that there is no direct and explicit instruction from Śrīla Prabhupāda regarding posthumous editing of his books. His last instructions about editing took place in June of 1977, and he passed away in November of that year. ISKCON leaders did speak with Śrīla Prabhupāda in 1977 about how initiations of disciples would continue after his passing and how the translation of Srimad *Bhāgavatam* would be completed.

But we have no record of anyone who broached the topic of whether, in what ways, and to what extent the next printing of his books should be edited when Śrīla Prabhupāda passed away. It seemed that it had become difficult even to discuss editing with Śrīla Prabhupāda after the June conversation:

> I don't think any of us want His Divine Grace to be burdened like this again.
> In any case His Divine Grace has not thought about this editing matter since the day of that conversation which was nearly a month ago.
> Please just try to make all the corrections in the new editions and everything will be alright, and of course don't make any unnecessary changes.[3]

On the same day, however, Tamal Kṛṣṇa Goswami wrote to Rāmeśvara on the same topic:

> I explained the contents of your letter, and Satsvarūpa's and Rādhāvallabha and he [Śrīla Prabhupāda] seemed satisfied that things were not being unauthorizedly changed, while at the same time whatever corrections needed to be done were being made.

The BBT goes beyond equating Śrīla Prabhupāda's desires for editing in his presence with posthumous editing. For example, in *Responsible Publishing* the BBT seems to rest the authority for posthumous editing outside of Śrīla Prabhupāda, as in the following statement: "Were his [Jayādvaita Swami's posthumous] corrections justified? Let's look at some of the words of Śrīla Prabhupāda's that Jayādvaita Swami restored, and you decide."[4]

The BBT thus declares that the justification for each edited change is for some undefined "you" to decide, rather than for the author of the book to decide. Indeed, some editorial decisions are based on input from various individuals.[5]

In the absence of any clear and explicit instructions for what Śrīla Prabhupāda wanted regarding posthumous editing, let us look at evidence from him in relation to each of five possibilities.

Option 1: Evidence for Śrīla Prabhupāda's Desire: No Change of Any Kind

The following was in reference to re-printing a book attributed to Śrīla Prabhupāda's own late spiritual master: a translation of, and commentary upon, the ancient scripture Brahma Samhita:

Prabhupāda: The system is: what ever authority has done, even there is mistake,[6] it should be accepted.

Radha-vallabha: Oh.

Prabhupāda: *Arsha prayoga* [*Arsha-prayoga* is a Sanskrit word meaning complete acceptance of what is left by the authorities, as it is, without any change at all] That is ha. . . . He should not become more learned than the authority. That is very bad habit. . . . Why finish it? Whatever is done is done. No more. . . .

Radha-vallabha: Well, now that this system of no corrections anywhere, that makes it very simple. Then he can't do anything. I don't think he wants to, either. It makes it more simple for him. It makes him very uncomfortable.

Prabhupāda: No corrections.[7]

Option 2: Evidence for Śrīla Prabhupāda's Desire: Proofreading but Not Editing

These excerpts from two letters provide evidence for this option. The first:

> We have to do things now very dexterously, simply we have to see that in our book there is no spelling or grammatical mistake. We do not mind for any good style, our style is Hare Kṛṣṇa, but, still, we should not present a shabby thing. Although Kṛṣṇa literatures are so nice that, even if they are presented in broken and irregular ways, such literatures are welcomed, read and respected by bona fide devotees.[8]

And: "Our editing is to correct grammatical and spelling errors only, without interpolation of style or philosophy."[9]

Option 3: Evidence for Śrīla Prabhupāda's Desire: Proofreading, Not Editing, and Corrections Prabhupāda Specifically Indicated

While reading his printed books or teaching from them, Śrīla Prabhupāda sometimes pointed out items that he wanted corrected in future editions, such as: "Cow protection. It has to be corrected. It is go-rakṣya, go. They take it cattle-raising. I think Hayagrīva has translated like this."[10] Śrīla Prabhupāda might have asked for a correction on one occasion and seemingly accepted the same section on other occasions. For example, regarding "The Blessed Lord Said," sometimes he commented that he did not like that translation of *śrī-bhagavān uvāca*, and other times he commented on its appropriateness.

There were also instances, such as those recorded in Hari Sauri's Transcendental Diary, Chapter Five, where disciples pointed out something confusing or inconsistent, and Śrīla Prabhupāda agreed to a change for the next printing.

Option 4: Evidence for Śrīla Prabhupāda's Desire: Proofreading, Explicitly Requested Corrections, and Attempt to Undo Earlier Edits That Appear to Deviate from Śrīla Prabhupāda's Intended Meaning

As we examine later in this paper, it is option four that the BBT promotes as describing their posthumous editing. Supporting evidence for this option is found in Śrīla Prabhupāda's conversation on June 22, 1977, in Vrindavana, India, when he brings up one Sanskrit translation mistake in his books. This conversation occurred at a time when Śrīla Prabhupāda's departure from this world was likely, though not certain. Disciples who were in the room discussed other problems editors had introduced where the meaning was changed. Śrīla Prabhupāda used the term "rascal editors" and said, "The next printing should be again to the original way." Some have interpreted this instruction to apply only to the specific Sanskrit mistake that started the conversation, in which case this conversation is evidence for option three. Others have interpreted it much more broadly as evidence for option four. Considering the timing of this conversation, such a broad interpretation might indicate Śrīla Prabhupāda's desire for posthumous editing also.

In 1972, Śrīla Prabhupāda had noticed a place where the first line of the Devanāgarī script was placed last and the last line placed first, a middle line of Devanāgarī script missing, and many, many English errors also, which were "very obvious." According to Pradyumna, Śrīla Prabhupāda said,

> One mistake will spoil or murder the whole book. . . . What's done has been done, but now we should try to do two things: make sure that errors like these won't occur again, and start a listing of past mistakes in each book so that we can correct them when they are reprinted.[11]

Option 5: Evidence for Śrīla Prabhupāda's Desire: Proofreading, Explicitly Requested Corrections, Attempted Undoing of Earlier Editing Errors, and Full Content Editing in a Wide Range of Areas

BBT editors quote Pradyumna's letter from 1972, as referenced for option four, as evidence for option five, using the broadest definition of "mistake." Additionally, the BBT references the following quote as support for the comprehensive posthumous editing that has been done:

> Concerning the editing of Jayādvaita Prabhu, whatever he does is approved by me. I have confidence in him.[12]

In assessing how to practically understand the above, we do well to keep the following in mind. This correspondence relates to a conversation where Śrīla Prabhupāda was heavily criticizing some editorial mistakes he found:

> as long as the editors edit everything perfectly they are "authorized" and when they make mistakes, whatever the reason is then they become "unauthorized." When you do everything nicely you are praised and when some mistake is there, you are a "rascal." This is true for all of us.[13]

Note about Defining *Proofreading* in Regard to Spelling, Grammar, Punctuation, and Usage

Usually, errors in spelling, grammar, and citations are unambiguously objective as to both the fact that there is an unintended error and the fix required. Sometimes, even in these three categories, there is uncertainty about what meaning was intended. For example, in the *Bhagavad-gītā* 1972 edition, 12.11, we find: "There are many descriptions of sacrifices and special functions of the pumundi or special work in which the result of one's previous action may be applied." While the word *pumundi* is clearly a misspelling of something, it took a lot of detective work on the part of Brahma Muhūrta Dāsa of the BBT to discover the intended phrase.

There are some instances of punctuation or usage where changes are in the realm of proofreading and are related to rules of grammar. However, because punctuation and usage changes can alter meaning, sometimes such changes are in the realm of content editing. An example is a case where Jayādvaita Swami changed "eye-to-eye" to "face-to-face."[14] His reasoning is that "eye-to-eye" has an idiomatic meaning of being in agreement rather than looking someone in the eye.

Nature of the Posthumous Editing

After considering five possible options for what posthumous editing Śrīla Prabhupāda might have wanted for his books, we turn to an examination of what BBT editors have done in option five.

BBT Posthumous Edits: Categories

There are no existing written BBT guidelines or principles for their posthumous editing. Therefore, the following categories come from conversations over the years with members of the BBT, explanations on the BBT website for various edits, along with analyzing editing not explained on their website:

- Copy editing or proofreading
  - English spelling, grammar, and punctuation
  - Inaccurate citations
  - Sanskrit that is not in scholarly form
- Fixing specific items Śrīla Prabhupāda requested to fix
- Attempting to improve Sanskrit translations
- Carrying out stylistic changes to more accurately communicate Śrīla Prabhupāda's intended meaning as the editors understand it
- Carrying out stylistic changes to improve English composition and usage (changes that are not addressing technical errors)
- Attempting to identify and reverse previous editorial mistakes by referencing earlier drafts, *ācāryas*' commentaries, statements Śrīla Prabhupāda makes in other places, and so on.
- Creating consistency between
  - Word-for-word and translation
  - Translation and purport
  - Language used in various places
  - Similar philosophical points made in various places
  - Śrīla Prabhupāda's purports and the *ācāryas*' commentaries
  - Versions of narratives about historical and sastric personalities

Sometimes edits are done to adjust inconsistencies, and other times inconsistencies are left as they are.

MOTTOS AND MISUNDERSTANDING

For many years after Śrīla Prabhupāda's passing away, there was little or no communication from the BBT about the rationale for, or nature of, the posthumous editing. As already mentioned, there exists no published (or unpublished) list of principles or guidelines for posthumous editing. While on the BBT website there are some quotes from Śrīla Prabhupāda about editing, there is not any comprehensive and analyzed research into Śrīla Prabhupāda's instructions that are, or reasonably could be, applicable to posthumous editing.

In at least one instance where the BBT sent out an email newsletter soliciting feedback, no one monitored the return email address provided.[15] In BBT correspondence with ISKCON members who submitted reservations about editing, there is often a minimization or denigration of their concerns. BBT materials question the character or loyalty of those with concerns about posthumous editing.[16]

After some time, the BBT adopted the motto of "Closer to Prabhupāda" to communicate the rationale for, and nature of, the posthumous edits. This quote from the BBT materials explains the meaning:

> After Śrīla Prabhupāda left [meaning: passed away], Jayādvaita Swami simply continued his prescribed duty finding and correcting errors, guarding against needless changes, and making sure that Śrīla Prabhupāda's books came as close as possible to Śrīla Prabhupāda's intended meaning and Śrīla Prabhupāda's original words.[17]

If this motto is understood in the sense of basing changes on Śrīla Prabhupāda's original unedited words, such a claim is difficult. First of all, most authors have the intent of editors improving upon their original words, at least in some instances. Therefore, a return to a pre-edited edition would defy both common publishing practices as well as Śrīla Prabhupāda's choice to employ editors.

Secondly, even if it is reasonable to return a published book to its manuscript state, in the case of Śrīla Prabhupāda's books—with the exception of the first canto of the Srimad *Bhāgavatam*, some *Bhagavad-gītā* chapters, and much of the Kṛṣṇa Book—such is literally impossible. Most of his books came from transcripts of dictations. Except for most chapters of the Kṛṣṇa Book, those dictation recordings were not preserved. The BBT readily admits that most of the transcriptions have errors from mishearing recordings,[18] and for large sections of books,[19] there are no existent transcriptions at all. Considering this situation, no one can consult a first draft in order to presumably go "closer to Prabhupāda." Rather, a tremendous amount of detective work, extrapolation, and educated guesswork is involved to approximate Śrīla Prabhupāda's original words.[20] Such investigation yields a result that particular editors feel is closer to what Śrīla Prabhupāda might have said or intended.

It should also be noted that, while BBT urges the general readers ("you") to decide on the validity of posthumous edits,[21] in most cases the public does not have access to "original" materials in terms of transcripts and so forth. Requests for such materials are denied.[22]

In any case, even a few hours spent going over the edits detailed on the BBT site make it obvious that the majority is not about getting "closer to Prabhupāda" in the sense of his original words nor in relation to his "intended meaning."

SOME POSTHUMOUS EDITING EXAMPLES

We can look at just a few representative examples of posthumous edits from *Bhagavad-gītā* Chapter 10. In the word-for-word to text 16, both the 72 edition and the manuscript read: "Yourself." The posthumous editing changed that word to the phrase "your own opulences" as a more accurate translation of the Sanskrit. In the purport to text 16, "as" is changed to "to be" because the latter is "idiomatically more clear," although "as" was in the manuscript. A correction to the purport to text 18 is interesting. The 72 *Bhagavad-gītā* has "Vedic hymns." The manuscript and Prabhupāda's *Bhagavad-gītā* from India had "good prayers" instead of "Vedic hymns." The posthumous editing has "excellent prayers." Here we see somewhat of a return to the manuscript, along with some idea of "improvement" by the editors.

A particularly interesting example of the fact that posthumous edits are often not guided by getting "closer to Prabhupāda" is *Bhagavad-gītā* Chapter 12 Text 12 purport. Jayādvaita had written to Prabhupāda regarding the sequence of items in verse 12.12, translation that to him "seemed inconsistent with the Sanskrit."[23] We may note that the sequence is also inconsistent with the *ācāryas*' commentaries. Śrīla Prabhupāda responded in a letter on March 17, 1971, "the order of supercession [*sic*] of these various indirect processes for approaching the Absolute Truth is not as much important as fixed understanding of the exalted position of devotional service rendered directly to Kṛṣṇa." He concluded: "So far changing the wording of verse or purport of 12:12 discussed before, it may remain as it is."

Jayādvaita followed Śrīla Prabhupāda's instruction in 1971 and did not make any changes to the verse or purport of *Bhagavad-gītā* 12.12. After Prabhupāda's passing, Jayādvaita Swami made a total of six changes in wording and four changes in punctuation to that two-paragraph purport. Because the changes were different from what he had asked Śrīla Prabhupāda about, his opinion was that he could make those changes.[24] The editing for that purport is not explained on the BBT editing site.

One interesting example of a philosophical change is in *Śrī Caitanya-caritāmṛta*, Madhya Līlā, 20.117, as follows:

> The transcript of Prabhupāda's dictation: "While staying in the marginal position he [the *jīva*] is sometimes attracted by the external, illusory energy, and that is the beginning of his material life."
>
> The 1975 edition: "He is sometimes attracted by the external illusory energy when he stays in the marginal position, and this is the beginning of his material life."
>
> The posthumously edited edition reads: "Being in the marginal position, he is sometimes attracted by the external, illusory energy, and this is the beginning of his material life."

Draviḍa Dāsa wrote Ramesvara in 2013:

> yes, such philosophical clarification is now part of the editorial decision making. But such clarification has always been part of the editorial decision-making. If for some reason the intended philosophical point Śrīla Prabhupāda is trying to make isn't clear, the editors make changes to clarify.

Perhaps no posthumous "clarification" was warranted, as we find this lecture substantiates the original text:

> marginal potency. . . . Just you go on the coast of the Pacific beach. . . . Sometimes it is covered by water and sometimes it is open land. This is marginal. Similarly, we spirit souls, although we are constitutionally one with God, but sometimes we are covered by māyā and sometimes we are free. . . . So we have to maintain that free state. . . . If you come little far away from the sea water, then there is no more water; it is all land. Similarly, if you keep yourself from the material consciousness, come to the land of spiritual consciousness, or Kṛṣṇa consciousness, then you keep your freedom. But *if you keep yourself on the marginal position, then sometimes you'll be covered by māyā and sometimes you'll be free.*[25]

This is from *Bhagavad-gītā* 2.13 purport, last sentence. We have Śrīla Prabhupāda's original writing that was done in India, so we know what his original words were. There is no explanation on the BBT website:

> Manuscript: "Under the circumstances it is admitted that Lord Kṛṣṇa is the Supreme Lord superior in position to the living entity Arjuna who is apt to be a forgotten soul under the illusion of māyā."
>
> The 72 edition: "Under the circumstances, it is admitted that Lord Kṛṣṇa is the Supreme Lord, superior in position to the living entity, Arjuna, who is a forgotten soul deluded by māyā."
>
> The posthumous edition: "Under the circumstances, it is admitted that Lord Kṛṣṇa is the Supreme Lord, superior in position to the living entity, Arjuna, who is a forgetful soul deluded by māyā."

The following is another example where the change in meaning is significant. The BBT explanation for it is grounded in correcting a previous editorial mistake.[26] I include it here as an example of the complexities of posthumous editing being done without the research to find out Śrīla Prabhupāda's own desire and thus to base all changes on that desire. From the purport of *Caitanya-Caritāmṛta*, Madhya Līlā 7.130:

> Manuscript (transcription): One should not try to become artificially advanced devotee. [unreadable word due to editorial mark-up] is best to accept any disciples. These things are not necessary.
>
> 1975 and 1996 editions: One should not try to be an artificially advanced devotee, thinking, "I am a first-class devotee." Such thinking should be avoided. It is best not to accept any disciples.
>
> 2013 edition: One should not try to be an artificially advanced devotee, thinking "I am a first-class devotee, so it is best not to accept any disciples." Such thinking should be avoided.

For context, in all the three editions, after the above, is the following (I do not have the manuscript for this):

> One has to become purified at home by chanting the Hare Kṛṣṇa mahā-mantra and preaching the principles enunciated by Śrī Caitanya Mahāprabhu. Thus one can become a spiritual master and be freed from the contamination of material life.

The BBT made the change because Bhakti Vikas Swami wrote to Draviḍa Dāsa in 2007, saying that this section of the purport was quoting directly from the commentary of Bhaktisiddhānta Sarasvatī Ṭhākura (no attribution is noted in the purport) and had been mistranslated. At least one Bengali expert agrees that the change accurately reflects what Bhaktisiddhānta intended.[27]

Examples Where Posthumous Editing Was Not Done

This example demonstrates that the BBT did not consistently edit for consistency.

David Buchta found this error in the Bengali of Caitanya *Caritāmṛta* Madhya 17.53. He writes:[28]

> The problem is that the Bengali text of the CC, in every edition that I have seen including Gauḍīya Maṭha editions, all read *bhinna-prāya* instead of *bhilla-prāya.* Note that in Bengali script ভিন্ন (bhinna) and ভিল্ল (bhilla) look a bit similar and might be confused with a hasty glance. . . . Note [also] that the Bheels don't (at least typically) live in Jhārikhaṇḍa. . . .
>
> If that is fixed, then Prabhupāda's translation becomes incoherent, since it is translating a different word. And, of course, his purport also becomes incoherent (though one can trace some elements of the commentary to Bhaktisiddhānta's gloss, to a different effect).

In the above example, BBT editors decided to leave the error as it is. In addition, this purport is problematic in terms of modern sensibilities, specifically because of the error in the Bengali.

An example where the BBT has not corrected an error is in Kṛṣṇa Book, chapter 35, where they have not posthumously replaced "flowers" in the original edition with Śrīla Prabhupāda's clear audio dictation of "flower-like snow."[29]

Earlier in this paper, we mentioned that "eye-to-eye" was posthumously changed to "face-to-face" to avoid the idiomatic meaning of being in agreement. However, there are still two instances of "eye-to-eye"[30] where the idiomatic meaning is most likely not intended. There are another two instances where "eye-to-eye" and "face-to-face" are used as appositives of each other[31] that remain unchanged.

Regarding inconsistency between editing in *Bhagavad-gītā* and *Nectar of Devotion*, the former has been extensively posthumously edited; the latter only lightly. This is the case, although the last three sections of the *Nectar of Devotion* are very difficult to understand, in part due to Śrīla Prabhupāda's choice of English for translating esoteric terms.

Artwork

A brief mention about artwork is necessary. While the BBT claims that Śrīla Prabhupāda was often only superficially involved with text editing, there is universal agreement that he was intimately involved with the detail of the illustrations in his books. He also had a variety of artists illustrate each book. Yet, posthumously edited books often replace paintings with new ones, and in some cases,[32] have an entire book illustrated by only one artist who employs a style never used in Śrīla Prabhupāda's presence. The BBT does not offer any explanation of their replacement of artwork in terms of Śrīla Prabhupāda's desire or instructions.

Costs of the Posthumous Editing

Even if every posthumous edit is some sort of improvement, and even if the editors feel confident that Śrīla Prabhupāda would have approved of each edit if done in his physical presence, "*phalena paricīyate*: one's success or defeat in any activity is understood by its result."[33] In this section, we examine some negative results of the posthumous editing for members of ISKCON and those who read the books of Śrīla Prabhupāda.

Verse Translations

BBT editors have noted that most objections to posthumous editing involve the verse translations.[34] ISKCON members who memorize scripture are most likely to focus on verses. And, once a person memorizes a translation, it can be disconcerting to find a very different translation in the posthumous edition, sometimes with a different meaning. Conversely, were the BBT to return to the translations used in the original books, those who memorized the current translations may be disturbed. This situation is magnified by the many languages into which Śrīla Prabhupāda's books have been translated.

Doubts about the Authenticity of Śrīla Prabhupāda's Books

The BBT asserts in the introduction to the 1983 *Bhagavad-gītā* that their comprehensive posthumous edit is "a work of even greater richness and authenticity,"[35] than the edition Śrīla Prabhupāda produced. Further, on the BBT website, it states:

> I appeal to all intelligent and sincere devotees to trust, support, and relish the latest BBT editions of Śrīla Prabhupāda's books, with all their valuable corrections and restorations. For those who still prefer the previous editions, I have this one word of caution: You're accepting a lot of "non-Prabhupāda" as Prabhupāda and missing a lot of what Śrīla Prabhupāda intended those books to say. Like many devotees, I treasure my Macmillan *Gītā*. It's redolent with the old blissful days of early ISKCON. Especially for anyone who grew up in devotional service reading it, the Macmillan *Gītā* is a priceless memento. I wouldn't trade mine for anything. But when I want to read what Prabhupāda actually said, I turn to the 1983 edition of *Bhagavad-gītā As It Is*.[36]

This mood of the BBT gains support from ISKCON leaders. For example, in support of posthumous editing, Saṅkarṣaṇa Dāsa, an ISKCON *dīkṣā-guru*, wrote publicly on Facebook[37] the 1972 *Gītā* is "an already proved flawed product."

The above assertions and rationale are astonishing in the light of Śrīla Prabhupāda's many statements about his books. In Śrīla Prabhupāda's recorded audio and correspondence, there are five hundred and two times he uses the term "my books." He exhorts his disciples to read his books in this typical example: "So I am requesting all of my students to read my books very seriously every day without fail."[38] He also wanted his books to be sold widely: "more than anything I want that my students should distribute my books and literatures profusely all over the world,"[39] and: "Please try to distribute my books in huge quantities more and more."[40]

Śrīla Prabhupāda strongly urged his disciples to translate his books in various languages. His desire and joy in having his books in many languages is evident in many places, such as: "you engage him full-time in translating my books, and he may train other Japanese-speaking boys also to translate and preach, then everything will be successful."[41] And: "It is so much important to me to have my books printed in all languages of the world."[42]

Yet, the BBT is informing us that the holy books, the scriptures, the sacred writings, the basis of ISKCON that members sold to millions of people, and read with great attention to every word, have "a lot of non-Prabhupāda" in them; in fact, they are not "what Prabhupāda actually said."

We hear that these problems with the original books were caused by editors. Yet, the posthumously revised editions rely on editors who must, obviously, work with zero direct input from Śrīla Prabhupāda. At best, their sources are transcripts, which the BBT editors say are flawed. We are left, therefore, with no edition we can fully trust. Every reader will logically question every sentence's authorship and authenticity in any edition. The implications regarding faith in Śrīla Prabhupāda's books are significant.

As predicted by Rāmeśvara:[43]

> Immature devotees cannot even be informed that editors are making changes—they will either doubt Prabhupāda's infallibility or else doubt the published books—and either way would cause a genuine crisis within ISKCON . . . what to speak of doubts instilled in devotees who hear rumors that the books are full of mistakes.

TRUST OF ISKCON MEMBERS MOVING FROM THE FOUNDER TO ISKCON LEADERS

One consequence of the posthumous editing is a moving of trust in Śrīla Prabhupāda to a trust in ISKCON leaders. The BBT is asking readers of its publications to trust something the original author is not here to approve and without explicit evidence of his prior approval. Such an appeal opens the door to all sorts of things ISKCON leaders might ask members and the public to trust over the words of its founder. Historically, it's not uncommon for the senior followers of a religion's founder to put on the robe of interpreter of the founder's words and intentions. Naturally, there are those who are not inclined to move their trust from Śrīla Prabhupāda to ISKCON leaders. As a result, factions have formed.

Questioning Śrīla Prabhupāda's Competency

Re-visiting *Bhagavad-gītā* 12.12 shows us a striking example of Śrīla Prabhupāda's attitude towards editing for consistency. In this verse, Lord Kṛṣṇa is explaining a hierarchy of processes for spiritual elevation. Previous *ācāryas*' commentary explains the rationale of this ranking. Yet, Śrīla Prabhupāda's translation seems to indicate a different ordering. When Jayādvaita pointed out the inconsistency, Śrīla Prabhupāda wrote back to express a lack of concern—as long as the reader understands bhakti as the supreme process, the order of inferior processes is unimportant. It would have been easy in 1971 for Śrīla Prabhupāda to have approved a change to achieve consistency. He was not rushing—he took the time to look over the verse, consider Jayādvaita's point, and write a reply. Regarding content editing other than dealing with consistency, Śrīla Prabhupāda did not want editing for "good style." Thus, it is reasonable to conclude that Śrīla Prabhupāda, overall, truly wanted his books as they were both stylistically and in terms of consistency, for his own reasons as the author.

Perhaps ironically, it is Śrīla Prabhupāda's attitude toward editing that is the BBT's stated rationale for broad posthumous editing. The BBT gives evidence that Śrīla Prabhupāda was not very concerned with editing in general or with supervising his editors.[44] His mood, they claim, caused many problems with the books—both problems with what Śrīla Prabhupāda dictated and with errors that editors introduced. After Śrīla Prabhupāda's passing, the BBT asserts, there was an opportunity to edit, as could have been done initially if the early editors had had more time and knowledge, and to undo editorial mistakes.

Their reasoning is that Śrīla Prabhupāda was putting out editions that he knew were deeply flawed just to do everything quickly.[45] Or he knew the books were flawed with serious mistakes but felt the situation was an emergency, that overall the books were good, and things could be fixed later.[46] Or that he unduly trusted the disciples who edited in his presence,[47] and so either didn't care or realize how flawed his books were, despite the fact that he read from them and lectured from them daily.[48]

But Śrīla Prabhupāda considered his books to be like spiritual medicine. He said: "If you simply read our books very carefully, then immediately this disease of heart palpitation, anxiety, will cease."[49]

If the BBT claims that Śrīla Prabhupāda knew his books were deeply flawed because the editors he trusted had introduced extensive errors, this claim indirectly accuses Śrīla Prabhupāda of deliberately misleading his followers and the millions who purchased his books. Analogously, the situation could be compared to knowingly selling tainted medicine. Or perhaps not informing patients of side effects.

And if, on the other hand, Śrīla Prabhupāda was not aware of the extensive problems with his books, such a view calls Śrīla Prabhupāda's competency as a spiritual leader and organizational manager into question. He made his books the basis of his entire society and mission. In such a situation, one would expect the author, founder, and leader to ensure that the books he gave such importance to were free of harmful errors that could mislead people. Analogously, the situation could be compared to selling tainted medicine because of a lack of care in the manufacturing process.

Any scenarios that describe the "original" books as less authentic or deeply flawed call Śrīla Prabhupāda's competency into question because of how he consistently categorized and promoted those books.[50] Such questioning cannot be avoided with the BBT's rationale for the kind and degree of their posthumous editing.

BBT Editing after the Current Editors' Deaths or Retirement

Jayādvaita Swami wrote guidelines in 2015, with examples, for "future editors" who lack "the benefit of having worked for many years under his [Śrīla

Prabhupāda's] personal supervision." All of the guidelines except one are objective and relate to minor fixes of obvious problems, such as spelling errors or incorrect citation references. Here is an excerpt from that paper:

> In principle, Śrīla Prabhupāda's books should be sealed. They should be left as is and never changed. In practice, we recognize that certain categories of revisions should be allowed. These should best be confined, however, to the correction of errors made by Śrīla Prabhupāda's editors, not to "transcendental errors" attributable to Śrīla Prabhupāda himself. Even more firmly, we admonish future editors not to "improve" Śrīla Prabhupāda's books by well-meaning additions, subtractions, or changes that merely guess at what the author "must have intended," "would have wanted," "would have approved of," or "would have done."
>
> Again: In principle, leave things alone.
>
> That said, the following list is meant to make plain the extent to which revisions should be allowed and the limits beyond which wise editors would best be advised not to go.
>
> We call upon future editors, when in doubt, to err on the side of leaving things as they are.

There is perhaps some puzzle in the fact that the BBT feels editing should be tightly constrained according to written guidelines after the retirement or passing of the current editors, but saw no need for any articulated constraints regarding editing after the passing of the author himself. And some puzzle in the current posthumous editing goal of "making sure that Śrīla Prabhupāda's books came as close as possible to Śrīla Prabhupāda's intended meaning"[51] as something that should not be done by future editors.

SUGGESTED SOLUTIONS

A pivotal meeting of some members of the BBT, facilitators, and concerned ISKCON scholars took place in Washington, DC, in September 2019. All members agreed to a solution to the controversy. The agreement reached in DC was to establish a scholarly board that would first research to find out Śrīla Prabhupāda's desires for his book editing. That research would have two parts—identifying records of what Śrīla Prabhupāda said and did directly related to the editing of his books, as well as identifying what he said and did that would indirectly relate to the book editing of scripture—his books and in the tradition in general. In addition, the scholarly board was to research academic standards on posthumous editing and any historical evidence in the Gauḍīya Vaiṣṇava tradition for how works of translation and scriptural commentary have been treated after an author's passing.

After the above comprehensive research is completed, the board will derive *principles* of posthumous editing of Śrīla Prabhupāda's books. Each principle would have generous backing from the research. Finally, the board would derive from the principles specific editing guidelines, with examples, for BBT editors to use. Theoretically, such editing could then result in book editions that would satisfy all but those with the most extreme views and once again unify ISKCON with Śrīla Prabhupāda's books as the basis. The one point that was left unaddressed in the DC agreement was how to determine the baseline version of a text for various books and portions of books.

However, the BBT in general discarded the entire conception of basing posthumous editing of Śrīla Prabhupāda's books on solid research into Śrīla Prabhupāda's desire for the editing of his books. They also discarded the step of extracting principles from that research. The BBT has convened a review panel but has only tasked them with the approval of guidelines.

Unfortunately, we are still left with the original problems, namely: Śrīla Prabhupāda's books should only be posthumously edited in ways that he clearly and explicitly wanted, the recognition that the books in the form they existed in Śrīla Prabhupāda's presence were "his" authentic books in every sense of the term, and that a resolution of this topic is essential for ISKCON harmony and clear direction.

If the BBT were to adopt the conclusions of the DC meeting, those problems would be addressed. Difficulties with the books that posthumous editing now seeks to address could instead be examined through the traditional method of commentaries and notes.

"We cannot change even one word in this Bhagavad-gītā. That is folly."[52]

NOTES

1. Clearly, a different standard exists for the posthumous finishing of incomplete and unpublished works. As the latter applies only to a very small amount of Śrīla Prabhupāda's works, we will not address that situation here.

2. p. 14.

3. Letter from Tamal Kṛṣṇa Maharaja to BBT editor Radhavallabha Dāsa, July 22, 1977.

4. p. 3.

5. The Great Soul can Import Knowledge Unto You: A BBT decision explained by Jayādvaita Swami, June 10, 2017, where the decision to revert to an earlier translation of *Bhagavad-gītā* 4.34 was sparked by a letter from Anuttama devi dasi (explained on page 3) and the example later in this paper of CC Madhya 7.130 sparked by a letter from Bhakti Vikas Swami.

6. This word "mistake" could be taken in the widest and most literal sense to include a spelling error, or in a broader sense to allow for changes to spelling but not to other areas that are incorrect usage of a term, for example.

7. February 28, 1977, Mayapur.

8. Letter to: Satsvarupa—Los Angeles, January 9, 1970, quoted in Responsible Publishing, p. 15.

9. Letter to Rupanuga Prabhu February 17, 1970.

10. Room Conversation with the Mayor of Evanston—July 4, 1975, Chicago.

11. http://www.bbtedit.com/node/260.

12. Letter to: Radhavallabha—Vrindaban September 7, 1976.

13. Tamal Krishna Goswami letter to Radhavallablha regarding Srila Prabhupāda's view of specific editors July 22, 1977.

14. Personal communication without a reference to the location of the change.

15. Personal correspondence with the BBT.

16. Such as: "I appeal to all intelligent and sincere devotees to trust, support, and relish the latest BBT editions of Śrīla Prabhupāda's books" Responsible Publishing, p. 13 (implying a lack of intelligence and/or sincerity of those who do not trust, support, and relish the posthumous edits).

17. Responsible Publishing, p. 19.

18. Responsible Publishing: "The transcript itself was flawed because the typists scrambled much of Śrīla Prabhupāda's Sanskrit dictation and misunderstood some of the English."

19. Such as Gita chapters 13–18.

20. http://www.bbtedit.com/.

21. Responsible Publishing, p. 3.

22. Correspondence between the BBT and Graham Schweig regarding transcripts of the Caitanya *Caritāmṛta* March 2020.

23. Jayadvaita Swami's letter to Govinda Dasi, undated.

24. Jayadvaita Swami's letter to Govinda Dasi, undated.

25. Lecture—October 2, 1968, Seattle.

26. The transcription is ambiguous in meaning, making it nearly impossible to know what Śrīla Prabhupāda intended. It's a reasonable assumption that he was quoting his own guru's commentary, and the transcriber misunderstood what he heard. The editors who worked in Prabhupāda's presence most likely did not have access to Bhaktisiddhanta's commentary that could have helped them decipher the ambiguous transcription.

27. Personal correspondence.

28. Personal correspondence February 2020.

29. commentary of Śrīla Viśvanātha Cakravartī Ṭhākura on this verse: "small particles of ice which are just like tiny flowers".

30. *Śrīmad-Bhāgavatam* 2.9.33 and 1.8.36 purports.

31. *Śrīmad-Bhāgavatam* 3.21.13 and Kṛṣṇa Book, chapter 23.

32. Such as one edition of Kṛṣṇa Book.

33. *Śrīmad-Bhāgavatam* 8.9.28 purport.

34. Personal discussion February 2020.

35. Notes to the Second Edition of *Bhagavad-gītā* As It Is. See appendix for the full note.

36. Responsible Publishing, p. 13.

37. April 2020.

38. Letter to: Bhargava—Los Angeles June 13, 1972.

39. Letter to: Sridama—Delhi November 17, 1971.

40. Letter to: Sons— Bombay December 28, 1974.

41. Letter to: Sudama—Mayapur February 28, 1972.

42. Letter to: Niranjana—Bombay January 21, 1975.

43. July 13, 1977 letter to Tamal Kṛṣṇa Goswami and other ISKCON leaders.

44. In http://bbtedit.com/editing-the-unchangeable there is a description of Satsvarupa telling Śrīla Prabhupāda in 1972 that "in numerous instances the edited version seemed to have low fidelity to Śrīla Prabhupāda's original work." Without any direct quote from Śrīla Prabhupāda, or anything in writing, the bbtedit website continues: Śrīla Prabhupāda responded, in essence: "Don't lose time. Just print it." This is a remembrance of Jayādvaita Swami who heard from Satsvarupa in Boston soon after this conversation took place.

45. In http://bbtedit.com/editing-the-unchangeable there is a description of Satsvarupa telling Śrīla Prabhupāda in 1972 that "in numerous instances the edited version seemed to have low fidelity to Śrīla Prabhupāda's original work." Without any direct quote from Śrīla Prabhupāda, or anything in writing, the bbtedit website continues: Śrīla Prabhupāda responded, in essence: "Don't lose time. Just print it." This is a remembrance of Jayādvaita Swami who heard from Satsvarupa in Boston soon after this conversation took place.

46. http://www.bbtedit.com/node/260.

47. You'll be glad now that Caitanya-caritāmṛta is now published.

> Devotees: Jaya! Haribol!
>
> Prabhupāda: Yes. It is the . . . Our Paṇḍitjī, Pradyumna, he has presented. Actually, he has worked for it, although I have translated. But I am very much indebted to him that he very carefully edits and makes the thing very perfect.

Śrī Vyāsa-pūjā Lecture—August 22, 1973, London.

48. http://bbtedit.com/editing-the-unchangeable: "Most of his books, however, he dictated on a Grundig dictating machine, using tapes that each afforded perhaps an hour of dictation. This enabled him to achieve greater speed. Yet the method had its drawbacks: he had less opportunity to review and revise his words, he sometimes spoke passages twice, and—most of all—he had to depend on the accuracy of his transcribers. Especially in the early years, accuracy was poor. The transcribers were not yet deeply familiar with his philosophy, they had difficulty with his strong Bengali accent, and most of his Sanskrit words and quotations were strange to their ears.2 Moreover, Śrīla Prabhupāda's frequent clicking of the switch to start, stop, and review his dictation clipped short many words or deleted them entirely. This resulted in numerous gaps and errors. Sometimes transcribers simply left things out—entire

Sanskrit quotations, for example—or gave only phonetic approximations. Sometimes they could only guess at what Śrīla Prabhupāda was saying, and often guessed wrong."

49. Śrīmad-Bhāgavatam 7.9.39—March 17, 1976, Māyāpur.

50. For example, if he thought there were serious problems with the books, it's not reasonable that he would want to duplicate them into a multiplicity of languages. Rather, he would have cautioned disciples to make the books more authentic and then translate them.

51. Responsible Publishing, p. 19.

52. Śrīla Prabhupāda's lecture on Bhagavad-gītā 7.1 [with Translator]—December 25, 1975, Sanand.

REFERENCES

Audio Recordings of Śrīla Prabhupāda (1966–1977), Los Angeles: Bhaktivedanta Book Trust.

Bhagavad-gītā As It Is (1993), (A.C. Bhaktivedanta Swami Prabhupāda, Trans.) [The Song of God]. Los Angeles, California: Bhaktivedanta Book Trust. (Original work published ~3000 B.C.)

Correspondence between the BBT and Graham Schweig, March 2020, shared in personal correspondence by email.

Correspondence between Tamal Krishna and Radha Vallabha, received from the Bhaktivedanta Book Trust in personal correspondence.

Kṛṣṇa, the Supreme Personality of Godhead (2012), A.C. Bhaktivedanta Swami Prabhupāda, Los Angeles, California: Bhaktivedanta Book Trust.

Letters from Śrīla Prabhupāda (five volumes), (1987), Culver City, California: The Vaisnava Institute in association with the Bhaktivedanta Book Trust.

Responsible Publishing, Bhaktivedanta Book Trust, Microsoft Word - Responsible Publishing.doc (jswami.info).

Śrīmad-Bhāgavatam (1972), (A.C. Bhaktivedanta Swami Prabhupāda, Trans.). Los Angeles, California: Bhaktivedanta Book Trust. (Original work published ~3000 B.C.)

Śrīmad Bhāgavatam: with Sārārtha-darśinī commentary (2008–2018 in several volumes), Viśvanātha Cakravartī Ṭhākura (Bhanu Swami, Trans.) Chennai, Tamil Nadu, India, Tattva Cintāmaṇi Publishing. (Original work published ~1704)

The Great Soul can Import Knowledge Unto You: A BBT decision explained by Jayādvaita Swami, June 10, 2017.

Chapter 3

Posthumous Editing and the Privilege of the Sages

Austin Gordon

In posthumously editing the books of an Acarya, the *arsa-prayoga* principle (translated by Srila Prabhupāda as the "privilege of the sages") calls for accepting the writing of great saints as it stands. This is the overriding editorial imperative when working with sacred texts. It forms the fundamental architecture of editorial policy and requires that modifications be permitted only when the need for correction is unambiguous and cannot be dealt with in a less intrusive way. Or, as Srila Prabhupāda himself stated, when the change fits within the Acarya's direct instructions to correct grammar, and so on: "Our editing is to correct grammatical and spelling errors only, without interpolation of style or philosophy."[1]

Arsa-prayoga demands profound deference on the part of editors, meaning that changing the text in any of the Acarya's published writings is permissible *only* when there is objective certainty that such a change is absolutely required, and with the recognition that revisions cannot be based on inference or supposition. When the *arsa-prayoga* principle is not strictly applied, it can result in unnecessary and unacceptable revisions. Therefore, in the absence of clear, incontrovertible evidence to the contrary, the following three principles, in combination, must govern:

THE AUTHORITY OF THE AUTHOR

A book should be revised only with the unambiguous consent of the author. In 1972, Srila Prabhupāda signed a detailed contract with Macmillan for the publication of *Bhagavad-gita As It Is* (MAC72), and this direct, documented approval of the final manuscript must be granted all due deference. The contract with Macmillan for the publishing of the 1972 edition even includes a specific clause, initialed by Srila Prabhupāda personally, prohibiting revisions without his expressed consent.

Claims that the author (Srila Prabhupāda) might have been inattentive to editorial errors are an unsatisfactory justification for wholesale revisions of the text. Such a claim is not only weak due to its speculative nature but also contradicted by numerous examples of the opposite: that the author paid a great deal of attentiveness to the manuscript submitted for publication. The following is but one such example of many, which demonstrates how meticulous Srila Prabhupāda was in his careful consideration of the contents:

> I noticed that on the carbon-copy [Macmillan] contract you neglected to initial the last clause (b) of Section XX Special Provisions, although you had done so on the original copy. In addition, I have added the phrase to XII. Competitive Material as follows: "as well as the 48 pages of illustrations for which the Author reserves the right to publish for any purpose he may determine."[2]

While the MAC72 may contain phrases or words that could fairly and rationally be considered "mistakes," a posthumous reconstruction of substantial portions of the MAC72 text is not the appropriate means to deal with this issue. There are other, far less intrusive means. Such vigorous content editing, even though it may appear to serve a valuable purpose, extracts too great a cost, ethically and spiritually.

THE ARSA PROYOGA PRINCIPLE

The *arsa-prayoga* principle has historically placed immense value upon the recorded words of great saints and sages. It is how lineages of very specific teachings have been kept intact and handed down from one generation to the next for millennia. It functions on the philosophical precedence that sacred knowledge descends from the Supreme Divine through the pure vessels of saints and sages. Unless this "privilege of the sages" is operative, the transmission of sacred knowledge risks being broken, along with the absolute authorship of the original authors.

Srila Prabhupāda's *own* authority as the author of his own works is further enhanced by this very principle of *arsa prayoga*, which requires that his words be preserved as initially approved by him. As a Vaishnava Acharya—or teacher by example—Srila Prabhupāda outlines a very clear directive of how this preservation "system" of descending sacred knowledge works:

> The system is: whatever authority has done, even there is mistake, it should be accepted. *Arsa prayoga.* That is ha . . . He should not become more learned than the authority. That is very bad habit.[3]

It is critical that Srila Prabhupāda has stated "even if there is mistake, it should be accepted," as it anticipates the inability of others to see the value of the knowledge that is being transmitted—and recorded—at any point in history by a Vaishnava Acharya. Since the "system" is to accept the complete presentation of the authority, including "mistakes," it follows that the mistakes also hold value—that the mistakes play an important role in illuminating the complete teaching, even—and perhaps, especially—when others want to obliterate the "mistakes."

In contrast to this preservation of sacred texts "system" that Srila Prabhupāda defines above, a team of editors at the Bhaktivedanta Book Trust took it upon themselves to posthumously produce a "new and improved" version of Srila Prabhupāda's *Bhagavad-gita As It Is* in 1993: the infamous BBT83, aimed at correcting the "mistakes." These editors stated that they felt at liberty to rewrite passages when *they* believed that a philosophical point was confusing and needed restating:

> If for some reason the intended philosophical point Srila Prabhupāda is trying to make isn't clear, the editors make changes to clarify. . . . So yes, philosophical clarification is part of editorial decision-making.[4]

Within the *arsa prayoga* paradigm, each intended word of the Vaishnava Acharya is sacred, even what may be considered a "mistake" to an ordinary person—or one who is bound by time, place, circumstances, and conditioning. The tendency of ordinary editors to want to change "mistakes" is akin to declaring that one's vision surpasses that of the pure sage or saint, who is being used as a transparent medium through which the Supreme Divine transmits sacred knowledge.

YEARS OF UTILIZATION WITHOUT REQUEST FOR REVISION

When an author has produced a manuscript, submitted it to a publisher, had it accepted by a publisher, reviewed and approved the edits provided by the publisher, entered into a contract with the publisher, saw the successful release of their published work, and then went on to engage that work, reading from it to audiences around the world for years on end, it is reasonable to assume that the author was pleased with the publication and didn't run into any "mistakes" that needed changing. Perhaps Graham M. Schweig states this best below, in the excerpt below:

> I cannot imagine that there exists any doubt in anyone's mind, even in the minds of the editing team, that Prabhupāda approved what was finally published as

> the MAC72. Prabhupāda not only joyously accepted the MAC72, but also read from the MAC72 for the five years he remained on earth, utilizing it for at least 250 classes on the Bhagavad Gita . . . Prabhupāda never gave any instruction to Jayadvaita Swami, nor to anyone else, that he wanted an improved and revised edition.[5]

During the entire time that Srila Prabhupāda was happily lecturing around the world from his original *Bhagavad-gita As It Is*, he also had at his disposal—had he wished to also engage them—the earlier drafts of his book. However, Srila Prabhupāda gave no importance to these earlier rough drafts. And who would have expected him to? After all, he had been through the very tedious, meticulous, and time-consuming process of carefully authoring, editing, and preparing a book for publication. A book, he appeared to be—for all intents and purposes—quite happy with, at least as demonstrated by his teaching and lecturing records.

Nevertheless, the editors of the BBT83 frequently hold that "re-writing" the published text is justified by referencing these earlier rough drafts, which Srila Prabhupāda himself gave no importance to, after his *Bhagavad-gita* was published. And in complete disregard of Srila Prabhupāda's own detailed instructions when authorizing the publication of his final manuscript,that it *not be modified* without the express consent of the author.

The BBT83 editors' strong reliance on an "original manuscript" is problematic for two important reasons: Firstly, it is unethical to draw upon earlier manuscripts as a basis for posthumous editing. Compounding this infraction is the fact that the author in question (Srila Prabhupāda) is a holy man, a saint, and a sage belonging to an ancient *arsa-prayoga* tradition intent on preserving the integrity of the presentation of sacred texts, in this case, the *Bhagavad-gita*. As such, this ethical mandate is considerably heightened. Regardless, how many authors, of *any* literature, would want a publisher to turn to early drafts to revise the content of their personally approved books after their passing?

The following excerpt is relevant, as it is on the topic of posthumous editing and discusses recognized boundaries for reconstructing literary works. Sappenfield uses the metaphor of a jigsaw puzzle to make his point:

> The simplest textual situation—a child's first puzzle—involves a minimum of three forms: the author's autograph manuscript, printer's page proof, and first published edition. I am not sure how many texts present a profile quite that simple. Hawthorne's *The Scarlet Letter* is one. Three pieces of the puzzle . . . permit a virtually definitive edition of Hawthorne's American classic. The novel was printed by Metcalf & Co. in Cambridge from the author's autograph manuscript. Hawthorne read and marked the proof. Ticknor and Fields issued

the first edition. Inasmuch as the author never intervened in a subsequent edition of *The Scarlet Letter* during the last thirteen years of his life, that text does in fact present the simplest possible textual jigsaw puzzle.[6]

Srila Prabhupāda's original *Bhagavad-gita* (the MAC72) was printed by MacMillan from the author's autograph manuscript, after Srila Prabhupāda signed the publisher's proof—including specific comments—and, henceforth, Prabhupāda never called for a revised edition while reading and lecturing from the book hundreds of times. However, in contrast to the example provided above, the Bhaktivedanta Book Trust (BBT) editors have intervened heavily and repeatedly since 1983 with the author's first and only published edition.

In some instances, earlier drafts can be useful in sorting out whether a word or passage was published in error. But it is a very delicate task, and basing editorial changes on previous drafts is fraught with difficulties—some unseen at first—and therefore should be used most sparingly. It is a plain and important truth that "you don't know what you don't know."

Secondly, the ethical problems of incorporating material from early manuscripts into editorial revisions are compounded by the fact that there exists no definitive "original manuscript". What we do find, in fact, is that the editors are relying on an unsystematic collection of *various* earlier drafts. In fact, for several chapters, there are no available manuscripts whatsoever. In spite of this, to enhance the authenticity of the BBT83 revisions, the BBT editors have publicly promoted the sense that there is a definitive, intact, "original manuscript" that reflects the pre-edited words of Prabhupāda.

In 1971, Hayagriva Dasa, Prabhupāda's principal editor, presciently spoke to this idea of turning to earlier manuscripts in a letter to—none other than—Jayadvaita (the editor of the BBT83 edition), who was assisting Hayagriva in his work on the *Bhagavad-gita*. Hayagriva wrote:

> I have some of the earlier manuscripts here. They appear to be pre-Rayarama, so in some instances I am consulting them. But in the majority of cases they require such extensive revisions that it is easier and generally better to consult the Macmillan version rather than get in a tangle of manuscripts. Srila Prabhupāda stated that the Macmillan version is all right; we simply have to revise for grammar.[7]

What the BBT83 editors refer to as the "original manuscript" is essentially a collection of typed drafts from various stages of the editing process, which can only be utilized for the purpose of posthumous editing with the greatest restraint, under the understanding that the real "original manuscript" was presented to Macmillan for publication.

EXAMPLES OF CHANGES MADE TO PRABHUPĀDA'S ORIGINAL WORK

Whether the BBT editors drew from Srila Prabhupāda's earlier drafts, or from their own minds—intending to clarify a philosophical point they felt their guru didn't express well enough—or from any other plethora of rationalizations for the changes they made to the work of a deceased Vaishnava Acharya, these editors, unabashedly, altered 75 percent of Prabhupāda's original, published *Bhagavad-gita As It Is.*

This is a shocking statistic that has, understandably, shaken the faith of many readers. When eager recipients of divine grace no longer have the assurance that the words they are reading actually originated with the Vaishnava Acharya who authored the book, a whole tradition becomes at risk of disappearing, as the *arsa-prayoga* principle evaporates.

To more specifically illustrate this dangerous risk, what follows is a critical analysis of editorial changes in the text of Prabhupāda's original MAC72 edition, which were introduced into the over-edited BBT83 edition. In selecting these examples, the intention is not to highlight the most substantial changes but rather to offer a cross-section of the different types of revisions, thus giving a balanced overview of how the BBT83 differs from the author's actual work: the MAC72.

As indicated above, there is certainly no shortage of changes to consider! One content analysis found 521 of the 700 verses (about 75 percent) altered by either deletions, insertions, or rearrangements. In chapter 6, for example, 43 of the 47 verses are changed; and in chapter 11, 50 of the 55 verses are changed. Significantly, the count referenced here does not include corrections of spelling or punctuation as revisions (these were rare). So clearly, extensive changes were made. The revisions themselves are varied and often nuanced, yet fall into two main types:

The first type, as might be expected, are simply corrections in spelling, punctuation, grammar, and so on—more or less proof-reading—and are therefore more likely to be objective and less controversial, although a careful analysis found many to be unnecessary and subjective. Prabhupāda, as a serious author, naturally did not want spelling or grammatical mistakes in his books and, in numerous statements insisted on this "error-free" standard, literary speaking. His principal editor, Hayagriva Dasa, recounts one such occasion:

> He (Prabhupāda) tells me. "By Krishna's grace, you are a qualified English professor. You know how grammatical mistakes will discredit us with scholars. I want them to appreciate this Bhagavad-Gita as the definitive edition."[8]

The second broad category of editorial revisions involves revisions to content. This is where the main source of the controversy over posthumous editing rests (although a fair amount of revisions do correct objective mistakes). The BBT83 editors deemed these content edits to be necessary due to perceived flaws either in the draft personally typed by Prabhupāda or the transcription of Prabhupāda's recorded tapes—perceived flaws that were inadvertently carried into the MAC72. In other cases, they discovered material that, in their judgment, somehow was wrongly placed or incomplete.

In implementing this type of revision, the editors frequently relied on the aforementioned earlier manuscripts to determine if, in their view, there was an error, as well as to subsequently support the claim that such a revision was needed to bring the text closer to what Prabhupāda had intended to communicate. Clearly, this is an entirely different project than correcting mistakes in spelling, grammar, and so on, as it introduces substantial subjectivity into the editorial work. Subjectivity that Srila Prabhupāda refers to as a very bad habit: "He should not become more learned than the authority. That is very bad habit."[9] The examples that follow offer a cross-section of the changes, along with some accompanying comments.

CONTENT EDITING: ERASING THE GURU'S VOICE

In this section, you'll be presented with a diverse collection of painstakingly selected, posthumous editing examples first executed by the BBT in 1983 to help illustrate the extent to which the original author's teachings and voice have been compromised over the decades in some of the verses. Before we examine this exhibition, let us carefully consider the following:

1. Translations of sacred texts are understood to bring out the unique spiritual insights and visions of the particular spiritual teacher translating them, via divine revelation and instrumentality.
2. Spiritual masters, like Srila Prabhupāda, possess the unique authority to translate sacred texts in a manner that will emphasize or deemphasize parts of the original Sanskrit, as they see fit, for trustworthy transcendental reasons beyond our grasp.
3. Translations of sacred texts by revered spiritual teachers (like Srila Prabhupāda) are understood to be transcendental and, therefore, just as sacred as the original Sanskrit texts. Changing them is out of the question.
4. The editing instructions left by the revered spiritual teacher himself, as the author of the work in question, need to be adhered to, under all

> circumstances. These are Srila Prabhupāda's: ". . . correct grammatical and spelling errors only, without interpolation of style or philosophy." And ". . . even there is mistake, it should be accepted. *Arsa prayoga.*"

Using the latter premises as the lens through which to examine the following content edits, let us now ask ourselves if any of the following changes to Srila Prabhupāda's original, 1972, published *Bhagavad-gita As It Is*, were really necessary. Worse yet, have they deprived the reader of valuable spiritual perspectives—reflected in Srila Prabhupāda's unique, original translations and commentaries—that were lost as a result of the irresponsible content editing of his sacred work?

To help orient the reader, listed first under the heading "Early Draft," you'll find any pre-publication manuscript the BBT editors utilized when posthumously editing that particular verse. Listed second, under "MAC72", are Srila Prabhupāda's authorized, final translations published in his *Bhagavad-gita As It Is*, by MacMillan Press in 1972—reviewed and approved by the author, regardless of who helped him edit them. Listed third under "BBT83" is the adulterated condition of the verse produced by BBT's editors six years after the author's demise, and eleven years after the publication of the author's original work.

Also offered below are commentaries and some potential arguments on both sides of the underlying issue of whether or not to justify changing the content based on the language used in earlier drafts. Nevertheless, bear in mind that such attempts at justification become moot points in light of the four premises for posthumous editing mentioned above. In the examples below, the bolded text is mine and highlights the text in question.

ATTEMPT TO COMPLETE AUTHOR'S VERSE TRANSLATION

The following is an example drawn from *Bhagavad-gita* 7.12 of a verse in which a full phrase—not found in the author's earlier drafts—was incorporated into Srila Prabhupāda's translation. The BBT83 editors tagged eight words onto the end of the verse, presumably in the name of translating Sanskrit that the author elected not to, as if to complete their guru's translation.

Early Draft:
No early rough drafts were found for these verses
MAC72:
All states of being—be they of goodness, passion or ignorance—are manifested by My energy. I am, in one sense, *everything*—but I am independent. I am not under the modes of this material nature.

BBT83:
Know that all states of being—be they of goodness, passion or ignorance—are manifested by My energy. I am, in one sense, *everything*, but I am independent. I am not under the modes of material nature, *for they, on the contrary, are within Me.*

The extension of the sentence with "for they, on the contrary, are within Me" originates with the BBT83 editors, as there are no early drafts presenting this verse. Trying to justify this by stating that the editors added on these words to make Srila Prabhupāda's translations more similar to the original Sanskrit is inadequate. Even if the Sanskrit text expresses something similar to what the BBT83 editors have added here, the proper placement of such information is in an endnote and not as part of Srila Prabhupāda's translation.

The fact remains that Srila Prabhupāda *did not* translate that part of the verse. It is unethical to make readers believe that he did. Srila Prabhupāda's choice to leave certain parts of a verse untranslated is his prerogative—and one protected by the *arsa-prayoga* principle.

TRANSLATING SANSKRIT VERSE THE AUTHOR ELECTED NOT TO

This is yet another instance that demonstrates the extreme liberties taken by the BBT83 editors by adding whole phrases to verses that did not originate with the author—either in his approved MAC72 *Bhagavad-gita As It Is,* or in any earlier drafts. Here, in *Bhagavad-gita* 1.20, a full phrase—not found in the author's earlier drafts—was incorporated into Srila Prabhupāda's translation: "drawn in military array".

Early Draft:
Oh the king, at that time Arjuna the son of Pandu who was seated on the chariot with flag marked with Hanuman and while just he was about to throw his arrows taking up the bow, he said unto Lord Krsna as follows after looking on the situated sons of Dhritarastra.

MAC72:
0 King, at that time Arjuna, the son of Pandu, who was seated in his chariot, his flag marked with Hanuman, took up his bow and prepared to shoot his arrows, looking at the sons of Dhrtarastra. 0 King, Arjuna then spoke to HrsTkesa [Krsna] these words:

BBT83:
At that time Arjuna, the son of Pandu, seated in the chariot bearing the flag marked with Hanuman, took up his bow and prepared to shoot his arrows. 0 King, after looking at the sons of Dhrtarastra *drawn in military array*, Arjuna then spoke to Lord Krsna these words.

As we see above, the sons of Dhritarastha are described in the BBT83 as "drawn in military array". Again, whether or not this information is found in the ancient Sanskrit text is of no consequence when the *arsa-prayoga* principle is honored; it still holds that this is information that the author elected not to include in his verse translation. That choice is entirely up to the author.

The *arsa-prayoga* principle requires that we treat the decisions made by great spiritual teachers as participating in a divine plan beyond our understanding. As such, Srila Prabhupāda has the privilege of either revealing or concealing specific parts of the ancient Sanskrit verses, as he is inspired to do so.

In other words, great sages are free to deemphasize sections of a text, even by omitting them, as we can observe here. Srila Prabhupāda has elected *not* to include the image of the enemy's sons in his translation. The reasons are meant to remain mysterious and awe-inspiring, and are certainly not viewed as an oversight in need of correction.

We find another example of this in verse 18.64. While the author's early draft and the MAC72 are identical, the BBT83 editors added the phrase "My supreme instruction" to translate the Sanskrit text, without including an explanation. Alternatively, a responsibly edited edition would include an annotation informing the reader that the author elected to omit that information from his own translation.

RADICAL RE-WORDING OF DIVINE EPITHET

In this first example of BG 2.2, note how "Blessed Lord" has been changed to "The Supreme Personality of Godhead." This is a highly visible alteration that the BBT editors decided to make throughout the entire book.

Early Draft:
The Supreme Personality of Godhead said, "Oh sinless Arjuna, I have already explained to you before that there are classes of men for realizing self."
MAC72:
The Blessed Lord said: "O sinless Arjuna, I have already explained that there are two classes of men who realize the Self."
BBT83:
The Supreme Personality of Godhead said: "O sinless Arjuna, I have already explained that there are two classes of men who try to realize the self."

Does the changing of "The Blessed Lord" to "The Supreme Personality of Godhead" meet the standard required for a posthumous revision? It is certainly not a correction of grammar or spelling. Does it constitute an "interpolation of style or philosophy"? Some may say it does. If so, is the need for the change objectively justifiable?

For example, some have argued that "The Blessed Lord" was actually based on the preference of the first editor (Hayagriva), who "slipped it past" the author (Prabhupāda). Is this accurate?

A thorough search on this topic uncovered four pieces of evidence to consider here, one of which supports the change, but rather indirectly. The other three are more direct and do not support the change, based on the language used in earlier drafts.

Evidence supporting the change in translation might be the following quote from a letter Srila Prabhupāda wrote in 1970:

> In the Gita Press edition you will see "Paramatma." They never say "Krsna." They're so much afraid that *If I say Krsna, He will at once capture me.* You see? [chuckles] So in a different way. "Param Brahman," "Caitanya," like this, so many impersonal ways they will say. But that is not required. Bhagavan *uvaca* means Supreme Personality of Godhead, Krsna. *Sometimes they say "Blessed Lord said." No. Why you say? The Supreme Personality of Godhead, Krsna, said.*[10]

The following may be considered as evidence not supporting the change in translation:

> *Be consistent and translate "Sri Bhagavan Uvacha" as "The Blessed Lord said",* which is stylistically more appealing and Srila Prabhupāda approved.[11]

> The Mayavadi atheists also interpret the *Bhagavad-gita.* In every verse of Srimad *Bhagavad-gita* it is clearly stated that Krsna is the Supreme Personality of Godhead. *In every verse Vyasadeva says, sri-bhagavan uvaca, "the Supreme Personality of Godhead said," or "the Blessed Lord said."* It is clearly stated that the Blessed Lord is the Supreme Person, but Mayavadi atheists still try to prove that the Absolute Truth is impersonal.[12]

> Just like here, "*The Blessed Lord said,* 'I instructed this imperishable science of yoga to the sun-god Vivasvan.'" What is difficulty there? Is there any word which you cannot understand? Is anyone here who cannot understand these lines? It is clear. *"The Blessed Lord said,* 'I instructed this imperishable science of yoga to the sun-god Vivasvan.'"[13]

Even if during the editing of the MAC72 book, Srila Prabhupāda actually approved consistently translating "Sri Bhagavan Uvacha" as "The Blessed Lord said," in the latter collection of quotes, it appears that Srila Prabhupāda used the phrase "The Blessed Lord" very deliberately in very specific instances, as a didactic tool. For example, we see the phrase "The Blessed Lord" appearing in instances in which Srila Prabhupāda sets out to disprove the Mayavadi atheists when he emphasizes the personhood of the "Absolute Truth".

When editors take the liberties of changing something as essential as how a holy man refers to God—limiting him to just one phrase for the sake of consistency—they deprive more careful readers of the joys of discovering where he chose a different phrase and for what reason. This is just one of many significant, cautious angles of consideration when preserving the integrity of an author's words that the BBT editors seemed to have entirely overlooked.

ENGAGING PHRASES FROM OLD DRAFTS

Here, in *Bhagavad-gita* 2.18, we encounter an eliminated word, and the replacement of a perfectly well-constructed phrase with another: "is subject to destruction" becomes "is sure to come to an end." An attempt by the BBT83 editors to match earlier drafts.

Early Draft:
The material body of the indestructible immeasurable and eternal living *entity is subject to be ended*: therefore you fight the descendent of Bharata.
MAC72:
Only the material body of the indestructible, immeasurable and eternal living entity *is subject to destruction;* therefore, fight, O descendant of Bharata.
BBT83:
The material body of the indestructible, immeasurable and eternal living *entity is sure to come to an end;* therefore, fight, O descendant of Bharata.

In the first adulteration, the word "only," with which Srila Prabhupāda begins the verse, is completely eliminated. The BBT83 editors felt compelled to return to an earlier draft in which the author doesn't use "only" at the start of the sentence. Yet, beginning a statement with "only" is powerful, as it immediately brings the reader's attention to the stark contrast between "the material body" and "the eternal living entity". It also sets a different tone. Was deleting "only" justified?

Similarly, although we can see that the BBT83 editors drew from Srila Prabhupāda's earlier drafts, where he wrote "is subject to be ended," to arrive at their "is sure to come to an end," nevertheless, it stands that in the published MAC 72 *Bhagavad-gita As It Is*, the author's final decision was to use "is subject to destruction" instead.

In his final choice of words, did the author intend for us to view our material bodies as "subject to destruction" (as happens to the bodies of warriors on the battlefield) rather than as merely coming to an end? Some might say that Srila Prabhupāda's final choice of words is much more dramatic than those chosen by the BBT83 editors. Perhaps they even communicate a sense of urgency. We might consider that not all things that "come to an end" have been necessarily "destroyed." Musical concerts, for example, come to an end, but would we say that they were "subject to destruction"?

Even if the BBT editors were to argue that their translation is closer to the original Sanskrit text, this is Srila Prabhupāda's translation, not theirs. Therefore, it is Srila Prabhupāda's prerogative, as an enlightened guru, to emphasize—if he so desires—that the body is "subject to destruction."

IMPROVING AUTHOR'S KEY TRANSLATED WORD

Please note how in the MAC72 final authorization of this verse translation (*Bhagavad-gita* 2.48), Srila Prabhupāda very succinctly defines yoga as "evenness of mind." Yet the BBT83 editors changed the author's definition of yoga in this verse to "equanimity," presumably to match an earlier draft, which defined yoga as: "to remain just in equipoised condition."

Early Draft:
Do your prescribed duty in equiposed condition. Do such duty without being attached to success or failure and to remain just in *equiposed condition* is called Yoga.
MAC72:
Be steadfast in yoga, O Arjuna. Perform your duty and abandon all attachment to success or failure. Such *evenness of mind* is called yoga.
BBT83:
Perform your duty equipoised, O Arjuna, abandoning all attachment to success or failure. Such *equanimity* is called yoga.

Was changing "Such evenness of mind is called yoga" to "Such equanimity is called yoga" a necessary change? How a Bhakti yoga teacher defines yoga is especially important. Even if an earlier draft engaged the phrase "equipoised condition," the author settled, ultimately, on "evenness of mind." It was, after all, a phrase Srila Prabhupāda used to explain yoga *prior* to the publication of the MAC72. The following is an excerpt from a lecture he gave at the Los Angeles Temple, in which he did just that:

> This is the explanation of yoga, evenness of mind. Yoga-samatvam ucyate. If you work for Krsna, then there is no cause of lamentation or jubilation.[14]

No one can presume to know why Srila Prabhupāda's final decision for his definition of yoga in this verse was "evenness of mind." But, as a means to illustrate one of the ways in which divine orchestration comes into play during the translation work of a great sage, we offer the following colorful hypothetical to help readers better appreciate the *arsa-prayoga* principle:

Note how the phrase "evenness of mind" reverberates with the popularity of "mindfulness" that spread all over the world after the author's departure. Though today mindfulness is a concept that is often ascribed to Buddhism, in this verse, readers learn that yoga is "evenness of mind": a quality often connected with "mindfulness."

As part of our illustration, we ask: could the author—who is considered to be divinely empowered by those in the tradition from which he emerged—have anticipated the "mindfulness craze", and adjusted his translation accordingly, with the intention of redirecting those interested in mindfulness to yoga?

While no one can claim this for certain, it warrants reflection on just how many forces are at play when an author such as Srila Prabhupāda approves his final copy of *Bhagavad-gita As It* Is for publication. In this hypothetical, we wonder if printing "Such *evenness of mind* is called yoga" might have been more potent in drawing readers to yoga during a time in the world when Buddhism is on the rise. We will never know because since 1983 the BBT has deprived its readers of that definition of yoga.

ARBITRARY REPLACEMENTS OF WORDS ALTERING MEANING

Here, in *Bhagavad-gita* 3.1, we have a case of changing the tone of a grammatically correct phrase, from an active one to a more passive one. The word "urge" is replaced with "want" in describing Krishna's feelings (as perceived by Arjuna) about Arjuna fighting in the war. Is the reader to understand that Arjuna perceived Krishna as *urging* him or *wanting* him to fight?

Early Draft:
Oh Janardana, Oh Kesava why do you *like to engage me* in this ghastly warfare if you think that intelligence (in Krsna consciousness) is better than fruitive work.
MAC72:
Arjuna said: O Janardana, O Kesava, why do You *urge me to engage* in this ghastly warfare, if You think that intelligence is better than fruitive work?
BBT83:
Arjuna said: O Janardana, O Kesava, why do You *want to engage me* in this ghastly warfare, if You think that intelligence is better than fruitive work?

As mentioned above, expressing a desire, or preference for someone to fight, differs in mood from *urging* them to fight. In the author's approved MAC72 translation, he portrays Krishna as urging Arjuna to fight. Then, later, Srila Prabhupāda uses a synonym for "urge", declaring "Krishna was *inducing* Arjuna to fight . . ."[15]

The earlier draft reads "*like* to engage me," which is more similar to the BBT83's "*want* to engage me." Yet, the author's final authorized copy of the manuscript reads "*urged* me to engage."

Whether the word "urge" originated with the author, or was proposed to the author via his trusted and appointed editor, Hayagriva, is irrelevant, as the author approved the use of "urge" for his final manuscript. In a letter to Satvarupa dated January 29, 1972, we find one of many examples in which the author, Srila Prabhupāda, expresses confidence in his choice of editor:

> Concerning Hayagriva, he is unquestionably a very expert editor, so you please try to help him and encourage him to perform that service.

On another occasion during a conversation Srila Prabhupāda had with the GBC on May 25, 1972, he said:

> So, Hayagriva Prabhu is taking charge of pushing this movement by help in editorial work. So that is most important because we are distributing books. Our writing will be gospel.

First, replacing words in a deceased author's work, such as replacing the word "urge" with the word "want," with the intention of restoring the author's original voice—as we see in this example—not only invalidates the author's choice of editor, but also presumes that the author did not carefully review and approve the editorial suggestions with which he was presented.[16]

Second, arbitrary replacements of author-approved words with words from early rough drafts rob the author of any authority he exercised when he approved the later, final edits. It also insinuates that the author did not review the manuscript carefully enough, and that the BBT83 editors have supposedly remedied this and improved it.

And, third, it certainly disregards the *arsa-prayoga* principle, or "privilege of the sages," suggesting that the BBT83 editors have not treated Srila Prabhupāda as a sage worthy of producing sacred books: books that, traditionally, are treated with reverence. Altering them is unthinkable, lest one risks losing sacred teachings, and suffering the consequences, as Srila Prabhupāda himself appears to suggest here:

> If you concoct, "I am more intelligent than my Guru," "I can make additions and alterations," then you are finished.[17]

ELIMINATION OF THE AUTHOR'S WORDS

In the example of *Bhagavad-gita* 3.21, we are presented with an eliminated word: "footsteps." Contrary to the previous example, in which the BBT83 editors appear to favor an earlier draft, here they disregard it—even when it engages a very similar word "footprints."

Early Draft:
Whatever and which action is performed by the respectable leader of human society common men follow the *footprints.* And whatever he sets as evidential act all the world also follow them.
MAC72:
Whatever action is performed by a great man, common men follow *in his footsteps.* And whatever standards he sets by exemplary acts, all the world pursues.
BBT83:
Whatever action a great man performs, common men follow. And whatever standards he sets by exemplary acts, all the world pursues.

We note that the early draft uses "footprints," which the MAC72 has, appropriately, replaced with "footsteps," under Srila Prabhupāda's authority. Why, then, was the phrase "in his footsteps" omitted from the BBT83 edition? Doing so changes the verse's translation.

One might argue that removing "in his footsteps" from the verse translation deprives readers of a more intimate view of the "great man" described therein. A literal reading of Srila Prabhupāda's approved MAC72 text potentially conjures up the image of a great man's feet as he walks. Given that the author represents a tradition in which the feet of great masters are regarded as holy, eliminating the phrase "in his footsteps," may be constituted as eliminating an opportunity for readers to meditate on the holy feet of great masters. This is a perfect example of how the author's expressions are being evaluated by the BBT83 editors as unnecessary, or "extra," and, consequently, deleted.

Another example of an unnecessarily eliminated word is found in verse 2.25, in which the author chooses to list four adjectives to describe the soul: "invisible, inconceivable, immutable and *unchangeable*." In the BBT83 revision, readers will find only three adjectives, as the word "unchangeable," has been inexcusably dropped. The same occurs in verse 2.20 when Srila Prabhupāda uses five words to describe the soul: "unborn, eternal, ever-existing, *undying* and primeval," and the BBT83 editors arbitrarily decide that "undying" is not necessary and remove it.

MUTING THE AUTHOR'S VOICE WITH RECONSTRUCTING PHRASES

In Bhagavad-gita 2.9, we find an example of a highly altered sentence from which thirteen words have been subtracted and ten words have been added, to the point that the author's original voice is nearly indiscernible.

Early Draft:
Anyone who thinks that the living entity is killing somebody or a living entity is being killed by others, does not know anything. One who is in the knowledge, he knows that no body kills no body and no body is killed by no body.
MAC72:
He who thinks that the living entity is the slayer *or* that he is slain, does not understand. One who is in knowledge knows that the self slays not, nor is slain.
BBT83:
Neither he who thinks the living entity the slayer *nor* he who thinks it slain is in knowledge, for the self slays not nor is slain.

Here, the early draft reflects that English is not the author's first language. Nevertheless, his grasp of English was more than sufficient to communicate his meanings clearly, which he did. In working with his editor, the author produces the MAC72 translation of this verse. It is a perfectly well-constructed, grammatically sound verse translation, and yet, the BBT 83 editors opted to alter it anyway with awkwardly worded English. What results—at least in my own reading—is a sense that I am not hearing Srila Prabhupāda's voice. There is, apparently, no justification for this change other than the BBT editor's subjective opinion.

STYLISTIC CORRUPTION BY REPLACING PHRASES

The following is an example of BG 1.21–22. Please note the three stylistic changes in the following example: The first replaces "who is" with "those." The second replaces "who is desirous of fighting" with "who desire to fight." The third replaces "great battle attempt" with "great trial of arms":

Early Draft:
Arjuna said, Oh the infallible please place my chariot in between the two armies. (Please keep the chariot) as long as I see who are present here with desire to fight and with whom I have to fight in this great attempt of strife.

MAC72:
Arjuna said: O infallible one, please draw my chariot between the two armies so that I may see *who is* present here, *who is desirous of fighting*, and with whom I must contend in this *great battle attempt.*
BBT83:
Arjuna said: O infallible one, please draw my chariot between the two armies so that I may see *those* present here, *who desire to fight*, and with whom I must contend in this *great trial of arms.*

Here, the writing was already free from spelling and grammatical errors, and the author's tone, emphasis, and manner of expression were intact. Nevertheless, the BBT editors felt it was necessary to alter this verse translation in three places:

The first change is the difference between seeing "who" is present to seeing "those" present. The latter paints a picture of the assembled warriors as a whole, while the former zeros in on the specific individuals who showed up for battle. Srila Prabhupāda's words "*who* is present here, *who* is desirous of fighting" emphasize personhood. Did Srila Prabhpada, as the original author, intend this emphasis? Readers deprived of the author's approved final manuscript will never even have the opportunity to ask themselves such a question or what such emphasis could mean.

The second alteration of "who is desirous of fighting" to "who desire to fight," does nothing to clarify the meaning. The original MAC72 phrase—though somewhat protracted—is nevertheless grammatically correct. Removing it from the verse translation has the effect of robbing the author of his manner of expression.

In the third change, the "great battle attempt" becomes "great trial of arms." For those BBT editors who argue that their edits draw from the author's "earlier manuscripts," preserving the author's voice, this is absolutely not the case here. As clearly demonstrated above, the unnecessarily added phrase "great trial of arms" is missing from the author's earlier drafts.

If this phrase did not originate with the author, it is reasonable to ask who it came from, and why? Oddly enough, "great trial of arms" is an expression that was mostly heard in medieval Germanic times, yet the BBT83 editors preferred it to Srila Prabhupāda's "great battle attempt," for whatever indiscernible reasons.

REMOVING AUTHOR'S DIDACTIC USE OF WORDS

The following two examples (*Bhagavad-gita* 3.25 and 3.38, respectively) show just how significant the sequential placement of the word "similarly" can be in a sentence. In reading these sentences aloud, one really gains a sense of how different the author's use of "similarly" was than that of the MAC72 editors.

MAC72:
As the ignorant perform their duties with attachment to results, *similarly* the learned may also act, but without attachment, for the sake of leading people on the right path.
BBT83:
As the ignorant perform their duties with attachment to results, the learned may *similarly* act, but without attachment, for the sake of leading people on the right path.
MAC72:
As fire is covered by smoke, as a mirror is covered by dust, or as the embryo is covered by the womb, *similarly,* the living entity is covered by different degrees of this lust.
BBT83:
As fire is covered by smoke, as a mirror is covered by dust, or as the embryo is covered by the womb, the living entity is *similarly* covered by different degrees of this lust.

In the MAC72 authorized edition, Srila Prabhupāda's placement of "similarly" is effectively engaged as a didactic divider between two states he is contrasting. Words such as "similarly" (or "therefore," "thus," etc.) indicate how to apply reason within the argument. Grammatically, the word "similarly" is placed as the first word to identify the beginning of a conclusive statement.

On the other hand, in descriptive statements, the word "similarly" is used simply as an adverb and placed in a different location, near the verb. In moving the word "similarly," the BBT83 editors turned it into an adverb, weakening the conclusive, logical force of the author's original statement. As part of the BBT83 phraseology, the word becomes less potent as a didactic tool.

WORD REPLACEMENTS ALTERING MEANING

In this verse, *Bhagavad-gita* 2.35, Krishna presents Arjuna with an unflattering view of what the great generals on the battlefield might develop of him if he leaves the battlefield. The word "coward" is replaced by the BBT83 editors with "insignificant."

Early Draft:
The great generals who has had very great estimation for your name and fame will consider that have had gone away from the battlefield out of fear only and thus they will think of you as *fig.*

MAC72:
The great generals who have highly esteemed your name and fame will think that you have left the battlefield out of fear only, and thus they will consider you *a coward.*
BBT83:
The great generals who have highly esteemed your name and fame will think that you have left the battlefield out of fear only, and thus they will consider you *insignificant.*

As is evident above, the early draft reads, "they will think of you as a fig." The author-approved verse uses the phrase "they will consider you a coward." The BBT replaces "coward" with "insignificant," perhaps to match the early draft's tone of men who wouldn't give "a fig" about Arjuna, thus thinking him insignificant. This is a reasonable conjecture. However, it still undermines the author's endorsed use of "coward." In fact, Srila Prabhupāda engages that very term in the purport preceding this verse (BG 2.34), perhaps in anticipation of this verse:

> The Lord says, Arjuna, if you leave the battlefield, people *will call you a coward* even before your actual flight.

There are also lectures in which we find the author engaging the term "coward" when speaking on this verse, such as the following:

> Now, you are so much honored as Arjuna the great fighter, Dhananjaya, and if you leave, you go away from this fighting and leave and people will say, *"Oh, Arjuna has become coward.* He did not fight," then what is the use of your living in such a way?

"Coward" communicates the idea of a shamed warrior and is the active cause of the loss of reputation. If the BBT83 editor's preference was to, instead, emphasize the ideas surrounding "insignificant" and felt justified in doing so because of the author's use of "fig" in the earlier draft, an annotation would be the appropriate place in which to share such information with readers.

AWKWARD USE OF BRACKETS WITHOUT EXPLANATION

This is another example of when whole phrases from the author's old drafts are reincorporated into verses that appear in the BBT83 revision. Here, in *Bhagavad-gita* 2.51, the added phrase is "by going back to Godhead."

Early Draft:
Thus by being engaged in devotional service of the Lord great sages or devotees are able to get free from the resultant actions of work in the material world and thus become from the cycle of birth and death and *go back to Godhead* where there is no more any miseries.
MAC72:
The wise, engaged in devotional service take refuge in the Lord, and free themselves from the cycle of birth and death by renouncing the fruits of action in the material world. In this way they can attain that state beyond all miseries.
BBT83:
By thus engaging in devotional service to the Lord, great sages or devotees free themselves from the results of work in the material world. In this way they become free from the cycle of birth and death and attain the state beyond all miseries *[by going back to Godhead].*

First, the sentence has been completely restructured, despite the MAC72 being clear and correct, and (at least, as I experience it) much more readable and poetic. Second, the added phrase "by going back to Godhead" is presented to the reader in brackets, a highly irregular practice. What is the reader to do with this information? It is missing an annotation explaining why it is in brackets.

Second, the author is on record as having engaged his MAC72 translation without the bracketed information in a *Bhagavad-gītā* lecture he gave in Los Angeles on December 16, 1968:

Tamala Krsna: "The wise, engaged in devotional service, take refuge in the Lord and free themselves from the cycle of birth and death by renouncing the fruits of action in the material world."
Prabhupāda: Yes. There is purport?
Tamala Krsna: No. There's a little more to that sloka.
Prabhupāda: All right. Finish.
Tamala Krsna: In this way they can attain that state beyond all miseries.
Prabhupāda: Read it again.
Tamala Krsna: The wise, engaged in devotional service, take refuge in the Lord and free themselves from the cycle of birth and death by renouncing the fruits of action in the material world. In this way they can attain that state beyond all miseries.
Prabhupāda: How easy it is. You take to Krsna consciousness, you act in Krsna consciousness, you overcome the cycle of birth and death. And as soon as you overcome the cycle of birth and death, you overcome all miseries. Because birth and death means this material body. The living entity, spirit soul, has no birth and death. And anyone who possesses this material body has to undergo the threefold miseries of the material world.

RESURFACING OF PHRASES FROM OLD DRAFTS

The following verse translation is another example of a verse in which we find phrases from old drafts resurfacing. In this particular case, the MAC72 *Bhagvad-gita As It Is* verse 2.24 was left unedited, except for replacing the "all-pervading" phrase with the phrase "present everywhere," found in an earlier draft.

Early Draft:
This individual soul is unbreakable, cannot be burnt,
insoluble, nondriable, everlasting, *present everywhere*,
nonchangeable, immovable and eternally the same.
MAC72:
This individual soul is unbreakable and insoluble, and can be
neither burned nor dried. He is everlasting, *allpervading*,
unchangeable, immovable and eternally the same.
BBT83:
This individual soul is unbreakable and insoluble, and can be
neither burned nor dried. He is everlasting, *present everywhere*,
unchangeable, immovable and eternally the same.

As mentioned above, the MAC72's phrase "all-pervading" was revised with the words "present everywhere," aligning it with an early draft. In this translation, the Sanskrit phrase in question is *sarva-gataḥ,* which not only describes the "individual" soul but simultaneously describes the Supreme Soul, who pervades over everything. It's not uncommon in the Sanskrit language for words to point to two ideas simultaneously.

Srila Prabhupāda actively accepted his editor's use of "all-pervading" by approving the Macmillan proofs, and again later, when he used the term "all-pervading" himself in lectures, such as the following:

> Neither you can burn with fire, neither you can moisten it with water, neither you can dry. In every respect, Krishna explains how soul is immutable. Another significance is *nityaḥ sarva-gataḥ. Sarva-gataḥ means all-pervading*; everywhere the soul is there.[18]

In the above lecture, the author clearly translates *sarva-gataḥ* as "all-pervading." The point made here is not that the individual *jiva* soul is "all-pervading," but that they (the *jiva* souls) are collectively "all-pervading" the material world. Also, the *Paramatma* is within each *jiva*, and as such, He is all-pervading as the Superself. Both ideas are simultaneously true. As such, the author was free to choose which philosophical perspective to emphasize in his verse translation. In this case, Srila Prabhupāda approved the use of "all pervading." The verse does not require a change to "present everywhere" to avoid philosophical confusion.

CONCLUSION

Posthumous editing that seeks to establish or preserve the legacy of a great sage or spiritual teacher doesn't exist within the ancient Vaishnava tradition, unless it strictly adheres to the principle of *arsa-prayoga.* This "privilege of the sages" demands a reverential treatment of literary works left behind by great spiritual teachers, such as those left behind by Srila Prabhupāda, the author in question.

As such, posthumously editing such sacred literature is a very delicate matter for which we've been given guiding perimeters designed to protect the teachings of deceased masters. Even if designated editors perceive "mistakes" in a deceased master's work—on principle—the deceased master's approved, published works are part of a trusted legacy. Breaching such boundaries of trust unquestionably risks muting the master's voice and participates in the desecration of sacred literature.

Readers cease being able to trust in the published words of great masters when posthumous editors go beyond correcting mere grammatical and spelling errors, and start venturing into the risky business of speculating what their deceased master was *actually* trying to say, or what he *meant* to say, or what he *should* have said, or what he *missed* translating, and so on. Even if the editors were appointed by the deceased master himself, the fact remains that the master is no longer here to consult with. "The privilege of the sages" simply does not extend to the master's editors once the master leaves. Thinking otherwise dangerously risks compromising the authenticity of the master's work—some might even say, to the point of expunging the sacredness from it.

The examples above were selected because they offer a peek into the kind of absolute authority the posthumous editors of Srila Prabhupda's work gave themselves to alter his approved and published *Bhagavad-gita As It Is* in his absence. The examples demonstrate that by eliminating words approved by the author, radically reconstructing phrases, carelessly removing the author's didactic use of words, denying the author his choice to leave parts of the verses untranslated, inserting bracketed phrases without explanation, engaging phrases from old drafts, and rewording, replacing, and restyling the author's manner of expression, the BBT editors have effectively changed the tone, mood, and meaning of Srila Prabhupāda's original published writings, resulting in a loss of his voice as the original author. If this is not a dangerous deviation from the principle of *arsa-prayoga,* I don't know what is!

For decades, since 1983, readers of Srila Prabhupāda's *Bhagavad-gita As It Is*, (and other works of his) have been let down by posthumous editors who have failed to declare where they have decided to alter their master's works in a scholarly way, in the books themselves. Consequently, readers are left to unfairly wonder which parts of the text are attributed to the author, Srila Prabhupāda, and which are the results of over-zealous editing executed after his departure. Unless actions are taken to remedy this, it is unreasonable to expect readers to place their full faith in books published under Srila Prabhupāda's name by the BBT, knowing the texts have been so altered—sometimes beyond recognition. This loss of faith is a sad testament to what happens when unique privileges that only holy men are entitled to are misplaced.

NOTES

1. Letter to Rupanuga Das on 2/17/70.
2. Srila Prabhupāda's letter to Rupanuga, 2/22/72.
3. Srila Prabhupāda's room conversation, Mayapur, 2/27/77.
4. These words were written by Dravida Das, Jayadvaita's primary protégé, in an email correspondence with Ramesvara Das, re: Sri Caitanya Caritamrita, Madhya Lila 20.117, December 15, 2013.
5. Graham M. Schweig, in his internet-posted statement, "Why I Am Looking into the BBT Editing" (2019).
6. James A. Sappenfield, University of Wisconsin, presented at the 9th Cooper Seminar at the State University of New York College, July 1993.
7. Hayagriva Dasa, letter to Jayadvaita and Satsvarupa, December 12, 1970. The Macmillan version referenced in this quoted text was the 1968 abridged edition of the *Bhagavad-gita As It Is.*
8. Hayagriva Dasa, *Hare Krishna Explosion*, "Edit for force and clarity." Date? Publisher?
9. Srila Prabhupāda's room conversation, Mayapur, 2/27/77.
10. Srila Prabhupāda, initiation lecture, Los Angeles, July 3, 1970.
11. Haya-Jaya letters: Installment 2. Hayagriva's letter to Jayadvaita Dasa, his assistant on the issue of using "Blessed Lord" or "Supreme Personality of Godhead", written during the editing of the MAC72.
12. Srila Prabhupāda, *Caitanya-caritamrta Madhya-lila 6*.132, purport.
13. Srila Prabhupāda, *Bhagavad-gita* 4.1–2 lecture in Columbus, Ohio, May 9, 1969.
14. Srila Prabhupāda, Bhagavad-gītā 2.46–62 lecture, Los Angeles, December 16, 1968.
15. A *Srimad Bhagavatam* lecture (January 9, 1974).

16. In *Bhagavad-gita* 2.30, the word "creature" is revised to "living being". The Cambridge Dictionary defines "creature" as "An animal or person—As fellow creatures on this planet, animals deserve respect". Perhaps the author intended for the reader to have the word "creature" conjure up images of the animals, which are so abused in our world today.

17. Srila Prabhupāda lecture on July 12, 1975 in Philadelphia, PA.

18. Srila Prabhupāda, Bhagavad-gita 2.23–24 lecture, London, England, August 27, 1973.

REFERENCES

Bhaktivedanta Swami Prabhupāda, A. C. *Bhagavad-gītā As It Is, Complete Edition* (First Printing). New York: The Macmillan Company, 1972 [Fourth Printing 1973 and Fifth Printing 1974 editions].

Bhaktivedanta Swami Prabhupāda, A. C. *Bhagavad-gītā As It Is, Complete Edition Revised and Enlarged.* Los Angeles: The Bhaktivedanta Book Trust, 1986 [Eighth Printing 2001].

Bhaktivedanta Swami Prabhupāda, A. C. *Bhagavad-gītā As It Is, Second Edition Revised and Enlarged.* Los Angeles: Bhaktivedanta Book Trust, 1989.

Bhaktivedanta Swami Prabhupāda, A. C. *Bhagavad-gītā As It Is, With Introduction, Translation and Authorized Purport.* New York: Collier Books, 1968 [Third Printing 1970].

Bhaktivedanta Vedabase. [https://vedabase.io/en/]

Chapter 4

On Restoring the 1972 Edition of the *Bhagavad Gītā As It Is*

Kenneth Rose

As[1] is well-known in ISKCON, there are three main editions of *Bhagavad Gītā As It Is* (*BGAII*), a situation that has sparked a controversy about whether the 1972 or the 1983 edition should be authoritative. (The 1968 edition can be set aside, as all would agree, except for historical purposes.) Given that Prabhupāda taught and preached extensively from the 1972 edition, which he helped edit and which he approved, it seems clear that it should be the standard, authorized text in ISKCON. This is underscored by the clear desire of Prabhupāda that this edition should not be changed and by the fact that he did not ask for a new edition of *BGAII*. The textual gap between the 1972 and 1983 editions has caused a crisis of confidence among ISKCON members, and many devotees are unclear about which of the two editions best reflects Prabhupāda's intentions. The 1972 edition is still available, but the 1983 edition appears to have become the standard edition. Because it is widely available and well-known globally, it would not be easy merely to reinstate the 1972 edition as the authorized text without raising several issues. The foremost issue is that readers familiar only with the 1983 edition might feel as if much is missing from the 1972 edition when they read it, while readers devoted to the 1972 edition may be uncomfortable with the changes adopted in the later edition. The second issue is that the 1972 edition may contain, along with small errors such as spelling and transcriptional mistakes, expressions and teachings that are not as well-received today as they were in the last quarter of the twentieth century. Restoring the 1972 edition unchanged might raise difficulties for people who are woke today to issues that people were not woke to in the 1970s.

One solution to this situation might be to determine, insofar as that remains possible, Prabhupāda's *ipsissima verba*—his very words themselves—in a new critical edition, which would be constructed in a group-based process conducted along text-critical and rule-governed lines, as in the case of the text of the Greek New Testament. This approach can be useful in establishing a base printed text of *BGAII*, which would allow users of the different editions to see how the 1968 and 1983 editions vary from the 1972 edition. This will be useful for scholars who may want to distinguish between the different readings in the different editions. It can also aid users of the 1983 edition in discovering Prabhupāda's actual textual choices.

Once the 1972 text has been clarified, it seems, given Prabhupāda's expressed wishes, that the only scope allowed to the editors of the *BGAII* in future printings is what one would expect in the reprinting of a classic work by any other author. This might involve fixing typographical errors and misprints, but it would rule out changing words, adding words and sentences, and rewrites by later editors. This includes changes that are made to reflect the changed social customs and attitudes of later generations of readers and editors. If a text is changed to reflect the woke stance of one generation, nothing will prevent later generations from making their own woke changes, and the text may slowly become unrecognizably as different from the original text.

A case study may help to clarify the situation. In 1948, a New York publisher published *The Seven Storey Mountain,* which is a memoir that was written by Catholic contemplative Thomas Merton. This book became a surprise bestseller and ignited an awareness of the contemplative life in countless readers. Merton wrote this book when he was still a young convert to Catholicism, but later in his life, he was embarrassed by some of the views that he expressed in the book. Yet he never revised the book, and when it was reissued on the fiftieth anniversary of its first publication in 1998, three decades after Merton's death, the publisher published the book in the same form as the first edition. Although the publisher added a couple of forewords to contextualize what was now a somewhat dated and partially unwoke book by the standards of the 1990s (the standards of wokeness have shifted dramatically since then), they are clearly separate from the text itself, which remains unchanged (barring the rectification of any possible typographical errors, which I haven't checked because that would require a word-for-word comparison of the two printings to verify).

There is nothing unusual about the practice of *not* changing an author's works posthumously in the literary world, and we expect that newer editions of classic works, at least as long as they are still under copyright protection, will not alter the work from the form in which it was fixed when it was published (this is the case in distinction to a work-for-hire, which may be changed at will by the publisher). After a work has gone out of copyright, altered editions are sometimes created, yet these editions cannot be said to reflect the intention of the author. If we want to read what the author intended, we will need to consult the original edition from which the altered edition was created.

One might, for example, rewrite a woke edition of F. Scott Fitzgerald's *The Great Gatsby* with a different ending and market it, but anyone knowing the original version will see it as an adaptation of *The Great Gatsby* and not actually that work itself. It should be the same with the *BGAII*: insofar as a later edition deviates from the first printing of the 1972 edition, excluding minor typographical and grammatical changes or changes authorized or requested by Prabhupāda, it should be classed as an adaptation of the original text. Given Prabhupāda's clear wishes on this matter and given the common editorial standard of not changing a published author's works without the author's approval, I suggest that the first printing of the 1972 edition be restored as the standard edition of *BGAII* with changes from this edition made by the editors in later printings and the 1983 edition and changes authorized or requested by Prabhupāda indicated in a critical apparatus at the bottom of each page, as, for example, in annotated critical editions of the Greek New Testament such as the Nestle-Aland Greek New Testament and the UBS Greek New Testament.

NOTE

1. Based on a paper presented at the ACADEMIC SYMPOSIUM. On the Challenges of Posthumous Editing: Focus on the Works of A. C. Bhaktivedanta Swami Prabhupāda. February 21–23, 2020. The Mira & Ajay Shingal Center for Dharma Studies. At the Graduate Theological Union, Berkeley.

REFERENCES

Merton, Thomas. *The Seven Storey Mountain.* New York: Harcourt Brace, 1948.

———. *The Seven Storey Mountain,* Fiftieth Anniversary Edition. New York: Harcourt, 1998.

Metzger, Bruce M., and Bart D. Ehrman. *The Text of the New Testament: Its Transmission, Corruption, and Restoration*, 4th ed. Oxford: Oxford University Press, 2005.

Nestle-Aland. *Novum Testamentum Graece,* 28th ed. Stuttgart: Deutsche Bibelgesellschaft, 2012.

Porter, Stanley E., and Andrew W. Pitts. *Fundamentals of New Testament Textual Criticism.* Grand Rapids, MI, Cambridge: Eerdmans, 2015.

Prabhupāda, A. C. Bhaktivedanta Swami. *The Bhagavad Gītā As It Is*. New York and London: Macmillan, 1968.

———. *The Bhagavad Gītā As It Is: Complete Edition.* New York and London: Macmillan, 1972.

———. *The Bhagavad Gītā As It Is.* Los Angeles: Bhaktivedanta Book Trust, 1983.

The UBS Greek New Testament, 5th ed. New York: American Bible Society, 2014.

Chapter 5

Issues Pertaining to the Editing of Prabhupāda's Books

Michael J. Gressett

Degree more than contrast comes to mind in considering the silence of two distinguished, but very different, writers—Maurice Merleau-Ponty and Śrīla Prabhupāda—after their passing. They are equally silent; it is we who continue to grieve forty-two years after the *mahāsamādhi* of Śrīla Bhaktisiddhānta's most illustrious disciple. Merleau-Ponty, an erudite phenomenologist known to (and understood by) few, and without the prestige of tradition, nevertheless inspired the following observations.

> All those who were bound to him by friendship knew the bitter truth of this affliction by the shock it sent into their lives. But now they have yet to hear the silence of a voice which, though it had always come to them charged with personal accents, seemed to them to have always spoken and to be destined to speak always. It is a strange silence to which the interrupted conversation abandons us—where we forget the death of the writer only to return to it by another route. The work has come to an end, and, simply because everything in it is said, we are suddenly confronted with it.[1]

Merleau-Ponty expired suddenly, but Śrīla Prabhupāda left us gradually. We were saddened, not shocked. In fact, we were prepared by Śrīla Prabhupāda himself and knew that unlike Merleau-Ponty, in a deeply spiritual sense he would be "living still in sound."[2] But although we were prepared for his passing and for the continuation of his books, we are still confronted with his work in the sense suggested above. Could we have been prepared for the division among us regarding the continuing *editing* of his books? I would submit that we were not prepared because we could not have imagined it, yet we are required to collect ourselves to imagine, now, the implementation of measures to protect Prabhupāda's books *after we are gone*. In addition to an author's rights, Prabhupāda's books have a special dimension that makes his silence particularly sacred, for they indicate *models of* and *models for* his metaphorical "body"—the International Society for Krishna Consciousness. As models, they can't be altered without altering the intention of the founder. They show us his own conception of what his society is and what it must be, and they show us how to achieve it, without requiring methods of textual criticism, for example, stemmatics (the process of determining a text by constructing a "family tree" of surviving manuscripts), higher criticism (examining the sources of a document to determine authorship, date, and provenance), or any copy-text he didn't personally approve. As he put it, "books are the basis" of his very body, which we are supposed to protect, not change.[3]

It falls to our generation to do this. Far more than the occasion of the passing of Merleau-Ponty, Prabhupāda's silence confronts us. This silence is especially valuable outside of India because he came to us as an ambassador from a Sanskrit, Vaishnava world that was formerly inaudible to our receptive ears. Think about the enormous implications of this situation, for when in history has an Indian religious leader left his own country to establish an entire religious tradition on foreign shores single-handedly? The monistic gurus who came to the West before Prabhupāda brought a hundred flavors of a similar teaching, but only Prabhupāda brought the personalist message. Will we honor the silence of his finished oeuvre? The history of editing suggests that we may have our work cut out for us. We shall presently return to this theme, but now some reflections on the present circumstances will situate the issue of Prabhupāda's right to silence within current thinking on editing.

Some voices in the academic study of editing support the silence without necessarily understanding the critical issues surrounding a self-realized author. Indeed, a Google search for issues pertaining to the posthumous editing of translators of religious texts offers very little because, realistically, there could hardly be a more esoteric issue. The closest I came to our concern was an account of contentious, continued editing after the passing of Paramhamsa Yogananda, whose disciples and grand-disciples have split into rival organizations.[4] The argument for continued editing seems to devolve to Paramhamsa Yogananda's expressed confidence in his editors during life, as if, post-mortem, there could be no question that continued editing was implied and necessary. In the situation with Prabhupāda's books, the same argument is being made. But such a presumption robs a self-realized author of the simple professional dignity enjoyed by even the most mundane of writers, as if the editor stood in the same rank as the author—and after his passing, above the author, changing his work without permission. I'm not actually expressing disdain for editors who have done this, for we all make mistakes.

However, there are scholars in the academy who readily understand the worth of any author's dignity, and I believe we should consider their arguments. Brian Mossop (Translation Studies, York University) insists that editors are only assistants who can make no demands.[5] So what can they revise? "Revision," Mossop declares, "deals with mistakes after they have been made." This is a simple statement of fact, for indeed, to err is human. But Prabhupāda revealed that the Lord wrote his books. And yet there were, at the very least, grammar and spelling mistakes, and at the most, technical errors resulting in misinterpretation of which translation or commentary Prabhupāda meant for publication. This situation means that we must consider carefully what Prabhupāda meant—what he could have possibly meant—when he declared that the Lord was the author. If the Lord is playing the role of an author, might he have enjoyed the sort of challenges more ordinary authors face? This could explain the "mistakes," but presumably only an advanced *bhakti-rasika* (aesthete) could know the answer to such a question. It seems prudent to consider something else if the Lord is the author; Prabhupāda, then, is the Lord's human scribe, and his editors mere human scribal assistants. This is where the editorial phase must end, for otherwise the endless "mistakes" of humanity, further and further from the fiery seed of inspiration imbibed by Prabhupāda, erode the sacred text. For the fire to blaze through the chain of custody, Prabhupāda's silence must be respected, with so-called errors—except for typos, spelling, and any misunderstanding of writing Prabhupāda intended, or not, for publication—included.

Yet some voices in academia counter the textual criticism of specialists like Mossop, who tend to privilege the view that the 'author" is the sole "authority," a position that Śrīla Prabhupāda would have endorsed, to the best of my knowledge. In his introduction to "Collaboration and Concepts of Authorship," M. Thomas Inge (English and Humanities, Randolph-Macon College) laments that Roland Barthes' effort to dismantle the very concept of an individual author—the infamous (as some would see it) "death of the author" theme—seems to encounter stiff resistance from the common-sense notion that an author alone is responsible for his or her writing. By seeing Prabhupāda in this (unreflective, as Inge would have it) way, we are going against the intellectual current, as Inge explains:

> It is commonplace now to understand that all texts produced by authors are not the products of individual creators. Rather, they are the result of any number of discourses that take place among the writer, the political and social environments in which the writing occurs, the aesthetic and economic pressures that encourage the process, the psychological and emotional state of the writer, and the reader who is expected to receive or consume the end product when it reaches print. Even if not intended for an audience or the publishing marketplace, a piece of writing cannot escape the numerous influences that produce it. All discourse is socially constructed.[6]

But we are fortunate, as Inge believes—because we can recognize that "the concept of the . . . divinely inspired author . . . is a myth" that necessitates no changes to the way that teachers teach and writers write—we can attribute part of any literary production to all the people that make it happen, perhaps even on the title page.[7] For instance, Ezra Pound's marginalia in T. S. Eliot's manuscript of "The Waste Land" stands in high relief for the treatment recommended by Inge. We are warned not to believe "the romantic myth of the author as solitary genius," especially a divinely-inspired genius. But must Śrīla Prabhupāda rank among the likes of Eliot and Pound, regardless of the relative worth of their work?

To the Lord (in Prabhupāda's view), Prabhupāda, although working honestly in his human situation—informed (in Inge's view) by "any number of discourses that take place within the writer," his own response to issues of power and social trends, and how he felt about his work and those who would read it—was a scribe. To us, Prabhupāda was a solitary genius with the Lord as his muse. But a review of the relationship of Prabhupāda with the Lord begs a further question, considering his editors. Are they solitary geniuses too, or something else? Forgive me the repetition, but perhaps they are only . . . scribal assistants?

Please allow me to frighten you a bit more, because Inge has confederates who would deny Prabhupāda his right to silence and entitle assistants to significant literary agency. The ideas of Jerome McGann (Department of English, University of Virginia) are fungible in relation to Inge's, and he wants us to consider where the authority lies in who can change a text and how. Authority should never be assumed because it must be divided between author and publisher. McGann believes this because "the fully authoritative text is . . . always one which has been socially produced; as a result, the critical standard for what constitutes authoritativeness cannot rest with the author and his intentions alone."[8] Not only the author, *but what he wants in her or his name*. McGann's solution is to introduce a "catholic" system of standards and prerogatives in which there is no absolute authority, only shifting policy based on changing circumstances.[9] For all we know, centuries from now, someone may claim the necessity to edit even further and cite the present or future circumstances as justification!

Because posterity exercises our dutiful concerns, we must try to imagine more than we have, heretofore, regarding potential future scenarios, when Prabhupāda's writings will be considered an ancient document and editorial philosophy and policy may be based on shifting circumstances. Critical editions are generally favored for ancient texts, yet even more recent volumes (for example, the work of Shakespeare) have been subjected to this treatment when there are questions concerning what was written or even intended. "Any edition that attempts to construct a text of a work using all the available evidence," Harvard's Geoffrey Chaucer's Website (n.d.) explains, "is 'critical' whatever its methodology."[10] It would seem that most of my readers would insist that there is no need for critical editions of Śrīla Prabhupāda's books; also, *there should be* no critical editions, and I agree, for according to the Harvard scholars, the essence of the critical edition is creativity—construction. But we can't improve on Prabhupāda's writing, nor do we need to ascertain its authenticity. So, like Lord Ganesha, Prabhupāda's editors must enjoy the sheer luxury of mere scribal service to a personage of immense prestige.

What about future generations? Will we protect the *parampara*, carefully handing down the work of a master, only for our descendants to decide that a critical edition is necessary? After all, some millennia from now, Prabhupāda's books will be ancient texts.

We don't know what issues will arise in the future, but we do know that we must not tempt future custodians by failing to establish uniformity and absolute authority now. We might think that the issue of Prabhupāda's authority over his own writing would be sacrosanct and non-negotiable, but what if textual critics of a different persuasion manage to enter the *sampradāya*? Such a development seems absurd to our twenty-first century minds, but what if Inge's view gets a purchase upon the Overton window—the accepted realm of discourse—in a thousand years from now? After all, the views of Bart Ehrman (an eminent scholar of the early Christian church that I deeply respect, regardless of our inner-circle, editorial concerns) fit within the Overton window in many "liberal" Christian churches, yet would shock the authors of the Synoptic Gospels, because, like Jefferson, Ehrman seems to accept only the moral teaching of Christianity and rejects almost everything else.

It may appear that there is nothing we can do to prevent further editing in the distant future—especially the unwanted critical edition—but perhaps a serviceable hypertext edition could provide guidance now and influence in the future. The hypertext edition is in some measure the opposite of a critical edition because "hypertext editing offers readers undigested data, not digested information" (and a lot of digesting may go into a critical edition!).[11] We might want to consider hypertext editing at the present time to get in front of future refinements, inasmuch as hypertext editing would actually leave the original intact and unadulterated. But some may argue that any sort of footnotes, endnotes, and so on would not be appropriate in a physical book because Prabhupāda did not order this to be done, so why the need for a hypertext edition? Yet, given that footnotes are commonly seen in ordinary (not only critical) editions of texts like the Bible, we should at least entertain the good in it. I have never met a Bible reader who thought footnotes infringed upon the right of Moses or Paul to remain silent down through the centuries. I could be wrong on this issue. We are certain that we can't divine the digital future in all its possibilities, but scholars of the future could have a hypertext record of what scholarly *bhaktas* of the twenty-first century, who lived and worked with the Founder, thought was important in hypertext and what was not.

However, I believe an even better possibility exists for those interested in a commentary on Prabhupāda. As long ago as the very beginning of textual criticism in Alexandria by Greek scholars in the third century BCE, efforts to construct critical editions set the example for conscientious editors through the ages. "Alexandrian editing was distinguished above all by respect for the tradition; the text was constituted from the oldest and best copies available, and conjectural emendation was rigidly confined to the commentary, which was contained in a separate volume."[12] There is nothing wrong with commenting upon a commentary; Sanskrit literature abounds in these, but like the Alexandrian Greeks, with "respect for the tradition." I would expect our living tradition, now represented in English, to produce an even greater interest in additional commentaries, using "conjectural emendation" or any other method. But correction of a text, according to the seminal school, "should be based on comparison with other copies, not on the unaided conjectural sagacity of the scribe."[13]

If we consider hypertext footnotes and/or separate commentary (in a separate volume) a valid way to respect Prabhupāda's silence while still fulfilling intellectual interests of our own, we may serve his purpose while explaining his meaning as we understand him, separating common mistakes in writing from issues regarding clarity. The recent controversy regarding Prabhupāda's intention in stating that "a woman likes a man expert in rape" stands, perhaps, as the best example of such a contextual necessity. When I researched this issue a few years ago, several questions struck me as vital. First of all, what did he mean by rape? What were the possible nuances of this word in late-Victorian Indian English? What were the sources of Prabhupāda's understanding, and what could be their relevance to our own time, place, and circumstance? After much research, it remained obvious to me that Prabhupāda most emphatically *did not* intend that a woman wants to be confronted by a violent man in a dark alley, and I would like Prabhupāda's readers to understand this, too. So, as you might imagine, I'm in favor of footnotes because these allow discussion without harming the text; and, allow me to repeat, I have never met a Christian who objected to the footnotes that one commonly finds in modern versions of the Bible. And separate commentaries published as separate volumes accomplish the same thing, which is quite handy because we can't know how long the digital world of hypertext will survive.

We are the arbiters of many issues regarding Śrīla Prabhupāda's books. Whatever we choose, it should follow—or at least not interrupt—the living tradition, deserving silence but living still in sound. Instead of preserving the specious right to continue attempts to improve upon what can't be improved—as if the Mona Lisa needed modification by students who mixed Leonardo's paints—preserving that silence is how we preserve the living sound.

NOTES

1. Lefort, Claude. "Editor's Foreword." In Maurice Merleau-Ponty, *The Visible and the Invisible*. Northwestern Studies in Phenomenology and Existential Philosophy. Evanston: Northwestern University Press, 1968, p. xi.

2. Common in 21st century Gauḍīya circles, the phrase comes from Bhaktivinoda Thakura, the father of Prabhupāda's guru, Bhaktisiddhānta Sarasvatī. The Thakura wrote:

> "He reasons ill who says that Vaishnavas die,
> When thou art living still in sound!
> The Vaishnavas die to live, and living try
> To spread the holy name around."

3. Prabhupāda approved this formula for his Society: "Books are the basis, preaching is the essence, utility is the principle, and purity is the force." It is difficult to see how the first and fourth item of this formula remain viable if the Founder's books cannot resist posthumous editing.

4. After his passing, the Self-Realization Fellowship decided that (formerly) *Paramhansa* Yogananda spelled his own name wrong, and inserted the letter "a" in his name for all future editions of their master's 1946 book *Autobiography of a Yogi*, to read *Paramahansa*. Prabhupāda—who preferred to spell his name A. C. Bhaktivedanta Swami instead of A. C. Bhaktivedānta Svāmi—could suffer the same posthumous editorial fate at the hands of errant disciples. So, what else could they do?

5. See Mossop, Brian. "Editing in Translation: Revision." In *An Encyclopedia of Practical Translating and Interpreting*. Chinese University Press, 2018. Mossop acknowledges the possibility of editors' conflicting loyalties. He writes, "Revisers who are responsible for the final wording of a translation may also find themselves facing questions of loyalty. Will they be loyal to the translator who prepared the draft? to the source text author? to the future readers? to the commissioner who is paying for the translation? . . . The demands made by one of these parties may conflict with the demands made by another." Ibid.

In the case of Prabhupāda's translations, it is difficult to imagine legitimate conflicts between his editors and source text authors like Vedavyāsa and Krishnadasa Kaviraja, and Śrīla Bhaktisiddhānta, who commissioned Prabhupāda to present the *sampradāya's* views in English. The future readers are the concern of this symposium. Note that the only party not considered to have legitimate demands are editors!

6. Inge, M. Thomas. "Collaboration and Concepts of Authorship." Modern Language Association. Source: *PMLA*, Vol. 116, No. 3 (May, 2001), pp. 623–30.

7. Ibid., p. 630.

8. McGann, Jerome J. *A Critique of Modern Textual Criticism.* Chicago: University of Chicago Press, 1983, p. 75.

9. Ibid., p. 94.

10. https://chaucer.fas.harvard.edu/types-editions.

11. Ibid.

12. https://www.britannica.com/topic/textual-criticism/History-of-textual-criticism.

13. Ibid.

REFERENCES

Harvard University. n.d. *Harvard's Geoffrey Chaucer Website.* Accessed July 15, 2023. https://chaucer.fas.harvard.edu/types-editions.

Inge, M. Thomas. 2001, May. "Collaboration and Concepts of Authorship." Modern Language Association. *PMLA* 116, no. 3: 623–30.

Kenney, Edward John. n.d. *Britannica.* Accessed July 15, 2023. https://www.britannica.com/topic/textual-criticism/History-of-textual-criticism.

Lefort, Claude. 1968. "Editor's Foreword." In Maurice Merleau-Ponty, *The Visible and the Invisible.* Northwestern Studies in Phenomenology and Existential Philosophy, p. xi. Evanston: Northwestern University Press.

McGann, Jerome J. 1983. *A Critique of Modern Textual Criticism.* Chicago: University of Chicago Press.

Mossop, Brian. 2018. "Editing in Translation: Revision." In *An Encyclopedia of Practical Translating and Interpreting*, edited by Chan Sin-wai, pp. 31–60. Chinese University Press.

Chapter 6

Los Angeles Devotees' Responses to ISKCON's Post-Charismatic Editing Crisis

Anna S. King

The editing controversy has been rumbling on painfully for many years and has its origins even in the lifetime of A. C. Bhaktivedanta Swami Prabhupāda (hereafter Prabhupāda). It is an emotive and complex issue which threatens to split the movement or, at the very least, to generate costly and damaging lawsuits. Often compared to the *rtvik* controversy, it is seen as far more fundamental because it strikes at the very heart of ISKCON by raising questions about the authenticity of Prabhupāda's translations, purports, and teachings. According to one of Prabhupāda's earliest disciples, "It endangers everything that Prabhupāda came to this world to do."[1] This chapter investigates devotees' opinions as to whether, and why, this controversy is consequential and significant for the entire movement, and whether and how there can be some sort of reconciliation and agreed outcome.

In the 2020 Berkeley Symposium "The Posthumous Editing of a Great Master's Works," participants on the whole deplored the post-charismatic (over)-editing of Prabhupāda's books as unscholarly and disrespectful and as setting the wrong precedent for the future. They wanted editing to reach the highest global standards and to conform to the instructions of Prabhupāda. They recommended meticulous research on both matters as a precursor to agreeing guidelines for the future. However, the symposium was not fully representative. In particular, Bhaktivedanta Book Trust (BBT) representatives were not there to explain why Prabhupāda himself had wanted his editors to revise his translations for accuracy of Sanskrit translation and transliteration, grammar, clarity, readability, flow, and connectivity, and more particularly why after his death they had continued to correct editorial discrepancies.[2]

Protagonists on all sides of the argument have approaches based on very different assumptions and criteria. It is this apparent incommensurability that appears so challenging. Devotee scholars like Graham Schweig, Edith Best, and Austin Gordon are concerned not only with fidelity to Prabhupāda but also with the damaging emotional effects of post-charismatic editing. They argue that the fruit of the controversy has been chaos and division within the society. The BBT editors, Dravida dasa and Jayadvaita Swami, on the other hand, believe that their authority comes directly from Prabhupāda and that they are safeguarding his legacy and scholarly dignity. Jayadvaita Swami writes that,

> As a matter of policy the BBT editors, mindful of Srila Prabhupāda's instructions, resist changes. But verified editorial errors are corrected in later printings or editions. This policy has brought the BBT some outspoken criticism, much of it, unfortunately, uncivil and badly uninformed.

Jayadvaita also argues that the indulgence in controversies that are needless, groundless, and baseless is not only "a loss to the world and to Chaitanya Mahaprabhu's movement but a gain for *maya*."[3] Dravida dasa, for his part, comments that the critics always go to principles: "And we have to go to examples. . . . They always like to go to the principles. We have to go to examples."

The situation as regards the editing of Prabhupāda's books is complicated. Not only did the publishing move process between various locations such as Ohio, Boston, Brooklyn, Los Angeles, New York, Philadelphia, and San Diego, but there are now different BBTs all over the world—North American, Indian, Northern European, Mediterranean, Western Pacific, African, and so on. Numerous editors, transliterators, artists, producers, Sanskritists, writers, marketers, publicity fundraisers, designers, IT experts, and distributors have been engaged in the publishing process both in Prabhupāda's lifetime and thereafter. The publishing industry has changed, production methods have become increasingly sophisticated, and standards of transliteration and Sanskrit translation are more exacting. BBT publications have multiplied to such an extent that even a panel of scholars would be puzzled to compare the different editions and translations of Prabhupāda's books without exhaustive historical research and detailed textual analysis.[4] While the BBT has attempted to provide a historical record of all the editorial changes and has set up websites (e.g., BBT.info, BBTedit.com) to explain the revisions and to invite devotees to report findings of further errors, there is no one universally accepted scholarly edition or authoritative commentary of Prabhupāda's books, particularly of the *Bhagavad-gita*.

When I was invited by Professor Graham Schweig to interview devotees in Los Angeles and record their views and perspectives on the crisis, I wondered whether such a project could throw fresh light on the debate. There is a vast, at times passionate and polemical, debate on various websites, internet forums, and message boards, and many devotees have written extensively and critically on the theological implications of post-charismatic editing. Moreover, the editing of Prabhupāda's books does not simply have an ethical element; it is an ethical commitment from the very outset. I was, however, mistaken. I received the warmest of welcomes in LA, and it was my great good fortune to interview some remarkable devotees and to have informal discussions and online exchanges with others. The outcome is a series of thought-provoking recordings that provide a wide spectrum of views.

THE LOS ANGELES COMMUNITY

The Los Angeles ISKCON community describes itself as

> a nonsectarian community dedicated to spiritual education and promoting unity and peace in the world through chanting the holy name, distributing sanctified vegetarian food and propagating spiritual knowledge and practices based on the great ancient scriptures, as presented by His Divine Grace A.C. Bhaktivedanta Swami Prabhupāda.

The Los Angeles New Dvaraka Temple was established by Prabhupāda in 1970, and his living quarters above the temple are a constant reminder of his presence. The Temple acts as the Western World Headquarters for ISKCON, and most importantly, Los Angeles was also the center of the Bhaktivedanta Book Trust publishing house in North America and the center of book production and book distribution for over forty-five years. No other ISKCON community in the world has the same detailed knowledge and understanding of the history of the editorial and publishing processes as these Los Angeles devotees.

The interviews immediately preceded the coronavirus lockdown, and having had time to reflect, I have realized that what was unique and precious about the interviews was that each devotee brought to the debate their entire life experience and their love and reverence for Prabhupāda. The interviewees contextualize the editing controversy in ways that touch upon a vast field of fluctuating and fluid associations, memories, and concerns about ISKCON's past, present, and future. All express a deep emotional and spiritual connection with Prabhupāda's books, but among those who are most upset are the first-generation disciples, for whom reading the *Bhagavad-gita* or the *Krsna Book* was critical to their joining ISKCON. In the 1960s and early 1970s, many were "hippies," part of the anti-establishment counterculture, and some were already exploring Eastern culture and psychedelics. The interviewees came from different backgrounds—Baptist, Episcopalian, Catholic, and Jewish—but were spiritually unsatisfied and "seeking the ultimate, the Absolute Truth." Prabhupāda's books were key influences in the life choices that they made, and many echo Balai dasi's statement that in reading Prabhupāda's books, "Every question I ever had or didn't even know that I had, everything was answered." Siddhanta dasa comments:

> But nothing really answered all my questions internally until I got that *Back to Godhead* magazine and read the main article by Prabhupāda, and it answered all my questions and more. It was like a light bulb went off, not only in my head but my heart. . . . If I hadn't come across that devotee handing me a *Back to Godhead* magazine, just a simple magazine, in Dallas, I wouldn't be here. I probably would have committed suicide by now.[5]

Vaikuntha Priya was brought up as a Catholic, but says that ISKCON offered God realization, "everything I wanted to know about the Divine Person I could finally have answers . . . because I'm French, I was very philosophical. So reading the Gita and other Vedic texts, that was very attractive to me." Purushottam Kshetra dasa reports that after first reading the *Bhagavad-gita* cover to cover he said to a friend: "This is an amazing book. Either it's the world's greatest fiction book, or it's all true and I better listen to what it has to say."

Book distribution (*sankirtan*), ISKCON's principal means of spreading Krishna consciousness, has strong spiritual and philosophical implications. Nearly all the interviewees had engaged in book distribution and believed that the books were "spiritual medicine," and that any contact, however fleeting and apparently inconsequential, with Prabhupāda's words would be life-changing. Purushottam Kshetra dasa maintains that "Even contact with edited books will have their eternally beneficial effect. This we have practically witnessed." However, many devotees had studied the Macmillan *Gita*, the "72 classic *Gita*, and today are mortified to find the original books "shunted aside." They feel as if "the chastity of the books had been violated."[6]

Several interviewees had specialized as copy editors, proofreaders, or transcribers, and most were familiar with the editing controversy's principal actors and protagonists. I was surprised at how often interviewees said, "Yeah, Garuda, I know him," or "Edith Best? Oh, you mean Urmila." "Yeah, I've known Jayadvaita Swami for decades' or "I heard Dravida Prabhu's temple presentation on the changes." "Yes, Austin Gordon, Bhutatma, we've had long conversations, and we're on the same page." Sometimes when I named a devotee, the interviewee would say something understated: "Yeah, I am familiar with him. I was married to him for about seven years." While the controversy is very much about scholarly standards, in LA it is also personal and political. Los Angeles ISKCON is a living, close-knit community, albeit with global networks. Despite what many devotees call "shenanigans," intimate association with, and service to, godbrothers and sisters remain cherished ideals and practices.[7] The interviews lead to the strong conclusion that the controversy has become a lightning rod or touchstone for many of the perceived ills and changes in contemporary ISKCON.

"Is the editing controversy a tempest in a teapot?"[8] Not everyone I met was exercised about the editing controversy. Govinda Datta dasa was not perturbed and did not see it as a crucial issue, while other devotees note that "we're distributing a lot of the edited books, and people are still reading them and coming to join the Hare Krishna movement." As I waited for *prasadam* in the distribution hall, Bhrigupati dasa, one of the most zealous and respected of all book distributors, told me that he was happy to distribute the traditional books as well as the edited ones. He commented that the spiritual message remains the same and regards the two BBT editors, Jayadvaita Swami and Dravida dasa, as "pure devotees who have performed this service faithfully." Karuna Dharani dasi reports that she respects the critics "because their hearts are dedicated to Prabhupāda and Prabhupāda is nondifferent from his words," but that she is not against the editing because Prabhupāda always wanted mistakes to be corrected. She adds that for her, loyalty and dedication, through thick and thin always trump anything else.

> One thing I have to say is I don't know the people so well who are in favour of turning it back to the originals. I don't know them very well. But I do know the people who have published the books from the get-go, from the beginning—people like Dravida, who did the editing—and I have faith and trust in them . . . in their sincerity, in their competence.

Other interviewees were torn and found themselves wavering: "I go back and forwards in my mind as I hear the arguments on both sides." Ratnabhusana dasa calls attention to the very important issue of translation in a globalizing world—something that very few devotees mentioned.[9] He observes that Prabhupāda's books are being translated into languages as different as Farsi, Arabic, and Chinese, and that translation necessarily involves cultural interpretation. He is also the only devotee to dare to suggest that there might be something of a bandwagon.

> Some of the people that are very angry may not even read that much and might not have even noticed the changes if someone hadn't told them. Then when they hear that "Oh, they changed the books," they're like "What?!" And then they go and look just for the changes.

There is also support for Jayadvaita Swami from interviewees, even from those who disagree with the BBT policies.

> Even Jayadvaita, they put him out as being evil or something, but I'm sure he had every good intention. And I know him personally. He's not someone who dislikes Prabhupāda and wants to destroy his books. He feels he's doing the best thing he could possibly do.

But there are others who think, "This is evil."

Prabhupāda's Heroic Pilgrimage to the West: Chaitanya's *Senapati-Bhakta*

Prabhupāda's voyage to the United States in 1965 to obey his spiritual master's instruction to bring global missionary Vaishnavism to the Western world is for ISKCON an epic event of legendary proportions and fulfills a prophecy made by Sri Chaitanya Mahaprabhu. In the *Chaitanya-mangala*, written by Locana dasa Thakur, Chaitanya describes the reason for his descent in 1486 in West Bengal, India: "With the powerful chopper of *harinama-sankirtan*, I will cut the hard knots of demoniac desires from the hearts of everyone." Chaitanya is then believed to predict the appearance and activities of Prabhupāda centuries later: "Even if the sinners reject religion or flee to foreign countries, still they will get My mercy. I will send My *senapati-bhakta* to go there and deliver them."[10]

Many interviewees recall the early days with Prabhupāda as gloriously wonderful. "It was just like a very close-knit and loving family." It is remembered as a time when Prabhupāda inspired a "ragtag band of transcendentalists" to abandon all "mundane" considerations. "As a devotee you gave up everything, you gave up your career, your education, working and your financial security, and you just dove in" (Ratnabhusana dasa). This creative and ecstatic era is compared with the events of the post-charismatic period and the power politics of contemporary ISKCON. Interviewees' personal experience of deviation and corruption, and of the "falling down" or "blooping" of so many gurus has cast a very long shadow. Kriyashakti devi spoke of the period after 1977, the time of the zonal acharyas, as "a devastating time, a time when power-hungry gurus wanted their guru's house, wanted their guru's fame, and usurped and hijacked his establishment."[11] Another interviewee commented that there are a lot of people "who love Krishna, who love Prabhupāda, who do not feel happy coming to ISKCON because of the history, and the amnesia and the whitewashing of the history."[12] The contrast between the "pure" devotee committed to the selfless service of Krishna and the wranglings and "shenanigans" of today had led several interviewees to remain on the fringes. They had left the temple community to avoid involvement in politics, but remained wholly absorbed in, and committed to, the life on the spiritual platform. For some devotees, the editing crisis is yet another sign that Prabhupāda's disciples have failed him. Prabhupāda's last instruction to his devotees was that they should prove their love for him by cooperating. "And we have not given him what he wanted. We're giving him our version of what he wanted."[13] The interviews make very clear that for some interviewees, the experiences of deviation from Prabhupāda's teachings have led to a lack of trust in the Governing Body Commission (GBC) and the gurus, which is projected onto the issues over editing.

ISKCON: A Society of the Book

Prabhupāda's greatest gift to the world was to bring to the West translations of the key texts of Vaishnavism—*The Bhagavad Gītā As It Is* (1968), *Śrī Īśopanishad* (1969), *Bhagavad-gita As It Is* (1972 unabridged), *Srimad-Bhagavatam* (1972–1977) (30 vols.), *Caitanya-caritāmrta* (1974–1975) (17 vols.), *The Nectar of Instruction* (1975). Prabhupāda also published summary studies: *Teachings of Lord Caitanya* (1969); *Krishna, the Supreme Personality of Godhead* (chapters 1–37), (1970–1971); and *The Nectar of Devotion* (1970). During the final twelve years of his life, Prabhupāda translated over sixty volumes of Vaishnava scriptures into English.

These texts are ISKCON's most precious resources. And while ISKCON is best known to outsiders for its exuberant and blissful *kirtan*, Prabhupāda was both a traditionalist and a reformer who initiated his followers into a disciplined knowledge of the sacred "Vedic" texts. The daily *Bhagavatam* and *Bhagavad-gita* classes ensure that devotees become familiar with the original Sanskrit slokas, the one-to-one translation of each word, and the interpretative purports. This rigorous spiritual formation within Chaitanya Mahaprabhu's tradition of *bhakti* yoga has produced devotees who are exceptionally textually literate and whose everyday conversation is peppered with Prabhupāda's words and phrases. Within LA's temple community, there are a great many devotees qualified to expound Gaudiya Vaishnava theology and the philosophy of *achintya-bheda-abheda* through the lens of Prabhupāda's teachings. It is this deep immersion in Prabhupāda's books and instructions that has enabled ISKCON to assume a brahmanical or priestly role to western Hindu diasporic congregations. And since ISKCON is literalist and lineal in its textual interpretation, the veracity and authenticity of the translations are of paramount concern. Several devotees felt that since ISKCON's philosophy comes down from the disciplic succession, any change is criminal and potentially illegal.[14]

Prabhupāda's commitment to translate, publish, and distribute the key Vaishnava texts can be compared to the resolve of Protestant reformers to produce accessible vernacular Bibles.[15] He established the Bhaktivedanta Book Trust in 1972 and, in 1974, appointed Hansadutta dasa BBT trustee for life with these words: "The devotees may fail, the temples might fail, but my books will live forever."[16] Many interviewees witnessed Prabhupāda's hands-on engagement in the editing and artwork of his books and recall that he called the American tendency to want change "the American disease." Prabhupāda believed that his books were divine revelations, and many devotees quoted this instruction verbatim:

> I speak what Krsna has spoken. That's all. Very easy. Everyone can do that. Not only I. Any of you, you can do this. Simply speak . . . what Krsna has said.

That's all. Don't make addition, alteration. Then you become rascal. Immediately you become rascal.[17]

However, others, some with publishing experience, also recognized that the mantra, "no change, no mistakes," is problematic, not only because Prabhupāda's remarks about his editors vary according to time, place, and circumstance, but because of the difficulties that the early devotees experienced.

Ekkehard Lorenz argues that Prabhupāda's work is neither text-critical nor systematic and that he drew from whatever sources were available to him. His books nowhere state the actual sources on which they are based.[18] Jayadvaita Swami in *Editing the Unchangeable Truth* (2005),[19] offers a remarkable overview of the editorial history of Prabhupāda's books and his own editorial responsibilities. He comments that any editor, typically, strives to bring out a work that is properly polished and yet stays as close to the author's language as possible. For Prabhupāda's books, this could be especially challenging. Jayadvaita notes that the books were dictated on a Grundig dictating machine, using tapes that each afforded perhaps an hour of dictation and which were afterwards re-used. While this enabled Prabhupāda to achieve greater speed, he had less opportunity to review and revise his words, he sometimes spoke passages twice, and—most of all—he had to depend on the accuracy of his transcribers. Especially in the early years, accuracy was poor. The transcribers were not yet deeply familiar with his philosophy; they had difficulty with his strong Bengali accent, and most of his Sanskrit words and quotations were strange to their ears. Moreover, Prabhupāda's frequent clicking of the switch to start, stop, and review his dictation clipped short many words or deleted them entirely. The transcribers gradually became well versed in his philosophy, accustomed to his accent, and familiar with his favorite quotations. And some of the transcribers learned the Sanskrit and Bengali alphabets to refer to the source texts that Prabhupāda was using. The most infamous examples of mistakes quoted by interviewees were the translation of *pitṛloka* by "land of trees" rather than "land of the ancestors," and the translation of *gorakṣa* by "cattle-raising" instead of "cow protection." (*Bhagavad-gita* 18.44). Balai dasi notes that she herself had made mistakes in transcribing Prabhupāda's words, writing that Mathura was surrounded by "canons" rather than "canals," and that "the city was decorated with horse heads and cow's heads" rather than "horse sheds and cow sheds."

The devotees recognize that during Prabhupāda's lifetime, his manuscripts were heavily edited for readability and accuracy by numerous editors, including Hayagriva, Rayarama, Satsvarupa dasa (later Satsvarupa Goswami), Purushottama, Hrishikesananda, Syamasundara, Gaurasundara Dasa, Pradyumna dasa (a Sanskrit scholar), and the most recent editors, Jayadvaita Swami, who began his editorial work in 1970, and Dravida dasa, who began in 1975. Of these editors, Hayagriva (Howard Wheeler), an associate professor of English literature at Ohio State University, is regarded as "Krishna-sent."[20] However, even he is criticized for his excision of some passages by Prabhupāda, particularly Prabhupāda's contentious remarks over the moon shot,[21] and his statements that the stars are moons reflecting our sun's light.[22] Hayagriva was also criticized for his use of the term "The Blessed Lord," rather than "the Supreme Personality of Godhead."

PRABHUPĀDA'S LANGUAGE AND "MOOD": HIS NON-DIFFERENCE FROM HIS BOOKS

Prabhupāda's mission was to bring about a complete cultural and spiritual transformation of the West, and his books are intended to bring about that purification of the heart. He says,

> As stated in the *Srimad-Bhagavatam* (1.5.11): "Literature that is full of descriptions of the glories of the unlimited Supreme Lord is a different creation, full of transcendental words directed toward bringing about a revolution in the impious lives of this world's misdirected civilization." Even if imperfectly composed, the *Bhagavatam* says, such literature is "heard, sung, and accepted by purified men who are thoroughly honest."

Prabhupāda promised to be always present with his disciples in his books. The editing controversy is therefore as much about the heart as the head. It cannot be disassociated from the emotions that devotees feel for Prabhupāda as Krishna's representative from the spiritual world and a self-realized soul. The editing controversy is viewed from the perspective of *guru bhakti* and *guru seva*. Prabhupāda is described by interviewees as "strong as a thunderbolt, soft as a rose," "fearless," "like a lion," "energetic, but always calm." Balai dasi commented, "You could just see anything Srila Prabhupāda touched or anything he did, how he ate, how he spoke, everything was just Krishna. And he had so much energy that he used every second to preach about Krishna consciousness." The devotees speak of Prabhupāda's books as imbued with his mood and presence—"full of spiritual potency." They cherish his poetic style, "alluring" presentation, "sweetness of heart," beautiful cadence, and flow of text. Many became devotees after reading the original Gita, "even with the typos and the errors, it's filled with love, and it comes through to your heart" (Siddhanta dasa). Rsabhadev dasa remarks on the living quality and vitality of Prabhupāda's language: "And {Prabhupāda} put his realisation into the text. So the language was living because it was imbued with his moods, with his consciousness. So to tinker with that is . . . what can I say?" Many devotees agree that the editing of Prabhupāda's books after his death in 1977 went "way too far" and was not *bhakti*-driven—it changed the "mood" if not the meaning of Prabhupāda's books. Siddhanta dasa reflects on the importance of transparency, "if you are going to edit the author who has left the planet, then that should be made clear that this is not the original, this is a second or third edition."[23] Kriyashakti devi dasi puts the same idea vividly. She says that the editing changes "erase a memory, erase an event, erase a time frame, erase history."

There are many reasons why the post-charismatic editing controversy is so emotionally charged.[24] Firstly, the supreme duty of the devotee is to please the spiritual master, and to obey his instructions (*vani*). It is disrespectful and shameful to believe that one could know better. The principle of *arsha-prayoga* states that one should not see mistakes in what the spiritual master has written or think that his writings may be changed to make them more effective or politically correct. To preserve his teachings in their originally published form is the way by which the Acharya is honored, and to do otherwise is to dishonor him. Thus, *arsha-prayoga* is a principle to which devoted followers of a bona fide spiritual master must adhere without deviation.

Secondly, Prabhupāda states with humility that his teachings come down unchanged from the whole line of disciplic succession. Kriyashakti devi dasi remembers him repeatedly saying, "I didn't write these books. These books were dictated to me." To alter his writings without his consent is very dangerous; it is to alter the instructions of a realized master whose lineal descent is from Krishna himself. It is "to jump over the guru."

Thirdly, editorial changes bring about a loss of Prabhupāda's unique charisma, mood, and voice. Prabhupāda's language, which even in his lifetime sounded archaic, has a solemnity, dignity, and "sweetness." "His words carry their own energy and unique and precise meaning or flair."[25]

Fourthly, ISKCON is a literalist movement that interprets Vedic texts through the lens of Prabhupāda's writings. Any change can therefore be catastrophic, leading to error.

Finally, post-charismatic editing sets a precedent for the future. Editors who find certain passages too intense or politically or socially incorrect could be led to delete or transform them without the recognition that the books must be understood by "the purified consciousness." Vaikuntha Priya dasi comments, "That's a very dangerous game, especially when the person is not there."[26] She speaks on behalf of those many devotees who see the post-charismatic editing crisis as emblematic of the way in which ISKCON has failed the spiritual master—the failure to cooperate, the failure to spread Krishna Consciousness in the way that Prabhupāda wanted, and the failure to develop *achar* (divine qualities) as well as *prachar* (the preaching mission).

> Talking about real compassion. Talking about having an open heart. Loving more fully. Connecting, being relatable, so that we can really have a real impact

on people and showing them that we care. We can't just talk about compassion and not live it. We practise spiritual life from the chin up. No! *Bhakti* is a process of the heart.

Bhutatma dasa's interview is illuminating in that he, like Garuda dasa, had changed his mind. For a time, he believed that the changes "weren't a big deal," but as he studied the changes his views altered:

> First of all, . . . you really shouldn't fool with it at all unless it's a clear mistake. . . . Prabhupāda approved it and he's invested his potency, and he's approved that as his voice. Which is the essence of any writing as it gives expression to the author's personality, right? So he's approved it. So that means he's OK that "This does express me accurately." So why change anything unless it's clearly a mistake? And . . . the changes are substantial. They're significant. These are verses that many devotees memorized, and all of a sudden, it's a different verse. Now, the meaning is still there, you could say, although you could even argue with that. . . . But I think the issue is . . . it's a loss of voice, it's a loss of a sense that this is Prabhupāda speaking to you.

Bhutatma dasa was concerned not only with the loss of Prabhupāda's voice and charisma but also with the implications for his life-transforming instructions (*vani*):

> It's a crisis in ISKCON. It's a crisis because people care so much and because these books are . . . the basis of his {Prabhupāda's} whole movement. And our philosophy says that the *vani*, the instruction of the guru, that these words, each word is a *bija*, it's a seed. . . . [Prabhupāda] said, specifically, I heard it many times, that "If you can understand one word, then you can be liberated," because each word is invested with *bija*, that seed potency. So if you really get it, if it really penetrates the ego, that word can illuminate you. So this is like the code. It's like behind all the word processing programs, this is the code for our movement and for Prabhupāda's preaching. So to me, I approach it in a reverential way.[27]

"NO ERRORS, NO CHANGES": THE CRITIQUE OF POST-CHARISMATIC EDITING

The most heartfelt cry about the editing crisis came from Kriyashakti devi dasi:

> Prabhupāda's books are not under protection, they're under slaughter basically. They're being torn apart. Instead of the King James version of the *Bhagavad-gita* we've got the King Jayadvaita Swami version of the *Bhagavad-gita*,

> drastically changed with hundreds of thousands of corrections, and the beautiful cadence is gone.

Many interviewees argue that the books published in Prabhupāda's lifetime were accepted joyfully by him, that he taught from them, and that he urged his followers to distribute them. They believe that authority has swung too far from Prabhupāda to the BBT. The multiplication of the versions of the *Bhagavad-gita* is bewildering for devotees and painful for the early disciples. They mourn the fact that the editing does not conform to universal publishing standards—as applied, for example, to the sacred texts of other religious traditions—and argue that if a book is substantially revised, it should have the name of the editor(s) prominently on the cover. They point to numerous alterations in the edited books that are not closer to the original taped lecture or transcription, and some suggest that, unlike Hayagriva, the later editors did not have the training, background, or scholarly skills to qualify them to undertake such a project. Their remedy is to stop further editing until agreement can be reached on a set of editing guidelines. Meanwhile, there should be transparency about the publishing and editorial history. The relation of the BBTI to copyrights on the books should be clarified legally. In many ways, these demands echo the suggestions that Jayadvaita Swami himself made earlier in the BBT booklet *Responsible Publishing,* in *Gita Revisions Explained*, *Bhagavatam Revisions Examined*, *Bhaktivedanta Book Trust Editorial Policies*.

Govinda Dasi, a senior disciple of Prabhupāda, was interviewed via a telephone link. A multitalented artist, communicator, and writer, she believes passionately that she has been given an order by her spiritual master to defend his books. She is a fearless critic of the post-charismatic editorial policies and argues that after Prabhupāda's demise in 1977, the BBT and Bhaktivedanta Book Trust International, Inc. (BBTI) have been publishing revised editions of Prabhupāda's books, heavily edited by disciples without his authorization. "Some of his leading disciples, such as Jayadvaita Swami, unauthorizedly changed and edited most of Prabhupāda's original translations and books, thus perverting and misinterpreting the real meaning and rendering them useless."

Govinda dasi speaks from very personal experience. She remembers that Prabhupāda was involved with every aspect of his book production process,

> I was one of the early devotees who transcribed some of his books from the original tapes. He would make tapes at night. And I transcribed *Nectar of Devotion*, I transcribed part of *Caitanya-caritamrta*, and also part of *Srimad-Bhagavatam*, not so much. My work was more with the other books. However, he {Prabhupāda} never wanted changes made to them other than light editing.

And light editing . . . I think he called it "no interpolation," those were his exact written words, and no . . . just make it smooth, typographical errors, that sort of thing."

Govinda dasi also points out that Prabhupāda was extremely happy with the books published in his lifetime:

When the 1972 Gita was published by MacMillan, Prabhupāda was overjoyed. He read his books daily and spoke from that original *Bhagavad-gita* for over 10 years! He gave lectures on nearly every verse in that original Gita, and he requested only a couple of corrections, such as "the planet of the trees," (to be changed to "the pitris"), and a couple of other small corrections. Had only those few changes been made, perhaps this controversy would never have occurred.

Govinda dasi recalls that Prabhupāda regarded the artwork in his books as having intrinsic spiritual, aesthetic, and ethical value, and that he was explicit that the paintings and drawings should never be removed. She is therefore fiercely opposed not only to the print editing but also to the withdrawal of the original artworks and the insensitive insertion of paintings that "don't have the same drama, the same excitement,"

I'm an artist, and art actually was very, very important to Srila Prabhupāda. Reading Jadurani, one of our godsisters who did artwork in the very beginning, he really encouraged artists to depict the spiritual world because he used to call them "windows to the spiritual world."[28] In other words, artwork that was of a spiritual nature that would lift people's consciousness. And that original Gita had many such paintings in it, but many of them were removed. In fact, the whole disciplic succession was removed. . . . [This] is the complete disregard, blatant disregard for Srila Prabhupāda's instructions that "don't remove the pictures, don't change my books." This brings about great ire to those of us who have dedicated our life to him.

For Govinda dasi, the resort to the law courts seems inevitable:

I won't say that there was a plot. I won't say anything like that because I'm not sure about that. However, if a person got carried away and over-edited a book and then 90 percent of all of the disciples are saying "why have you done this," it would seem normal, it would seem reasonable that they would want to work it out and talk about it, and they would want to figure out what the best solution was. But unfortunately, BBTI has stonewalled all of the disciples, even the senior ones like me, and Garuda, Graham Schweig, has also been stonewalled. And so that in itself leads us to believe that they don't want to work this out. They want to work it out in court, and that's right where we're going.

The BBTI's perceived intransigence, together with the weakness of ISKCON's leadership, is seen by Govinda dasi as leaving committed devotees no choice:

> Obviously, BBTI is not willing to make any concessions. They've made that clear to Garuda, they've made it clear to everyone. I think the only way to get them to do anything is to go to court because what they've done is illegal. And what they're doing is now becoming a big wart on your nose, the elephant in the room that smells so bad that you can't even ignore it anymore. And that is what's kind of happening because most of Prabhupāda's disciples, with the exception of the handful that are running the movement, that are running ISKCON . . . and even including some of those that are running ISKCON, but they can't say so. I've had people tell me, "Oh, Govinda dasi, we don't read anything but the original books at home, but I can't say that publicly because I'll lose my position," or "My real estate company will suffer," or "My kid goes to school there, I'll get . . . he'll have some kind of problems." It's that serious.

Govinda dasi, like many interviewees, claims that the Bhaktivedanta Book Trust International, Inc., is not the authentic Bhaktivedanta Book Trust (BBT) founded by Prabhupāda. She argues that "the BBT and the BBTI are two different animals entirely. They're not even the same species." Prabhupāda's Bhaktivedanta Book Trust is a legal trust with no connection with ISKCON, whereas the Bhaktivedanta Book Trust International, Inc., is a California corporation formed in 1988, eleven years after Prabhupāda's death. Govinda dasi is intensely critical of "a kind of plan, underground plan which some people would call a conspiracy, to redo Prabhupāda's books completely, and to take the editions from the BBT Trust and put them in a corporation called BBTI, BBT International Incorporated."

> And so this actually has created a huge rift in the Krishna consciousness movement because most of the early disciples, myself included, think that this was an unethical, immoral, and probably illegal thing to do. So that is kind of what's happened here in a nutshell, I might say.

Govinda dasi refers to the court case of 1998, when Prabhupāda's original *Gita* had been out of print and unavailable for about twenty years. The BBTI sued one of the trustees of the BBT Trust for printing the original Gita. However, the judge forced a settlement, licensing the defendant to print the original books.

> Now after so many years, people are seeing the vast differences between the edited Gita . . . and, by the way, there are about six different editions of them. I wouldn't say that there's 21 percent change in all of those editions, but there's

definitely more than 20 percent change in the 1983 and the original "72 version, the original version. So now those are available. And as people read them and discover the huge difference, they want them. But BBTI is committed to only the edited versions. And what many of us find very ironic is that in Srila Prabhupāda's ISKCON temples, the original books that made most of these people devotees, that actually we read when we were younger, they're not even allowed to be sold. Only the BBTI versions are allowed to be sold. So now it comes down to money, which is always the bottom line. BBTI is a corporation for making money. The BBT Trust was not.

Sri Jagadish dasa, from a very different perspective, also believes that the book changes are unforgivable because "the books are the foundation, the embodiment of Prabhupāda." Sri Jagdish dasa is shocked that ISKCON does not allow the distribution of the original books and considers that since the BBT became the BBTI, it has made editing changes that are illegal and result from "deviant business purposes." He admits that he was initially reluctant to be interviewed, but,

> I decided after a long think that I should come because I think I represent a lot of people who totally do not trust anything about ISKCON given the history. When Jayatirtha was the big guru, he fell down. They all turned into nightmares. And all the ducking and diving and hiding and covering, why trust anything? Especially now that the book changes are being made.

Sri Jagadish dasa in his interview, narrated something of his life history, which went far to explain his response to the editing crisis. He was born John Joannou in South Africa to Greek parents. In 1980, when he was eighteen years old, he was a "thoroughly confused young man" about to start his mandatory two years in the military, despite his principled opposition to the apartheid government. In the same year, he began to read the *Bhagavad-gita As It Is*, the Macmillan 1972 version, and spent his two years in the military studying Prabhupāda's books. He remarks that, "In South Africa the entire system of government was based on body type so to hear the profound philosophy that 'we're not these bodies, we're spiritual beings, these bodies are simply vehicles' was amazing." He comments,

> I ingested that *Bhagavad-gita* and studied a lot of the verses, particularly the second chapter, those verses I knew by heart. And I can't tell you how this totally changed my life around completely because it was so profound, it made so much sense.

In 1985, Sri Jagadish left South Africa for good, traveled to the USA, and, since he had heard of New Vrindavan, made his way there. His experience of "the fanatical, zealous, crazy cultish behavior of over-enthusiastic devotees'" and their devotion to Kirtanananda continues to haunt his view of ISKCON.[29] He left New Vrindavan and traveled to Los Angeles, where he was supported by two "wonderful" devotees, Nrsinghananda and Siddhanta. Given the importance of Prabhupāda's books in his life, Sri Jagadish is shocked by the fact that anyone dared to change his work and believes it to be a criminal offence,

> I will never listen to an ISKCON class, and I haven't in a long time because—and here's the point. I don't trust. I don't trust, and I think that the changing of these books, the changing of these books kills me. It kills me to see the new verses. Of course, I don't have those books, but I've looked up these verses, there's a lot spoken about this. They are atrocious. I think that they are dumbed down. What Jayadvaita has done is like *The Gita for Dummies* . . . . He is not a scholar, and you read his translations and they are flat, one-dimensional, and just dumbed down. And what they've done is they've changed the *siddhanta*, the ultimate conclusions of the philosophy.

A RADICAL APPROACH TO POST-CHARISMATIC EDITING

While devotees are united over the need to "get closer to Prabhupāda," outsiders, especially scholars, are likely to be as, or more, interested in the actual content of Prabhupāda's writings.[30] This is particularly so in the aftermath of the "Me Too" movement and the "Black Lives Matter" campaign. Professor Julius Lipner[31] had already suggested in the Berkeley symposium that controversial passages in Prabhupāda's writings that were irrelevant to ISKCON's spiritual message should be deleted. Krsna Avatar dasa went much further; he refused to condone any sectarian, sexist, or racist statements made by Prabhupāda on the grounds that they must be editorial interpolations.

Krsna Avatar was one of only three devotees who referred to the extant scholarly literature on ISKCON or the disturbing accounts of ex-devotees.[32] He asked, in particular, whether I had read *The Hare Krishna Movement.*[33] I had. It caused a stir at the time because one of the contributors, Ekkehard Lorenz, examined selected polemical statements made by Prabhupāda about Mayavadins, women, race, and gender, while other authors explored the reality of child abuse, gurukula, and a highly publicized child abuse scandal.

Krsna Avatar's approach emerges from his early experiences. His parents met Prabhupāda when he was five years old and became disciples. His father, who owned a chain of pharmacies, was a generous donor to the local Miami temple. Krsna Avatar, like many second-generation children, was sent to gurukulas, first in West Virginia, and then, when he was twelve years old, to Vrindavan. He narrates a harrowing story of sexual, emotional, and physical abuse made still more unbearable by the abuse he received as the child of black parents. Dhanurdhara Swami (Dennis Winiker), the head principal of the Vrindavan Gurukula Boys School from 1979 to 1986 and again from 1989 to 1995, told him to "go back to Africa with the rest of the monkeys." Dhanurdhara justified this abuse by reference to Prabhupāda's writings, particularly those passages that denigrate "black"/African people as sudra and deficient in the higher qualities. They reflect deep-seated Hindu beliefs that dark-skinned peoples represent the very bottom of the hierarchy of humanity—a direct reflection of India's ancient color-based *varna* system. Krsna Avatar argues that the frequent repetition of derogatory and controversial statements about black people in Prabhupāda's commentaries has desensitized ISKCON devotees to the reality of structural injustice and has had a very negative effect on their attitudes and behavior. Since Prabhupāda's purports are believed to be revealed by Krishna himself, they are the ideas and values that his followers imbibe and live by.

In the wake of Black Lives Matter and the murder of George Floyd, an African-American man, Krsna Avatar has found that many ISKCON leaders, even supposedly liberal gurus, express hateful racial bias and scathingly dismiss the idea that black people in the United States are the victims of violence and discrimination that compromise their ability to live with dignity and safety. He argues that this is a time when ISKCON should be showing its commitment to anti-racism and black liberation and developing an international agenda that promotes and incorporates solidarity of action to protect all minority groups across the world. Krsna Avatar asks rhetorically whether any black, woman, or Jewish millennial reading Prabhupāda's Purports could possibly be attracted to the movement, and since he cannot accept that these are Prabhupāda's own views or that Prabhupāda could ever justify racism, sexism, or anti-Semitism, he believes that *all* the commentaries are editorial interpolations and should be removed.

Krsna Avatar's conviction that the Purports are editorial interpolations is not shared. Indeed, the opposite tends to be true. Other interviewees often considered the Purports more personal and more expressive of Prabhupāda's thoughts than the word-for-word translations or interpretations of the verses. Siddhanta dasa points out that

> when you get into the Purports, then it gets really personal. These are Prabhupāda's words. . . . When you start to change the flavour of the Purport and the writing, then that's like stepping on toes, Prabhupāda's toes.[34]

However, many interviewees *did* discuss Prabhupāda's controversial statements as a contemporary issue that they recognize and want to respond to.

Overall, most devotees attribute statements likely to cause offence to Vedic cultural concepts, Indian societal influences, or to the fact that Prabhupāda was on a different transcendental plane. They recommend that Prabhupāda's negative statements about women, black people, or sudra should be carefully interpreted and contextualized by editors. Many devotees try to reconcile Prabhupāda's most uncomfortable pronouncements, particularly about women, with his behavior, which could be tender and celebratory. One interviewee, referring to Prabhupāda's notorious statement that "a woman likes a man who is very expert at rape" (SB 4.25.41), stresses that Prabhupāda empowered women in a way that many Indians of his generation found offensive.

Ratnabhusana dasa comments:

> Yes, there are some statements like that that are pretty heavy . . . but if you compare that with his life and how he treated people. He put things like that, but he had black disciples and women disciples who he respected the same as anyone else. . . . But what's written there is a little different than how he acted in his life. You could read that and say, "Wow, this person is racist. He says women are less intelligent."

Rsabhadev dasa also notes that:

> It reflects the time and place, something in Prabhupāda's upbringing . . . the culture that he came from. But in Prabhupāda's personal dealings, he was so different. . . . He had no racism in him. Insofar as women are concerned, he said so many things that were so positive . . . . And even in the first books he wrote, *Srimad-Bhagavatam,* before he even came here, that women have more natural devotional aptitude than men and in some ways they are superior.

Unlike Krsna Avatar, Bhutatma dasa fully accepts that Prabhupāda said those things ("and worse"), but "Prabhupāda is Prabhupāda." "You cannot sanitise him." Bhutatma argues that Prabhupāda was not mean-spirited—social conventions and bodily distinctions were simply not relevant to his thinking:

> He [Prabhupāda] was very respectful to women. I don't know how to perfectly explain it, some of these things. But on the other hand, Prabhupāda's greatest message was "you are not this body." So if you really take that to heart, then none of that matters very much at all because Lord Chaitanya was a complete revolutionary. He said, "I don't care whether you were born a brahmana, here or there, if you take this up, the soul will overwhelm any material consideration, any *karmas.*" And just do that. And your soul is part of God, it has every divine quality, that's going to overwhelm everything. So from that perspective, none of it matters that much because it's quite trivial and transitory. So I think that,

in a sense, was just how I understand Prabhupāda saying things like that, that in a way it was just all so trivial to him.

Vaikuntha Priya dasi also explains that a spiritual being like Prabhupāda, who is in communion with God, and with the Divine all the time, lives in a different world. He sees life from the perspective of many, many lifetimes and from a different consciousness, and he teaches that people could be so much more if they do not identify with the body, if they go beyond all bodily designations.

Krsna Avatar dasa's solution to the editing crisis is unorthodox. He advocates total generational change: "I would just fire the whole staff and put the BBT under the second generation and let us figure it out. So they should all go." He explains that while the first-generation devotees achieved positions of authority in their early twenties or even in their teens, the second generation, who had been trained to be priests and "pure" devotees, are entirely absent; "there's no one who's a temple president, there's no one on the GBC, there's no leadership position for us because they want all the power."[35] He claims that the editing controversy would only be finally remedied when his generation inherits responsibility and the older devotees obey Prabhupāda's instruction to retire at the age of fifty to become *vanaprastha* (retired and renounced).

Krsna Avatar's understanding of a missing generation *is* widely shared. Many devotees concur that real change will come about only with the retirement of the present editors, and nearly all interviewees accept that the movement needs to engage the energy and idealism of the young.[36] Conversely, however, many highly qualified interviewees lament that they are eager to train up young people to follow them, but the young generation is not interested.[37] A few speak of a corrupt hierarchy within ISKCON that privileges men, the older generation, and those attached to the temples.

THE POST-CHARISMATIC CONTROVERSY: "A MISDIRECTION OF PRABHUPĀDA'S MISSION?"

Kriyashakti devi in her interview takes a very different approach to many of the devotees. She testifies to Prabhupāda's modernity and reminds us of his appeal to youth.

> [But] Prabhupāda saw that this is not a Vedic culture. . . . This is Hare Krishna for the new age. This is not an archaic system. It's dynamic. It's evolving, it's growing, and Prabhupāda saw it like that . . . his international society, of course, was started in the United States and it was based on the temperament and mood of the youth at the time.

Similarly, while most devotees argue that ISKCON has failed Prabhupāda by not "protecting" his books, Karuna Dharani dasi courageously maintains, on the contrary, that the controversy takes attention away from the mission of ISKCON and from Prabhupāda's instructions.

> I think that if we really want to do the right thing, then we have to think of what Prabhupāda would do in this situation. We're here now; we can't go backwards. We're here now and we've got some books that are edited and some books that are not edited, and we're trying to make some decision or compromise or go extreme right or left. But if Prabhupāda stepped into the situation at this moment as it is, I don't think that he would put very much emphasis on this.

Karuna Dharani dasi explains her thoughts very persuasively:

> Prabhupāda was very much a man of action. He went around the globe in 10 years maybe 12 times, they say. And he wasn't so much a person of scholarship, although everyone applauds his scholarship. He wasn't so much of a man of writing and reading and study, although he was like that. But he was a man of action, about implementing things and starting many, many projects, and pushing things through so that they would be accomplished by his disciples—so many different programs and temples and farms and cow protection and *varnashram-dharma*, and different things having to do with art and culture. He said we would make a cultural conquest. So him being like that, and this is just me, but if he stepped into this situation right now, I don't think he would be very happy with this contention, and he would want us to go forward with his movement in reaching out to people and giving them Krishna consciousness as the first and foremost thing that is to be offered by us. And if haggling and quibbling over this word or that word would slow that down, he would put a stop to it immediately and he would do it in a second, and everyone would pay their obeisances and just go forward according to his instruction. They wouldn't have the time to do all this. It wouldn't be in their daily schedule to even think about this anymore. That's just how I feel.

Karuna Dharani dasi also notes that there are not only Prabhupāda's books, but thousands of his lectures and conversations that we can listen to. She argues that when we hear him speak and the way he speaks and the things he speaks about, we definitely get an impression of a person who didn't have much patience for people who wanted to quibble about details. He wanted action. He wanted solid progress for his Hare Krishna movement and success and a world conquest. Prabhupāda was not in favor of haggling and contention over long periods of time. "He didn't want us to spend our energies in that way."

> I try to always look at it through Prabhupāda's eyes, knowing his great desire for the BBT to be as strong and potent as possible. I think I should define what the

BBT is as an entity for the mass distribution of literatures that he wanted every person in America to have—his books. And he wanted that to be a function of every temple, that we send out soldiers to go and fight against *maya*, out in the precincts of the material energy, giving books to people who are unaware of anything about Eastern precepts, the scripture of *Bhagavad-gita*. He wanted us to be on the front line and to do that, and I've enjoyed that very much throughout my life. I like going and meeting people who have never heard about it and giving them a *Bhagavad-gita* and discussing it. So to take his BBT and turn it into an entity for making retro presentations, that's OK, but it goes against what his purpose is. It's not that it's wrong or bad or that it couldn't be supported in some way. But it goes against the original purpose and function of the Bhaktivedanta Book Trust, and I don't think he would be very pleased. I just don't think he would be very pleased. He would consider it a kind of diversion.

"CLOSER TO PRABHUPĀDA": THE DEFENSE OF POST-CHARISMATIC EDITING

Over the past decades, there has been a rising tide of opposition to the "unauthorized" editing of the works of Prabhupāda (e.g., adi-vani.org). Yet, as Lorenz points out, the "shastric principle of arsha-prayoga" cannot protect against scribal errors. He adds, "There is little evidence that Prabhupāda's pre-1978 books are more authentic . . . than later editions based on tapes, manuscripts, or transcripts."[38] Many devotees accept that Prabhupāda's instructions to his editors are that they should be loyal to the meaning of what he wrote and at the same time make whatever corrections were necessary to remove all mistakes and make his message clear and forceful.[39] There are letters in which Prabhupāda specifically requests his editors to revise and edit all copies meticulously and perfectly before publication. He does not want to present "a shabby thing," and he wants "erudite and deep-thinking men of the world to be able to enter into the intricacies of meaning in each verse."[40] He wants: "everything perfect for Krsna." In an exchange between Ramesvara and Tamal Krsna Goswami on July 13, 1977, Ramesvara says,

> The conclusion is that the editors have a very unique position, and are directly empowered by Srila Prabhupāda to work on his books . . . if the editors, like Jayadvaita, keep faith that Prabhupāda is infallible and edit only as a sacred act of devotion trying to be Prabhupāda's instrument, then the results we all want are achieved.[41]

The underlying question for all devotees then is: "Would Prabhupāda have wanted his disciples to continue the editing process after his death?"

Dravida dasa has been fielding questions on the editing controversy for decades both in face-to-face contact and in the technology-mediated worlds of cyberspace.[42] I asked him how he felt about the criticism thrown at him. He answered, "It may have been thrown at me, but I don't really get on Facebook so much. I know it's out there. I try not to dwell on it too much because it'll disturb my mind and I won't be able to do my work. But I know the issues." Dravida dasa and Jayadvaita Swami (who has now retired) are known to be committed and faithful devotees, but their approach is also that of editors interested in the whole publishing industry, the BBT online website, the BBT archives, the Digital Repository Project, the website BBT.info. Unlike any other interviewee, Dravida asked me to give him the questions in advance. In the interview he spoke as someone dedicated to producing books as error-free and as close to Prabhupāda's actual words as possible. He refused to make sweeping statements, preferring to consider the corrections individually case by case.

Dravida dasa is a Vaishnava intellectual, musician, and poet. He was born into a Jewish family but raised as a Communist. His father, a Marxist, was very active in the 1930s in the New York labor movement. Dravida protested against the Vietnam War, and, like many eligible young men, resisted the draft, finally gaining a medical deferment exempting him from military service. He studied philosophy at New York University, meeting others in the peace movement, but in 1969, after a serious bout of hepatitis, he began exploring different spiritual traditions—hatha yoga, Satchidananda's Integral Yoga, the Ramakrishna Mission, and so on. In 1973, he was introduced to Prabhupāda's books and was particularly attracted to the more philosophical publications such as *The Teachings of Lord Chaitanya*. He moved into the Brooklyn ashram, then a thriving center of book production and devotional art, and in 1974, he was initiated by Prabhupāda by letter. By this time, he had already started work as a proofreader. At the end of 1974, there was a crisis in the temple, and Prabhupāda decided to consolidate the whole press in Los Angeles. In 1975, Dravida had "the great blessing' of being part of the 17-books-in-two-months publishing marathon miracle. With editors, proofreaders, typesetters, and artists working 24 hours a day, all 17 books were printed within the two months.[43] In 1979–1980, he undertook some production managing and composition when he worked on the *Back to Godhead Magazine* (*BTG*) with Jayadvaita Swami in New York and Philadelphia. Since then, he has edited the *BTG* and books published by the BBT. From 1983 to 1989, he was a member of the team that produced the last six volumes of the *Srimad-Bhagavatam* (*Bhagavata Purana*). He also helped edit the revised version of the nine-volume *Caitanya-caritamrita* during 1995–1996 and the Krsna book from 1994 to 1995.[44]

Dravida dasa's position on the post-charismatic editing crisis is that the great majority of the alterations are not only defensible, but necessary. He says that he cannot see something that is obviously wrong in Prabhupāda's books and simply ignore it, and questions why a grammatical mistake, or the mishearing of a typist, should be immortalized forever. "What can I say? I'm steeped in this. I see something that's egregiously wrong, and it may have been wrong for 40 years. And I think, "Well, this has to be fixed for eternity."'

However, Dravida accepts that editing is not an exact science and that he and Jayadvaita are not infallible.

> Well, I'm not so fanatical that I think that we didn't make any mistakes. . . . So it's not that we're like this infallible thing. But we have a different perspective on. . . . Well, always you have what did Prabhupāda want? What was his standard? What would he be pleased with? If the original editor omitted, or distorted, some original content, by what logic shouldn't Prabhupāda's original, intended meaning not be restored?

I asked about some of the mistakes that had been made, giving as an example the abbreviated description of Prabhupāda as the Founder-Acharya of ISKCON in some publications. In most of Prabhupāda's books there is a frontispiece with a portrait of Prabhupāda, usually sitting on a *vyasasana*, with the words, "His Divine Grace A.C. Bhaktivedanta Swami Prabhupāda, Founder-Ācārya of the International Society for Krishna Consciousness and greatest exponent of Krishna consciousness in the Western world." Dravida was disarmingly apologetic about the fact that "and greatest exponent of Krishna consciousness in the Western world" had not been included in all the current printings:

> That's being fixed. That was a mistake on my part. . . . That's being fixed now. If you look at the latest printings of the Bhagavad-gita, for instance, Prabhupāda's always [described] . . . as the greatest exponent of Krishna consciousness in the Western world. Leaving that last phrase out on some printings was a mistake on my part. We were always told that we always must have the Founder-Acharya line. There were some books in the early days that didn't have that. So that's what we were focusing on, and I didn't bring that line about him being the greatest exponent of Krishna consciousness in the Western world in for . . . several of the printings of the Bhagavad-gita. I'm very sorry about that.

I then asked the key question: Did Prabhupāda give explicit instructions that the editing should continue after his demise?

> So the question, "Did Prabhupāda want editing to continue after his disappearance?" And the answer is yes. And the support for that comes in the conversation

> with Srila Prabhupāda on June 22nd, 1977. Now, if you know the history, that was just . . . less than five months before he passed away. This is in Vrindavan.[45]

This conversation is often referred to as the "Racal Editors'" conversation.[46] Prabhupāda's clear instruction in this conversation is that the next reprinting of the books should wait until all the corrections had been made. While critics dispute the claim that it follows that Prabhupāda intended that editing would go on for decades into the future, the discussion shows that Prabhupāda trusts Jayadvaita and invests him with a certain authority. Prabhupāda agrees to Tamāl Krishna's assertion that the other editors should not make any changes without consulting Jayadvaita. Dravida dasa emphasizes that Prabhupāda trusted Jayadvaita Swami completely and worked with him for years on Cantos 5–10 of the *Bhagavatam*. On September 7, 1976, Prabhupāda wrote to Radha Ballabha dasa, the production manager of the BBT offices in Los Angeles, saying, "Concerning the editing of Jayadvaita Prabhu, whatever he does is approved by me. I have confidence in him."[47] On July 22, 1977, about four months before Prabhupāda's disappearance, Tamal Krishna Goswami sent a letter to Radha Ballabha dasa concerning Prabhupāda's instructions on fixing the mistakes in his books. Tamal Krishna Goswami wrote that Ramesvara Maharaja, then leader of the North American BBT in Los Angeles, had pointed out that discrepancies in Prabhupāda's books were due to three reasons: (1) typographical errors, (2) mistakes made by English and Sanskrit editors, and (3) transcendental mistakes dictated by Prabhupāda himself. Tamal Krishna Goswami states unequivocally that Prabhupāda wanted ***all*** mistakes to be rectified, although he adds significantly, "Please just try to make all the corrections in the new editions and everything will be alright, and of course don't make any unnecessary changes."[48]

Dravida dasa acknowledges the criticism that Jayadvaita is not a Sanskrit scholar but argues that he possesses something unique - experience. He points out that help was always available, and that Jayadvaita was able to consult Bengali and Sanskrit scholars, scholars who included Santosh, Nitai, and Pradyumna.

> First of all, we always have Sanskrit scholars who we can consult. And he {Jayadvaita} had Gopiparanadhana Prabhu, who was an excellent Sanskrit scholar, for the *Bhagavad-gita*. Gopiparanadhana Prabhu produced a wonderful translation of *Brhad Bhagavatamrta* and several other books—*Tattva Sandarbha*, *Laghu Bhagavatamrta*. And he was the Sanskrit editor on the completion of the whole *Bhagavatam*.

Dravida foresees that the editing will come to a natural end,

> There were tons of changes. . . . But I'm saying that, practically speaking, the last several years there's practically nothing being done with the *Bhagavad-gita*.

> And we are getting to the point where we can talk about finalizing these books and there's no more changes. Certainly when I leave, because Jayadvaita has retired.[49]

I asked Dravida Prabhu why Prabhupāda's works shouldn't be treated in the same way as an editor might treat the work of Shakespeare or Goethe by producing a critical edition. The answer was illuminating. Dravida said,

> But, you see, this is the fallacy. First of all, you have to look into how the books were first produced. They were not produced at all the same way that Goethe or other . . . or today, a commercial or academic editor would write a book. Today there is a collaboration between author and editor during which the manuscript is discussed and revised, but the situation is very different with Prabhupāda's translations. They can't be fixed by moving a few commas here and there, or by going back to the original publications.

Dravida, quite as much as his critics, always turns the discussion back to Prabhupāda's wishes and instructions:

> But what would Prabhupāda want? Would he want an accurate translation based on his translation, or would he want what was printed in 1972 because of the tremendous rush and we couldn't consult with Prabhupāda, he was in India? That's what you're facing. And you have the whole ISKCON movement now—millions and millions have been sold of this 1983 Gita, over 30 years now. More than 30 years, almost 40 years. And the thesis here [of those opposed to the changes] is that . . . it's a huge offense against Prabhupāda, and it has to be righted because . . . this is why ISKCON, it's failing here and there, which is not true. There's all kinds of reasons.

THE WAY FORWARD? THE BBT TEXTUAL REVISION REVIEW PANEL (RRP)

The interviewees generally spoke of what *should* happen rather than proactively suggesting the means to make it happen. This was perfectly sensible given that very few knew that steps had already been taken to bring all sides together. A meeting between the BBT and their scholarly critics, mediated by Vraja Vihari dasa from ISKCON Resolve,[50] took place in Washington DC in September 2019, in which there was a joint decision to set up a panel to identify Prabhupāda's instructions, research universal scholarly publishing protocols, and finally formulate editing guidelines and principles. Participants at the Berkeley Symposium were told that subsequently the BBT had reneged on this agreement. Dravida dasa, when interviewed, denied that he had reneged, and explained that the two BBT trustees present, Nareshwar dasa and Brahma Muhurta dasa, had exceeded their mandate.[51] Subsequently, a BBT Textual Revision Review Panel (RRP) was appointed to advise on editing guidelines produced by Dravida as the BBT editor. The only interviewees who knew the details of this development were Bhutatma dasa and Dravida dasa himself. I therefore refer to their comments.

Dravida states that he was encouraged to travel to Tirupati, have discussions with the GBC, and "come up with this Review Panel."

> The GBC would propose some members and the BBT would propose some members, and it's a very qualified board. They're not all BBT loyalists by any means. You've got Bhanu Swami, who has translated tons of . . . he's very familiar with the Sanskrit language and translation; and Bhakti Vijnana Swami, a very wise, educated former member of the GBC; Radhika Raman, who is the world authority on Jiva Goswami's *Tattva Sandarbha*; Kalachandji, who has been a professional editor for many, many years, the brother of Tamal Krishna Maharaja; and several others, like Keshava Bharati Maharaja, . . . and Krishna Rupa devi dasi, who is a professional editor. So, these are not at all BBT plants or anything. They are going to look at these edits, and we set up a whole bunch of criteria and examples the best that we could do. I've never done this before. . . . But that's what we have to work with.

Dravida spoke of his confidence in the Review Panel,

> I have more faith in this Review Panel than they [the critics] do because they're not BBT loyalists. They're very intelligent devotees and some of them, at least two that I know right off the bat, are Ph.Ds., and they can have an input on this. If anyone can figure it out, how we're going to resolve it, they can help us.

Bhutatma Dasa Prabhu (Austin Gordon), one of the BBT's most determined and scholarly critics, also welcomed the Review Panel as symbolizing a new dawn and the passing of the previous age when editors acting alone could make all the decisions. "It's a new day. It's time to look at it with fresh eyes, neutral eyes":

> So let's review it, let's make sure every change is justified, and let's have a standard that reflects Prabhupāda's instructions, which I would see as the *arsha-prayoga* principle, basically the first take on it is don't change it. That's the default position. Now, if it's a misspelled word, that's going to pass muster, right? No one will argue, we don't want misspelling. But as we move to this other stuff, we want to have to have it reviewed by, so to speak, uninvolved people. I would consider myself uninvolved because I didn't have a position. But let's review each and every change. And if all the changes are better, then they'll all stand. What are you afraid of?

Bhutatma accepted that the BBT Review Panel was not exactly what the critics had initially planned, but it was "an evolving dynamic process and a work in progress." He said that he and Garuda dasa were working on formulating principles and guidelines to submit to the panel.

> That's how things work in the real world—two steps here, one back. To me it's inconsequential. Because the fact is, inter partes the panel was created. Now, obviously, what's the panel going to decide and what are the principles and guidelines, and how will those interact with the revisions that are in place? That remains to be seen. But my argument, Graham's argument. is based on everything Prabhupāda said and the principle of *arsha-prayoga*, which he instructed us to follow. . . . The argument is you have to be very deferential, very conservative. And so when these changes are reviewed, it shouldn't just be that Dravida is sitting there saying Prabhupāda's over his shoulder approving everything. That doesn't wash. I don't buy that for a moment. . . . That's not the way Prabhupāda operated, that "Oh, yes, here is my disciple and Krishna is telling him everything." Such independence was Prabhupāda's personal prerogative. But he told us to work conjointly because, "You'll check and balance each other, and your imaginations and all these things will not be able to carry the day because you'll be checked." Like "What are you . . . what is that?" And that's what we need. And I think that panel, if it can be established in the proper attitude of deference, conservatism, and as John Trimble wrote, "The burden of proof is on those who want to change." We haven't had that. We've had Jayadvaita, who's had free-range editing, editing at will. And I'm not saying he didn't feel he was right. . . . That's all true. I don't disparage him. But I think it was inappropriate the way he did it. I think he got carried away, and that's why so many people object. So let's review it. Those changes which are justified will stand, and those that aren't will be reverted back to the original. What's so hard about that?

SUMMARY OF FINDINGS: RECOMMENDATIONS AND SOLUTIONS

I often ended interviews with a question, "How would you transform this crisis?" "How would you build bridges?" Most respondents favored a middle path. They felt that even where the editorial corrections were technically correct, there was a gradual loss, a "blurring," of Prabhupāda's "authentic" voice by the continuous posthumous editing since 1978. They believed that the original texts and the original printings authorized by Prabhupāda in his lifetime should be preserved and protected with the proviso that obvious mistakes in grammar and transliteration be rectified. All the original artwork should be restored. Any book that had been edited after Prabhupāda's death should retain the original title but include the editor's names on the cover. The more militant wanted to ensure that the devotees had control of the books so that the BBT editors could not simply "go their own way," and are prepared to achieve this, if necessary, by legal action. However, there were also interviewees who thought that the debate was a massive distraction from Prabhupāda's mission of global spiritual transformation, others who were happy with both the authorized and the edited books, while several felt ambivalent and puzzled, or skeptical that any agreement can be reached. The position of "no errors, no changes" is articulated by many, but was unlikely to provide a long-term solution. It was difficult to undo what had been done since 1977—reverse the tide, unpack the work of decades. Moreover, while some interviewees wanted a very light editing touch, others wanted the entire process of editing from Hayagriva onward sifted, probed, and clarified and *all* "corrections" signalled in a scholarly commentary. This commentary would also contain extensive cultural and historical contextualization of Prabhupāda's statements which may now be considered insensitive or offensive. There were also devotees in the wider ISKCON world who opposed the setting up of a board or panel to deliberate on the editing changes on the grounds that this further extended the editorial process.

Purushottam Kshetra dasa offers one of the most detailed solutions to the crisis: "Let me be the archaeologist that's going back into history and digging up these artifacts and have full access, as though I was going into a museum that collected all of the artifacts." He envisages a scholarly edition of each book containing Prabhupāda's original manuscripts or links to his original recordings and the various edited versions. Readers would then be able to flip from page to page and see for themselves all the different versions together with relevant audio or video links. The book for mass distribution would then simply footnote or reference the scholarly concordance.

> [We] should acknowledge our actions and take responsibility. We should put into print a concordance—showing each and every differing version side by side, published and un-published. . . . If this mea-culpa is prepared by the BBT, as opposed to an independent, outside agency, and particularly if the rationale for each change is clearly presented, there will at least be a record for anyone to appreciate the historical influences and other reasoning which led to each change, allowing the reader to judge for themself what Srila Prabhupāda's original intent was.

Purushottam Kshetra dasa urges that the BBT should allow unfettered access to scholars and that all this must be done immediately before all Prabhupāda's disciples leave, "before it becomes hearsay instead of first-hand testimony, before memory is lost."

Recommendations

The devotees generally want ISKCON to put into place measures at every level of the Society that will encourage dialogue, transparency, and inclusion. The majority believes that a harmonious outcome can only be reached through consultation, civility, and dialogue. The most favorable outcome would be:

- a statement of agreed guidelines and principles for future post-charismatic editing.
- a decision by the BBT to enable the original books to be distributed and made available in all temples and communities.
- the creation and publication by the BBT of a detailed editorial history, an "audit trail" for scholars, BBT staff, and other interested readers.[52] This would enable scholars to view and compare the original and revised manuscripts, editorial notes, the first and subsequent editions, and the Sanskrit and Bengali commentaries consulted by Prabhupāda. Also included for each title would be a production history, the names of the original editors, typesetters, proofreaders, layout and other production staff, and information on the prepress work, the size of the first print run, and the names of the printers and binders for the original edition.
- an agreed mass publication volume for each book, which would not be burdened with all the scholarly apparatus, but would refer to the concordance in footnotes.
- Consultation should range widely, be open to new ideas as well as traditional understandings, and engage devotees from different backgrounds, generations, and positions within ISKCON.
- the review panel should be driven not only by scholars and legal advisors, but by devotees with guru-bhakti, love for the spiritual master.

Reframing the Crisis

The editing controversy creates ambivalent, conflicting feelings. On the one hand, it highlights the gratitude devotees feel for Prabhupāda's continuing presence in his books, yet it can also come to symbolize all ISKCON's perceived failings and internal struggles. "This is why the movement is suffering, because we've deviated from the books." "If we went back to how Prabhupāda did things and the *ritvik*, the temples would be full of devotees again." There is a shared perception that, while Krishna Consciousness is attracting thousands of new devotees in many countries (including India, Eastern Europe, the Middle East, South America, and Africa), numbers are hemorrhaging in the United States and Western Europe. Los Angeles devotees show strong awareness of the "Hinduisation" of ISKCON, and ISKCON's dependence on Indian heritage donors. They feel that a movement that appealed initially to American converts, has over time become a religious home for many immigrant Indian Hindus in search of "traditional Hinduism" in diasporic environments.[53] They welcome LA's Indian disciples, considering them highly qualified, committed devotees capable of excellent leadership. However, there is also anxiety that Prabhupāda's mission to the West is weakening, and that the devotees, particularly the leadership, have "failed" their spiritual master. They have not obeyed his direct instructions to preserve and protect his books. They have not obeyed his specific instruction to cooperate. They have engaged in internal struggles, or alternatively, they have not confronted and dealt with problems, they have not spoken out, they have played safe, they have not wanted to "rock the boat."

Rsabadev dasa rightly reminds us that Chaitanya's movement began as a civil disobedience movement:

> For this movement to remain dynamic and purposeful, it should also be challenging the dominant culture. There should be religious plurality, and there should be evolving of an ethic of nonviolence. Until humans start to evolve that ethic within themselves, there's no hope for this planet.

As an outside observer, the recipient of so many acts of kindness, I have become acutely aware of the integrity of devotees on all sides. All support their arguments with reference to Prabhupāda's authority and authorization, quoting directly from conversations, letters, books, or recorded talks. I am reminded of the Jain doctrine of *anekāntavāda* ("many-sidedness") and wonder what we can learn from appreciative inquiry—the idea that we flourish by emphasizing the positive aspects and potentials of a society or organization rather than, or as well as, its weaknesses and failings. The controversy revolves to some extent about how to handle disagreement, and this paper seeks to reflect ISKCON's multiple voices and internal complexity. Prabhupāda's ideal of a peaceful, unified community identified by devotees' mutual love and service, which models something of great beauty to those outside it, is, for many devotees, difficult to reconcile with a seemingly recurring descent into acrimonious dispute. However, in intellectual, and perhaps even in devotional life, constructive disagreement can be considered a gift. By means of disagreement and dialogue, theologians, scholars, and devotees clarify, order, and develop their thought. Their interpretations will enter ISKCON's intellectual life and gradually the errors, confusions, and imprecisions will fall away. Many devotees will disagree. They will point out that the debate over the post-charismatic editing is not an intellectual game. However, I suggest that the post-charismatic editing debate can be positively reframed. Often presented in polemical, polarized terms, it could be reframed to reassure devotees that, as a young religious movement, ISKCON is encountering and negotiating the inevitable challenges that every religious organization faces as it institutionalizes, globalizes, transforms, and diversifies. ISKCON's present trials can be compared to the early Christian scriptural debates and to ongoing attempts to revise the language of the scriptures and liturgy. While the interview transcripts reflect diverse, and sometimes very emotional and combative views, they also reveal devotees' willingness to understand the viewpoints of others, and to seek clarification and guidance on the legal and institutional barriers to resolution and reconciliation. If the recommendations above are implemented, they may not satisfy all devotees, but they will enhance ISKCON's reputation for exacting scholarship, spiritual authenticity, and cooperative harmony, all dear to the heart of Śrila Prabhupāda. This will enable ISKCON to celebrate fully the achievements of all those whose lives have been, and are, dedicated to the editing, publishing, and distribution of Prabhupāda's books, and to recognize their crucial role in spreading the message of Krishna Consciousness to all corners of the world.

> I want to hear directly from Krishna, I want to hear from His pure representative, Srila Prabhupāda. And we did a great job. . . . We did better than any other religious organisation on the planet throughout history in recording the thoughts, words, and deeds of a saint. And now we should take advantage of that honestly and straightforwardly. (Purushottam Kshetra dasa)[54]

ACKNOWLEDGMENTS

I am profoundly grateful to Professor Graham Schweig, who invited me to the Berkeley Symposium on Post-Charismatic Editing and who arranged my stay in Los Angeles; to Sacinandana dasa and Patrikananda dasa, who set up the interviews; and to Jeanne Clausen (Dinadayadri dasi) for her expert transcription of the recordings. Above all, I acknowledge my indebtedness to so many wonderful devotees, and in particular: Balai dasi, Bhutatma dasa, Dravida dasa, Govinda dasi, Govinda Datta dasa, Karuna Dharani dasi, Krsna Avatar dasa, Kriyashakti devi dasi, Purushottam Kshetra dasa, Ratnabhusana dasa, Rsabhadev dasa, Siddhanta dasa, Sri Jagadish dasa, and Vaikuntha Priya dasi.

NOTES

1. Govinda dasi, "To Edit or Not To Edit—That Is The Question," at www.govindadasi.com.

2. The Bhaktivedanta Book Trust (BBT) is the world's largest publisher of India's classic books of spirituality and serves as the official worldwide publisher for the books of Swami Prabhupāda. For the BBT's editorial policies, see https://bbt.org/editorial-policies.

3. Rsabhadev dasa (Roy Richard), however, claimed that the only Prabhupāda disciples that he had ever met who agree to the post-charismatic editing are those who have some position or support within ISKCON. "Everyone that lives free and independent of ISKCON, they all concur that the books should definitely not have been changed. So you have the vast majority of Prabhupāda disciples not agreeing with these changed versions."

4. Bhutatma dasa (Austin Gordon) described the hours he had spent discussing the editorial alterations to just one or two verses.

5. Siddhanta dasa is the creator of the acclaimed "Prabhupāda Memories" series of books and DVDs [https://Prabhupādamemories.com/index.html; https://www.youtube.com/channel/UC-Ajeil3NjKKgeN9-fxeWwQ/videos]

6. Dravida dasa interview.

7. Even during my very short stay in LA I heard many stories of the devotees' mutual support and kindness during illness and personal hardship and witnessed the selfless hospice service and end-of-life care given to dying devotees.

8. Bhutatma dasa interview.

9. Dravida dasa is also very aware of the challenges of sympathetic, idiomatic translation, and the fact that mistakes can easily be made. He quoted one of the arguments of the editors that, "We're translating the books in other countries, and they look at it and they say, "We can't understand the sentence, the grammar's not right."

10. This prophecy will come to be accepted by all devotees as proof that Prabhupāda is the person empowered by Chaitanya to spread Krishna consciousness all over the world. *Senapati-bhakta* means he is the Commander-in-Chief of Lord Chaitanya's *sankirtan* army (Govinda dasi).

11. "When Srila Prabhupāda left in 1977, there were over 10,000 members in the movement worldwide. . . . Years later, I think by 1982 or so, there were 500 Srila Prabhupāda disciples left in the movement." Kriyashakti devi dasi interview.

12. Sri Jagadish dasa describes his stay in New Vrindavan as "mad, completely scary."

13. Vaikuntha Priya dasi interview.

14. E.g., Sri Jagadish Dasa interview.

15. Srila Prabhupāda arrived in New York with only his books, and even as he lay dying Yadubara's wife was holding a microphone to Prabhupāda's mouth, and he dictated a purport to the 10th Canto of Srimad-Bhagavatam with practically his last breath. (Dinadayadri dasi by email).

16. Siddhanta dasa's interview of Hansadutta dasa in *Memories: Anecdotes of a Modern-Day Saint*, Volume 3, Tape 35. Prabhupāda writes in a letter to all temples dated March 14, 1974: "I specifically formed the BBT to invest in it exclusive rights for the printing of all literature containing my teachings, writings, and lectures. In this way, the collections are to be divided fifty percent for printing new books and fifty percent for construction of temples." The funds from book distribution have enabled

millions of books to be published and vast temples to be built in India, including those of Vrindavan, Mayapur, Mathura, and Mumbai.

17. *Srimad-Bhagavatam* Lecture 1.5.29, Vrndavana, August 10, 1974.

18. Ekkehard Lorenz. 2004. "The Guru, Mayavadins, and Women: Tracing the Origins of Selected and Polemical Statements in the Work of A.C. Bhaktivedanta Swami." In Edwin F. Bryant and Maria L. Ekstrand, eds., *The Hare Krishna Movement: The Postcharismatic Fate of a Religious Transplant.* New York: Columbia University Press. pp. 112–128.

19. Jayadvaita Swami. 2005. "Editing the Unchangeable Truth: An Overview of the Editorial History of the Books of His Divine Grace A. C. Bhaktivedanta Swami Prabhupāda," *ISKCON Communications Journal*, Volume 11. See also Jayadvaita, July 24, 2009, BBT Talk with Pandavasena Group.

20. Rsabhadev dasa interview.

21. Hayagriva thought that Prabhupāda's conviction that the moon landing had not taken place would discredit Prabhupāda. Prabhupāda personally chastised Hayagriva for removing a passage concerning the 1969 moonshot from *Easy Journey to Other Planets*, the first book Prabhupāda wrote in India. See *Transcendental Diary: Travels with His Divine Grace A.C. Bhaktivedanta Swami Prabhupāda* 1992, an account by Hari Sauri Dasa, of his days with Prabhupāda. See the entry for May 23, 1976, Honolulu, Hawaii.

22. Dravida dasa noted that he and Jayadvaita Swami had to fix editorial mistakes and omissions, including those of Hayagriva: "But if you're trying to stick as close as possible to what Prabhupāda said, if that's what the critics are really concerned about, then they would have to agree with us that Hayagriva did some things that were out of bounds. He took things out that he didn't agree with. For example, in the second paragraph of the purport to Bhagavad-gita 10.21, Prabhupāda writes that the stars in the sky are like moons, that they're reflecting the light of our sun . . . and Hayagriva just took practically that whole paragraph out. He said, "People will not believe this. It'll reflect badly on Prabhupāda."'

23. Siddhanta dasa, who has made an extraordinary contribution to the Gaudiya Vaishnava movement by documenting the testimonies of Prabhupāda's disciples about their spiritual master, further states, "I would feel offended if someone changed my editing of the audio transcriptions from which my books are based, over and above obvious spelling and punctuation mistakes after my demise, unless I appointed someone to do so prior to my departure."

24. Bhutatma dasa recalls with emotion that Sravanananda dasa, even as he lay dying, asked Garuda dasa to make sure that Prabhupāda's books were protected (interview).

25. Vaikuntha Priya dasi interview.

26. Vaikuntha Priya dasi interview.

27. Bhutatma dasa goes on to say, "Even as an author myself, if someone changed my book without consulting me. . . . If they fixed errors, I'd be happy. But if they start making material changes, I wouldn't like that." "Even when I had the cancer, people wrote me and said, "Don't die because you have to fight this." I said, "Thanks," you

know, a little utilitarian. But it's incredibly meaningful to many, many devotees. For many, it's the most important thing going on. And it's not that they're dropping their *sadhana*, but they want the books to be as close to Prabhupāda's approved editions. So there's that side."

28. Jadurani devi dasi was the first Art Director of ISKCON and has painted over 200 works for ISKCON's temples and publications. Her painting style combines influences from both India and the West.

29. Sri Jagadish dasa advised me to read *Killing for Krishna: The Danger of Deranged Devotion* by Henry Doktorski, himself a former ISKCON devotee, CreateSpace Independent Publishing Platform (January 8, 2018). This tells the story of the most notorious crime in the history of ISKCON, the murder of Steven Bryant (Sulochan dasa) in 1986.

30. "The purpose of religion is to kindle faith, and to achieve this end there may be an emphasis on those facts and interpretations that nurture faith and a tendency to disregard the data that do not." Shukavak N. Das. 2004. "Bhaktivinoda and Scriptural Literalism." In Maria Ekstrand and Edwin H. Bryant, eds., *The Hare Krishna Movement: The Postcharismatic Fate of a Religious Transplant*. 97–111. New York: Columbia University Press. p. 97.

31. Emeritus Professor of Hinduism and the Comparative Study of Religion, Faculty of Divinity, University of Cambridge.

32. Rsabhadev dasa mentions his friendship with Dr. J. Stillson Judah of the Graduate Theological Union, and their discussions of Vaishnava literature and culture.

33. Maria Ekstrand and Edwin H. Bryan. 2004. *The Hare Krishna Movement: The Postcharismatic Fate of a Religious Transplant.* New York: Columbia University Press.

34. Siddhanta Dasa interview.

35. Jayadvaita Swami affirms in his talk to a Pandava Sena group on July 24, 2009, that skills are being passed down the generations. He notes that Krishna.com is practically run by second-generation people, and that there are bright young people learning Sanskrit from Gopiparanadhana Prabhu, the chief translator in the Sanskrit school in Vrindavan, and Vrindavan art seminars where young artists train under veteran BBT artists, Dhriti and Ramdasa.

36. Rsabhadev dasa, for example, explains that efforts to give the second generation more responsibility in ISKCON had often been thwarted, and cites a legal case brought by his daughter in Hawaii on behalf of her entire generation, her fellow *gurukulis*.

37. Many interviewees feel that even if young people are interested, their families persuade them not to abandon their education or the possibility of a well-paid job to live in the temple. They contrast this behavior with that of the early disciples who "just threw caution to the wind." Ratnabhusana notes that "We have young men coming now, and they really want to come and join. But they listen to their parents, and their parents might be right: So if you're going to come and surrender in the temple like the devotees did in those days, everyone, they just left school, left their job, came and moved into the temple and got in a van and drove around the country selling books. And they didn't worry about "What am I going to do when

I'm 60?" That seemed . . . when you're 20 years old, 65 seems like 5,000 years from now before that happens. They don't know it's a blink of an eye and you're there. . . . And so people like to blame things like the book changes and they're not following Prabhupāda, and that's why people aren't joining like they did back in the day. But I don't think that's it. We have people coming and they're interested. They come and they're here for a few months, and then they go back to get a job. They still want to be devotees, but they can't do the full-time in the temple like we did in those days."

38. Ekkehard Lorenz. 2003. "Who Needs Authentic Books?" http://www.adi-vani.org/articles.php?articleId=9.

39. See Lalitanātha dāsa *No More Cattle Raising in the Planet of the Tress: A Study of Srila Prabhupāda's last instructions on book editing.*

40. Letter to Pradyumna, October 13, 1969. Letter to Satsvarupa, January 9, 1970.

41. July 13, 1977 exchange between Ramesvara and Tamal Krishna Goswami. See *No More Cattle Raising on the Planet of the Trees: A Study of Srila Prabhupāda's last instructions on book editing.* Lalitanātha dasa. Appendix 2.

42. For example, the website BBT.info. contains a section called "Gita revisions explained."

43. This was the occasion when Prabhupāda instructed Ramesvara to produce seventeen books in two months. Ramesvara replied, "Prabhupāda, that's impossible." Prabhupāda responded, "Impossible is a word in a fool's dictionary."

44. See also http://bbtmedia.com/en/narrator/dravida-dasa

45. https://www.vanisource.org/wiki/770622_-_Conversation_-_Vrndavana

46. Conversation, "Rascal Editors," and Morning Talk. June 22, 1977. https://Prabhupādabooks.com/conversations/1977/jun/conversation_rascal_editors_and_morning_talk/vrndavana/june/22/1977

47. 760907 - Letter to Radhavallabha written from Vrndavana, September 7, 1976. https://www.vanisource.org/wiki/760907_Letter_to_Radhavallabha_written_from_Vrndavana

48. 770722 - Letter to Radha Ballabha from Tamal Krsna, July 22, 1977. https://vanisource.org/wiki/770722_-_Letter_to_Radha_Ballabha_from_Tamal_Krsna

49. At the time of the interview, Dravida dasa was still working on the huge project of the *Bhagavatama* which ended soon after. On November 1, 2023, Dravida reported that the sole project remaining was the *Bhagavad-gita.*

50. An Ombuds and Mediation Service.

51. Dravida dasa explained, "But I am not the BBT. I came there at the insistence of my BBT bosses, who were also there—Nareshwar Prabhu and Brahma Muhurta Prabhu. And it was supposed to be an exchange of views, and it turned into a negotiation with a press release which turned out to be not authorized by the BBT. . . . I didn't renege on anything. I'm just the editor. . . . So the fact of the matter is they may point out that we reneged, but I didn't renege. The other two representatives of the BBT authorities, Nareshwar Prabhu and Brahma Muhurta, they agreed to something that they didn't have authority to agree to."

52. See Jayadvaita Swami (2005).

53. See Larry D. Shinn. 2004. “Foreword.” In Edwin F. Bryant and Maria L. Ekstrand, eds., *The Hare Krishna Movement: The Postcharismatic Fate of a Religious Movement*, pp. xv–xix.

54. Purushottam Kshetra dasa adds poetically, “For aspiring and initiated devotees, there is a continuum of developing faith. Some may initially appreciate our philosophy, our food, our association, our purity, and so on; yet become disillusioned by discrepancies they find in our books. Even so—their effect on the course of their life will remain forever. For the sincere devotee, these discrepancies will be tolerated as ‘spots on the moon’ are for lovers of the moonlight. For the scholar, discrepancies will, in the future, be a source of endless debate.”

Chapter 7

Challenges in Constituting the Written Works of a Post-Mortem Author

Jonathan Edelmann

This chapter is about the traditional commentarial Sanskrit style of writing and the usefulness of it for constituting the typographical features of a contested text. The focus of this study is the *Bhagavad Gītā As It Is,* published by Bhaktivedanta Swami Prabhupada in 1972, and another edition of the *Bhagavad Gītā As It Is* that was published in 1983—about six years after Prabhupada's death—by his students at the Bhaktivedanta Book Trust (BBT). How are the differences between these two editions to be reconciled? This chapter is backward looking and forward looking: I argue that for hundreds of years, the way Sanskrit authors dealt with contested readings (*q.v.*, *pāṭhaḥ*) of a text was through commentary, and that commentary is also a way forward today, even after the birth of modern print and online publishing.[1]

TWO PROBLEMS FACING AN EDITOR OF A *GURU'S* WRITINGS

This section looks at two problems that exist in contemporary religious discourse with regard to editing and interpreting the texts within a religious tradition. Both these problems face the students of Bhaktivedanta Swami Prabhupada and the editors at the Bhaktivedanta Book Trust, and given the larger patterns in the history of religion, there is no reason to believe that these trends will cease at any point. My discussion here is about editing texts, and the problems I discuss are only amplified when the author—as in the case of Prabhupada—has died.

Problem One: Making a Root Text

How does one make a root text, or an authoritative edition of a text, when there are contested readings between various published editions of a text? The first choice facing the Bhaktivedanta Book Trust (BBT) is to decide which version of the printed editions of Bhaktivedanta Swami Prabhupada's *Bhagavad Gītā* is the most authoritative. The consequences of the choice will impact the larger world of lived global Hindu traditions since the Hindu group that he established is international. Making a root text might entail the formation of a so-called critical edition, but there are additional options I explore below. By root text I mean the most certain rendering of all aspects of the language in a way that best reflects the intended meaning of the author, accompanied by a critical apparatus that demonstrates the various options.

Ideally, the root text would be based on the oral recitation of the teacher or a printed (or written) edition of a text that the teacher directly approved. This is the most immediate and certain evidence of the author's intended word choice and typography. In the conclusion, I suggest that philologists (who study and preserve texts) and the lived religion of contemporary Hindus (who also study and preserve texts) both revere language as giving access to authorial meaning.

Specifically, the problem here has to do with the production of the MacMillan 1972 edition of Prabhupada's *Bhagavad Gītā As It Is* and the changes that were then instituted in, but not limited to, the BBT 1983 edition of the *Bhagavad Gītā As It Is* by his disciples working within the Bhaktivedanta Book Trust. There is the further problem of how the 1972 and 1983 editions relate to what remains of the recorded versions of the *Bhagavad Gītā* spoken by Prabhupada and the many pre-publication editions of his *Bhagavad Gītā* with notes and comments. The 1983 edition is currently used and in print with the BBT, and it is clear from the other chapters in this book that the contested readings bring up theological, legal, and typographical issues, many of which are not unlike the problems faced by scholars in other religious traditions.

A "contested reading" refers to some aspect of the language or typography—the use of letters, words, punctuation, typeface, diacritics, and so on—for which there is more than one representation in different editions of the text. Are *all* the differences important? In this book, David Buchta argues that the only changes that should be made from the original edition(s) of a text (in this case, I believe this would be the 1972 edition) are those for which there is a clear grammatical or typological problem. Such problems might exist, in my estimation, if an oral recitation was clearly misunderstood, if a word or letter was clearly mistranscribed, if a word is misspelled, or if a well-known grammatical, theological, or philosophical principle was clearly violated (e.g., if a negation was omitted). Other considerations might be if some form of punctuation was erroneously applied, and so forth.

I believe that the only changes that should be made by editors of a text that has been ratified by the author are those that correct a clear grammatical or typological problem. One might call this the "parsimonious principle" since it provides a standard by which editorial choices can be made.

Let us suppose we do have a set of contested readings based on a parsimonious principle. I believe they can be grouped into two categories:

> *Contested Reading Type A.* These are changes that relate to *expression.* For example, this sentence appears in the 1972 edition: "There is also a planet of trees presided over by Aryama, who represents Kṛṣṇa." (*Bhagavad-gita As It Is,* purport to verse 10.29). The error arose because the editor, who was working from an oral recitation made by Prabhupada and recorded on a tape, misheard the word "pitṛloka" as "planet of the trees." Pitṛloka is term in the that refers to the world of the ancestors; the editors filtered the word through their own linguistic structure and out came "planet of trees" from "pitṛloka." This is a humorous homophone, but it is also an obvious mistake in expression and it was rightly corrected by the editors in the Bhaktivedanta Book Trust in the 1983 edition. Other issues in expression might involve clear violations of English grammar, the use British or American spelling, or the misplacement of punctuation.

> *Contested Reading Type B.* These are changes that relate to *meaning.* For example, in the 1972 edition the word *bhagavān* is translated as "The Blessed Lord" and in the 1983 edition it is translated as "The Supreme Personality of Godhead"; the latter term has become a signature mark of the International Society for Krishna Consciousness. Does this matter? One could argue that the two translations express different theological and philosophical import, that is, they have different meanings. This kind of contested reading might significantly impact the theological and philosophical interpretation of Prabhupada's teachings and the *Bhagavad Gītā* itself. One could argue that the difference between "The Blessed Lord" and "The Supreme Personality of Godhead" is merely a difference of expression and that the difference does not change the meaning of Prabhupada's theology. In reply I would say that that Prabhupada sought to connect himself with the commentaries on the *Bhāgavata Purāṇa, Bhagavad Gītā*, and related texts, and he was aware of how deeply invested commentators were in defining the nature of god's being using precise language. Even a little investigation into the works of Śrīdhara Svāmin, Jīva Gosvāmin, Rūpa Gosvāmin, Viśvanātha, Baladeva, and other Gauḍīya Vaiṣṇava theologians reveals the intensity of attention they gave to defining the nature of *bhagavān.* I believe that because of his interest in the Gauḍīya Vaiṣṇava commentarial tradition, Prabhupada would also see the difference between "The Blessed Lord" and "The Supreme Personality of Godhead" as one of *meaning.*

The problem of multiple editions of a text faced the editors of Charles Darwin's work. Darwin published *On the Origin of Species by Means of Natural Selection, or the Preservation of Favoured Races in the Struggle for Life* in 1859. In 1959, Morse Peckman edited and produced a "variorum text" of *The Origin of Species* by Darwin because, even within Darwin's own lifetime, Darwin had edited and republished at least five editions of the text.[2] The variorum of *The Origin of Species* reproduces the edits that Darwin introduced for each page of the *Origin* in each published edition of the *Origin*. While this particular publication is not without controversy,[3] it nevertheless demonstrates the importance, urgency, and interdisciplinary nature of this discussion. One possible option in the production of a "root text" could be a variorum of all available edits made on the *Bhagavad Gītā As It Is*. The difference between Darwin's text and Prabhupada's is that the variorum was produced by Darwin himself, whereas the variorum in Prabhupada's text includes his own edits and those produced by his students after his death.

Problem Two: Interpreting the Root Text

Once one has established something like an authoritative text (an *urtext*, *mūla*, or critical edition), then there is the problem of deciding how to interpret and develop the ideas in this text; in this regard, one might look at Prabhupada's statements about women, sexuality, race, gender, politics, aryans, and so forth, but there are also issues relating to science, theology, and philosophy that might also be given attention. Both problems have been faced by the editors of Prabhapada's work. In both cases, there is a way forward by the writing of *commentary*, a style of writing that can address and evaluate the competing readings of a text (Problem One) and the possible interoperations of a text (Problem Two).

COMMENTARY IN THE INDIAN TRADITION

In the section above, I argued that the problems faced by a new religious tradition often reside in forming the authoritative text(s) of the tradition and in interpreting them. Indeed, this is an essential aspect of the lived religious experience across the globe; in the case of this particular school of Hinduism, this is a global issue in the contemporary world since the scope of Prabhupada's influence on Hinduism is itself global or international.

In the case of the Indian traditions (Buddhist, Jain, Hindu, etc.), commentary was the place in which contested readings and contested interpretations of an authoritative are explored and dealt with. For example, in the commentary on the *Bhāgavata Purāṇa* by Śrīdhara Svāmin called the *Bhāvārthadīpika*, or *Lamplight on Sense and Meaning* (c.1400), he notes that in the first verse of the text there were (and continue to be) contested readings on the words: *amṛsā* and *mṛsā*. Kṛṣṇa Śaṅkara Śāstrī has *mṛṣā*, and an unnamed gloss has *amṛṣā (satyaḥ)*.[4] Bhaktivedanta Swami has *amṛṣā—almost factual*. Kṛṣṇācārya Tamanācārya, however, has *mṛsā*.[5] Śrīdhara Svāmin was aware of the different possibilities and provided an interpretation of both *amṛsā* and *mṛsā*. This is one example in which a contested reading—in this case, a word of great theological importance—is dealt with in a commentary. It brought Śrīdhara Svāmin into a discussion not only how which word is the correct word but also what each word means.

There are other examples of contested readings. In the *Tattvasandarbha* §31, Jīva Gosvāmin discusses variant readings of key verses in *Bhāgavata Purāṇa* 1.7.4-7 having to do with the words *pūrva* and *pūrṇa*[6]; while less theologically significant than contested readings of *mṛṣā* and *amṛṣā*, the *Tattvasandarbha*'s contested reading example demonstrates that commentary is an appropriate space to discuss all types of disparities. It is also not uncommon for printed editions of Sanskrit texts to note the different readings. For example, J. L. Śāstrī's *Bhāgavata Purāṇa of Kṛṣṇa Dvaipayana Vyāsa: With Sanskrit Commentary Bhāvārthabodhinī of Śrīdhara Svāmin* (1983: 719, footnote 9) notes that on *Bhāgavata Purāṇa* verse 12.7.19 that the compound *māyā-mayeṣu* is *māyā-mayāsu* in some readings (*iti pāṭhaḥ*); this minor difference points, however, to the attention and detailed awareness of the Sanskrit editors like Śāstrī. Such notations are numerous on each page of his edition, and this sort of contribution is common among editors of Sanskrit texts. One could easily reproduce many examples of contested readings discussed in the *Bhāgavata Purāṇa* commentaries.

As a style of writing, commentary provides a traditional technique and linguistic art that stands in its own right as a unique form of writing. It is helpful in many contexts, not just the interpretation and explication of religiously authoritative texts. For the scholar of intellectual history, however, they offer remarkable insight into the process by which a single text was scrutinized over time. There are many types of Sanskrit commentary, each distinguishable in their own way, for example *bhāṣya, ṭīkā, dīpa, prakāśa, tātpārya, kaumudī, candrikā, ṭippaṇī, vyākhyāna,* and so on. Commentary can also mean "sub-commentary." Sometimes a well-known commentary will garner one, two, or many sub-commentaries. Śaṅkara's *Bhāsya* (a comprehensive commentary that argues for a particular thesis) on the *Vedāntasūtra*, for example, is often read by scholars along with multiple sub-commentaries, for example, the *Pañcapādikā* of Padmapāda, the *Prabodhaparisodhinī* of Ātmasvarūpa, the *Tātparyārthadyotinī* of Vijñānātman, the *Pañcapādikāvivaraṇa* of Prakāśātman, the *Tātparyadīpikā* of Citsukha, the *Bhāvaprakāśikā* of

Nṛsiṃhāśrama, the *Bhāṣyaratnaprabhā* of Govindānanda, the *Bhāmatī* of Vācaspatimiśra, the *Nyāyanirnaya* of Ānandagiri, or the *Tattvaśuddhi* of Jñānaghanapāda, but there are many others.[7] One might argue, then, that more sub-commentary on a commentary is evidence of its influence and power over time. It is not uncommon for an author to write a sub-commentary on their own work; Jīva Gosvāmin, for example, wrote the *Sarvasaṃvādiṇī* on portions of his *Bhāgavatasandarbha*.

If commentary on the *Bhagavad Gītā As It Is* is the way to deal with textual problems, what might it look like? What would it do? How would it be composed? The sort of commentary that I am discussing here is not ideal to give a full and complete discussion of all and every "contested reading" (defined and discussed above) between various editions of a text. Traditional commentaries focus primarily on contested readings related to theological and philosophical meaning. It might draw from a critical edition of a text, but commentary as I am examining it here is focused on the contested readings relevant to meaning-making, for instance, those that are directly related to the tradition's theology, philosophy, ritual, ethics, aesthetics, and so on (i.e., *Contested Reading Type B*).

It is no wonder that followers of Prabhupada today are thinking about how and in what ways to discuss his writings in a detailed and informed manner. This is to be welcomed by scholars and practitioners of the religion alike, and it is a feature of religion across the globe and across time. The authority of the commentator lends authority to the text upon which he comments; thus, the more commentary on Prabhupada's work, the more authority it gains. The commentator also lends authority to the text. In this case, people read Prabhupada's *Bhagavad Gītā* precisely because it is Prabhupada's *Bhagavad Gītā*—the authority of the author shines light on the authority of the ancient text. While Prabhapada did not write in Sanskrit, his Purports do in many ways follow the commentarial style of writing in the sense that he deals directly with the root text, gives voice to previous commentaries, and also engages constructively with his own interpretations. These are but a few reasons it should receive a sub-commentary.

TYPOGRAPHICAL STYLE AND COMMENTARY

For many years, I have been reading and writing about Sanskrit commentaries, especially those by Vaishnavas and Advaitins on the *Bhāgavata Purāṇa*, *Bhagavad Gītā*, and many other texts. This study has revealed a massive body of literature that is sophisticated and unlike other styles of writing in Sanskrit. This section examines the typography of commentary, especially the editing and reproduction of commentaries using modern print technology.

There is no doubt that present and future scholars in a tradition will want to comment on the words of their teacher; this is the way of religion and intellectual history more broadly. In Sanskrit commentary like those of Śrīdhara Svāmin or Jīva Gosvāmin, the aim is to further explain the words of the *Bhāgavata Purāṇa* with their own theoretical framework in mind, and this is accomplished in a number of different ways. The typographical style discussed below helps one see how a commentator is engaging the root text, the previous commentator(s), and the reference material(s).

There are color coding systems used by Dr. Jan Brzezinski (Jagadananda Das), Sacinandana Dāsa, and Vraja Mohana Dāsa at the Gaudiya Grantha Mandira, an online collection of transcribed Sanskrit texts, but my goal here is to develop a style for black and white print books. Thus, while their system is helpful in my own work and ideal for color printing or electronic mediums, my approach here is closer to that of Gary Tubb and Emery R. Boose in *Scholastic Sanskrit* because they use black and white print.[8]

The typographical style discussed here facilitates the reading of and the writing about Sanskrit commentary, and this is particularly true for those new to Sanskrit commentarial style or those who read with the intent to parse the philological details of a commentary. Part of what is involved in elaborating on a root text is to bring other texts—dictionary definitions, supporting scriptural statements, supporting commentarial statements, reference manuals, grammar books, and so on—and the commentary style also accommodates such moves.

(1) The word(s) of the commentary that are written by the commentator are in regular typeface.

(2) The word(s) of the commentary in which the commentator quotes from the root text upon which the commentary comments are underlined. For example, when Jīva Gosvāmin is commenting upon *Bhāgavata Purāṇa* verse 11.3.16 (*cf. Paramātmasandarbha* §48), he wants to make an interpretive move to support his overarching theology, arguing that the word bhagavat from the verse in fact means paratmātman:

> bhagavataḥ svarūpa-bhūtâiśvaryādeḥ paramātmana I eṣā taṭa-stha-lakṣaṇena pūrvoktā jagat-sṛtyādi-kāriṇi māyākhyā śakti I
>
> The Supreme Personality of Godhead means the Indwelling Lord, whose lordliness is part of his inherent being. This, a power called māyā, is the cause of the creation, etc. of the universe, was referred to previously as an incidental characteristic.[9]

(3) The word(s) of the commentary in which the commentator quotes from a previous commentary are in *italic* typeface. For

example, when commenting on *Bhāgavata Purāṇa* verse 11.24.1 (*cf. Paramātmasandarbha* §49), Jīva Gosvāmin is again making an interpretive move to show that the meaning of a word in the commentary of Śrīdhara Svāmin supports his own overarching theology:

> *prastauti* atha *iti* [. . .] atra pradhāna-paryāyaḥ *prakṛti*-śabdaḥ ǀ
>
> Now, *he praises thus*. Here the word *material nature* is a synonym for primordial nature.[10]

(4) The word(s) of a commentary in which the commentator quotes from reference material, e.g., *śruti, smṛti, sūtra, kośa, nyāya, tantra*, and so on, are in *SMALLCAPS* typeface. For example, when commenting on *Bhāgavata Purāṇa* verse 11.24.4 (*cf. Paramātmasandarbha* §49), Jīva Gosvāmin bolsters his interpretation by quoting from *Viṣṇupurāṇa* 1.2.42 and Śrīdhara Svāmin's commentary thereupon:

> evaṃ śrīviṣṇupurāṇe *VIṢṆOḤ SVARŪPĀT PARATO HI TE'NYE RŪPE PRADHĀNAṂ PURUṢAŚ CA VIPRA* ity atra teṣām eva ṭīkā ca PARATO *nirupādher* . . . ǀ
>
> Thus it is said in the *Viṣṇupurāṇa*: *O BRAHMIN, THE TWO OTHER FORMS, THE PRIMORDIAL NATURE AND THE SPIRIT, APPEARED FROM THE INTRINSIC BEING OF VIṢṆU WHO IS TRANSCENDENT*. On this Śrīdhara Svāmin comments that *TRANSCENDENT* means *devoid of limiting conditions*.[11]

Thus, (1) the commentary is in regular font, (2) quotes from scriptures are in underlined font, (3) quotes from other commentaries are in *italics*, and (4) quotes from reference texts are in SMALLCAP font.

Commentaries, as demonstrated here, involve intertextual elaborations and arguments about how words from root texts, previous commentaries, and reference materials should be interpreted and understood. The use of different typefaces can assist in distinguishing the various forms of text that are commented upon, especially the root text, previous commentaries, and supporting material.

TEXT AND TRADITION: WHEN THEOLOGY MEETS ANTHROPOLOGY

Having examined the problems in forming a canon and in interpreting it, and having looked at some larger contextual and typographical issues, in this section I examine the specific religious issues that further justify the commentarial style of writing.

More often than not, when I walk from my office to lunch at my university, a follower of Prabhapada will offer me a copy of Prabhupada's *Bhagavad*

Gītā As It Is "for a small donation." Sardonically, one might ask whose words are in the *Bhagavad-Gītā As It Is*? Are they the words of Prabhuapada, the spiritual master who founded a new Hindu religious movement in 1965? Are they the words of his disciples? Is there a difference? Is the difference important? What kinds of theological, philosophical, liturgical, or ethical implications are involved in the differences between the two *Bhagavad Gītās*? Or are the differences superficial and inconsequential?

The advantage of this study is that scholars get to see the complexities of editing religious texts and the complexities of canon formation in our own age, one in which the preservation of many documents is involved in the process, e.g., multiple published editions of a single text, audio recorded words of teacher and student conversation, multiple drafts with written marginal notes on the text, legal documents related to copyrights and ownership, letters and recorded testimony about the author's intent, published recollections about the author's intent, and in some cases, contemporary conversation with the editors and other direct witnesses. Given the complexities of this discussion, scholars of Indian religion may wonder—and perhaps even draw inductions about—what was behind the production of books and commentaries by authors of antiquity like Rāmānuja, Madhva, Jīva Gosvāmin, Viśvanātha, and others. Thus, perhaps this study of canon formation in the Bhaktivedanta Book Trust can shed light on what might have been but is now lost in the past.

Those familiar with the worship of the teacher in Hindu traditions will recognize this song recited daily in the temples established by Prabhupada: "Make the teachings emanating from the lotus mouth of our spiritual master one with your heart, and do not desire anything else" (*guru-mūkha-padma-vākya, cittete koriya aikya, ār nā koriho mane āśā*).[12] This is the second verse of "Śrī Guru Mahimā" from Narottamadāsa's *Premabhakticandrikā, Moonlight on Spiritual Love*. It is widely held within the Hindu tradition that the words of the *guru* are like the words of God; they are the heart and soul of the disciple.

While many Hindus memorize and internalize their *guru*'s words without any change or distortion, editing is nevertheless a part of the mythology of *Bhāgavata Purāṇa*. This text tells of an interaction between Nārada and Vyāsa, two widely known personalities in the Hindu pantheon of sages. After speaking with Nārada, Vyāsa was inspired to sit down in a meditative and devotional state, one in which he "saw" the true nature of reality, and after which he made (*cakre*) a book called the *Sātvasaṃhitā*, another name for the *Bhāgavata Purāṇa*. What I wish to focus on here is that after seeing and then composing the *Bhāgavata Purāṇa*, the text also says that Vyāsa's work was not done: "Having made that collection called the *Bhāgavata*, he edited it" (*sa saṃhitāṃ bhāgavatīṃ kṛtvânukramya, Bhāgavata Purāṇa* 1.7.8). Śrīdhara Svāmin says anukramya, or edited, means that he *purified or reduced the initial composition* (*śodhayitvā*). Even Vyāsa edited his own work, so the devotee can hardly say editing is unimportant.

My point in examining these verses is not to give a history of the *Bhāgavata Purāṇa* or to suggest that these events happened in historical time. My point, rather, is that even within the tradition, there is the recognition that comprehending, composing, and editing are each necessary parts of any author's process, even one with the mythologically epic status of Vyāsa.

CONCLUSION

The focus of the conference from which this chapter emerged was on editing the work of Bhaktivedanta Swami Prabhupada after his death. I have argued that the best way to deal with the problems of contested readings between different editions and the issues of interpretation is the use of a style of writing called commentary, one which I outlined above and which stands in its own right as a powerful technique for conveying the intellectual history of a text.

NOTES

1. My argument in this chapter was precipitated by the conference on *The Posthumous Editing of a Great Master's Works: Special Focus on A. C. Bhaktivedanta Swami Prabhupāda* at the Graduate Theological Union in Berkeley, California, organized by Professor Graham Schweig. I wish to thank him and the conference participants for their helpful comments, and for an enriching discussion on text editing.

2. Peckham, M., editor. 1959. *The Origin of Species by Charles Darwin: A Variorum Text*. Philadelphia, PA: University of Pennsylvania Press.

3. See, for example, Bordalejo, Barbara. 2009. "Online Variorum of Darwin's *Origin of Species*." Available at: John van Wyhe, editor. *The Complete Work of Charles Darwin Online*, http://darwin-online.org.uk/Variorum; Shillingsburg, Peter. 2006. "The First Five English Editions of Charles Darwin's On the Origin of Species." In *Variants 5. Texts in Multiple Versions: Histories of Editions*, edited by Luigi Giuliani, Herman Brinkman, Geert Lernout, and Marita Mathijsen, Brill Publishers: Leiden, The Netherlands, pp. 221–243.

4. Śāstrī, Kṛṣṇaśaṅkara editor. 1965. *Śrīmad Bhāgavata Mahāpurāṇam. Contains Śrīdhara Svāmin's Bhāvārthadīpikā, Śrīmad Jīva Gosvāmin's Kramasaṃdarbha, Śrīmad Viśvanātha Cakravartin's Sārārthadarśinī and Many Others*. Ahmedabad: Śrībhāgavata Vidyāpīṭha, p. 1.

5. Pāṇḍuraṅgi, Kṛṣṇācārya Tamanācārya, editor. 2009. *Śrīmad Bhāgavata*, with the *Śrīmadbhāgavatatātparya* of Ānandatīrtha (Madhva), *Bhāgavataprakāśika* of Yadupatyācārya, as well as Satyadharmatīrtha, Ceṭṭī Veṅkaṭādri, Vyāsatatvajña

Tīrtha, Chalāriśeṣācārya, and Liṅgerī Śrīnivāsācārya. Bangalore: Dvaita Vedanta Studies and Research Foundation, p. 1.

6. Dāsa, Satyanarayana, translator and commentator. 2015. *Śrī Tattva Sandarbha: Vaiṣṇava Epistemology and Ontology by Śrīla Jīva Gosvāmī.* Jīva Institute of Vaishnava Studies. German: Kösel GmbH & Co. KG, Altusried-Krugzell, p. 230.

7. Chandrasekharan, T., S. Śrīrāmaśāstrī, and S. R. Krishnamurthi Śāstrī, editors. 1958. *Pañcapādikā of Padmapāda, with Prabodhaparisodhinī of Ātmasvarūpa, Tātparyārthadyotinī of Vijñānātman, Pañcapādikāvivaraṇa of Prakāśātman, Tātparyadīpikā of Citsukha, and Bhāvaprakāśikā of Nṛsiṃhāśrama.* Madras: Government Oriental Series Library, Number CLV; Maha, M. and Anantakṛṣṇa Śāstrī, editors. 1938. *The Brahmasūtra Śānkara Bhāsya with Commentaries Bhāmatī, Kalpataru and Parimala and with an alphabetical index of quotations occurring in the bhāṣya index of sūtras, etc.* 2nd edition by edited Bhāgvav Śāstrī Śāstrācārya. Bombay: published by Pāṇḍuraṅg Jāwajī, Propriotor of the Nirṇaya Sāgar Press; Śāstrī, J. L., editor. 2000. *Brahmasūtraśāṅkarabhāṣyam, with Bhāṣyaratnaprabhā of Govindānanda, Bhāmatī of Vācaspatimiśra, Nyāyanirnaya of Ānandagiri.* Dehli: Motilal Banarsidass; Suryanarayana, Sastri and E. P. Radhakrishnan, editors. 1941. *Tattvaśuddhi of Jñānaghanapāda.* India: University of Madras.

8. Tubb, Gary A. and Emery R. Boose. 2007. *Scholastic Sanskrit: A Handbook for Students.* Treasury of the Indic Sciences Series. New York: The American Institute of Buddhist Studies at Columbia University and Columbia University's Center for Buddhist Studies and Tibet House US.

9. Dāsa, Satyanarayana, translator and commentator. 2016. *Śrī Paramātma Sandarbha: The Living Being, Its Bondage, and the Immanent Absolute by Śrīla Jīva Gosvāmī.* Jīva Institute of Vaishnava Studies. German: Kösel GmbH & Co. KG, Altusried-Krugzell, p. 319.

10. Ibid., p. 321.

11. Ibid., p. 325.

12. Dāsa, Narottama. 2000. *Śrī Prema Bhakti Candrikā with Comments of Viśvanātha.* Translated by Bhumipati Dāsa. Īśvara dāsa and touchstone Media, p. 29; Dāsa, Narottama. 1963. *Śrī Śrī premabhakticandrikā o sri sri prārthanā*, edited by Sundarananda Dasa. No. 639 in Śrī Śrī Jayanti-granthamāla, Nadiya: Śrī Nabin Krishna Das.

REFERENCES

Bordalejo, Barbara. 2009. "Online Variorum of Darwin's *Origin of Species.*" Available at: John van Wyhe, editor. *The Complete Work of Charles Darwin Online* http://darwin-online.org.uk/Variorum.

Chandrasekharan, T., S. Śrīrāmaśāstrī, and S. R. Krishnamurthi Śāstrī, editors. 1958. *Pañcapādikā of Padmapāda, with Prabodhaparisodhinī of Ātmasvarūpa, Tātparyārthadyotinī of Vijñānātman, Pañcapādikāvivaraṇa of Prakāśātman, Tātparyadīpikā of Citsukha, and Bhāvaprakāśikā of Nṛsiṃhāśrama.* Madras: Government Oriental Series Library, Number CLV.

Dāsa, Narottama. 1963. *Śrī Śrī premabhakticandrikā o sri sri prārthanā*. edited by Sundarananda Dasa. No.639 in Śrī Śrī Jayanti-granthamāla. Nadiya: Śrī Nabin Krishna Das.

Dāsa, Narottama. 2000. *Śrī Prema Bhakti Candrikā with Comments of Viśvanātha*. Translated by Bhumipati Dāsa. Īśvara dāsa and Touchstone Media.

Dāsa, Satyanarayana, translator and commentator. 2015. *Śrī Tattva Sandarbha: Vaiṣṇava Epistemology and Ontology by Śrīla Jīva Gosvāmī*. Jīva Institute of Vaishnava Studies. German: Kösel GmbH & Co. KG, Altusried-Krugzell.

Dāsa, Satyanarayana, translator and commentator. 2016. *Śrī Paramātma Sandarbha: The Living Being, Its Bondage, and the Immanent Absolute by Śrīla Jīva Gosvāmī*. Jīva Institute of Vaishnava Studies. German: Kösel GmbH & Co. KG, Altusried-Krugzell.

Maha, M. and Anantakṛṣṇa Śāstrī, editors. 1938. *The Brahmasūtra Śānkara Bhāsya with Commentaries Bhāmatī, Kalpataru and Parimala and with an alphabetical index of quotations occurring in the bhāṣya index of sūtras, etc.* 2nd edition by edited Bhāgvav Śāstrī Śāstrācārya. Bombay: published by Pāṇḍurañg Jāwajī, Propriotor of the Nirṇaya Sāgar Press.

Pāṇḍuraṅgi, Kṛṣṇācārya Tamanācārya, editor. 2009. *Śrīmad Bhāgavata*, with the *Śrīmadbhāgavatatātparya* of Ānandatīrtha (Madhva), *Bhāgavataprakāśika* of Yadupatyācārya, as well as Satyadharmatīrtha, Ceṭṭī Veṅkaṭādri, Vyāsatatvajña Tīrtha, Chalāriśeṣācārya, and Liṅgerī Śrīnivāsācārya. Bangalore: Dvaita Vedanta Studies and Research Foundation.

Peckham, M., editor. 1959. *The Origin of Species by Charles Darwin: A Variorum Text*. Philadelphia, PA: University of Pennsylvania Press.

Śāstrī, J. L., editor. 2000. *Brahmasūtraśāṅkarabhāṣyam, with Bhāṣyaratnaprabhā of Govindānanda, Bhāmatī of Vācaspatimiśra, Nyāyanirnaya of Ānandagiri*. Dehli: Motilal Banarsidass.

Śāstrī, Kṛṣṇaśaṅkara, editor. 1965. *Śrīmad Bhāgavata Mahāpurāṇam. Contains Śrīdhara Svāmin's Bhāvārthadīpikā, Śrīmad Jīva Gosvāmin's Kramasaṃdarbha, Śrīmad Viśvanātha Cakravartin's Sārārthadarśinī and Many Others*. Ahmedabad: Śrībhāgavata Vidyāpīṭha.

Shillingsburg, Peter. 2006. "The First Five English Editions of Charles Darwin's On the Origin of Species." In *Variants 5. Texts in Multiple Versions: Histories of Editions*, edited by Luigi Giuliani, Herman Brinkman, Geert Lernout, and Marita Mathijsen, Brill Publishers: Leiden, The Netherlands, pp. 221–243.

Suryanarayana, Sastri and E. P. Radhakrishnan, editors. 1941. *Tattvaśuddhi of Jñānaghanapāda*. India: University of Madras.

Tubb, Gary A. and Emery R. Boose. 2007. *Scholastic Sanskrit: A Handbook for Students*. Treasury of the Indic Sciences Series. New York: The American Institute of Buddhist Studies at Columbia University and Columbia University's Center for Buddhist Studies and Tibet House US.

Chapter 8

Guru, Śāstra, Anubhava

The Triumvirate of Gauḍīya Vaiṣṇava Authority

Barbara A. Holdrege

In this essay I would like to begin by reflecting on the sources of the authority of a *mahā-guru*, a "great master," and by extension the authority of his works, as articulated in the Gauḍīya Vaiṣṇava tradition, an important Kṛṣṇa *bhakti* tradition that was inspired by the Bengali leader Caitanya (1486–1533) in the sixteenth century and that flourishes today in a variety of forms in India and in the worldwide International Society for Krishna Consciousness (ISKCON) that was founded by A. C. Bhaktivedanta Swami Prabhupāda (1896–1977) in 1966. I will then raise a number of questions pertaining to the central focus of the present volume: the posthumous editing of a great master's works, and more specifically the works of Prabhupāda.

PRAMĀṆA: SOURCES OF THE *GURU'S* AUTHORITY

Tamal Krishna Goswami, in *A Living Theology of Krishna Bhakti* (2012),[1] provides an illuminating theological analysis of the life and teachings of his own *guru*, A. C. Bhaktivedanta Swami Prabhupāda. Goswami emphasizes that Prabhupāda's goal was to transplant the sacred wisdom of India, and more specifically Gauḍīya Vaiṣṇava teachings regarding Kṛṣṇa as the supreme Godhead, into the fertile soil of the West,[2] and he suggests that "the daunting task of transplanting an entire cumulative tradition depended entirely upon his ability to establish its canonical literature"[3] through writing commentaries on the Bhāgavata Purāṇa, Bhagavad Gītā, and other authoritative *śāstras* (scriptures) of the Gauḍīya Vaiṣṇava tradition. Goswami notes, moreover, that in his scriptural commentaries, Prabhupāda is particularly concerned to clarify the spiritual master's position and qualifications and "to define and establish not only his own authority but also the principle of disciplic succession, the dynamic agency responsible for transmitting the tradition."[4] I would suggest that Prabhupāda's understanding of the authority of the *guru* can be illuminated through an analysis of the Gauḍīya Vaiṣṇava understanding of *pramāṇa*, the means through which valid knowledge is acquired.

Among the immediate disciples of Caitanya who came to be known as the "six Gosvāmins of Vṛndāvana," Jīva Gosvāmin (ca. 1516–1608) is acclaimed as one of the principal architects of the Gauḍīya Vaiṣṇava theological edifice. He devotes the first part of the *Tattva Sandarbha*, the opening volume of his six-volume *Bhāgavata Sandarbha*, to epistemological concerns regarding *pramāṇa*, the means of acquiring valid knowledge, which he explicates more fully in his commentary, the *Sarva-Saṃvādinī*.[5] After initially listing ten *pramāṇa*s, he collapses the *pramāṇa*s to three—*pratyakṣa*, sense perception; *anumāna*, inference; and *śabda*, the verbal testimony of the Vedas, which are ascribed the status of *śruti*, "that which was heard." He concludes that *śabda* alone is the only authoritative source of valid knowledge in which epistemological certainty resides. In this context he expands the domain of *śabda* to include not only the Vedic texts—Saṃhitās, Brāhmaṇas, Āraṇyakas, and Upaniṣads—but also the Itihāsas (epics) and Purāṇas, which the Gauḍīya authorities invest with the transcendent authority of *śruti* even though they are generally relegated to a secondary status in the brahmanical canon of *śāstra*s as *smṛti*, "that which was remembered" rather than "that which was heard." In the first phase of his three-phase argument in the *Tattva Sandarbha* (sections 10–11), Jīva is concerned to establish the transcendent authority of the Vedas and invokes the terminology and arguments of the two formal schools of Vedic exegesis, Pūrva-Mīmāṃsā and Vedānta, in order to establish that the Vedas are *apauruṣeya*, uncreated; *nitya*, eternal; and *svataḥ-prāmāṇya*, intrinsically authoritative. In the second phase of his argument (sections 12–17), he extends the Vedic canon beyond the circumscribed corpus of *śruti* texts and ascribes Vedic status to the Itihāsas and Purāṇas. In the third and final phase of his argument (sections 18–26), his principal concern is to establish the transcendent authority of the Bhāgavata Purāṇa as the "sovereign of all *pramāṇa*s"[6] and the "sovereign of all *śāstra*s"[7] that contains the essential meaning of the Vedas, Itihāsas, and Purāṇas.[8]

Jīva deploys a series of arguments to establish that the Bhāgavata Purāṇa, like the Vedas, is *apauruṣeya*, uncreated, and *nitya*, eternal, and is therefore a transcendent and infallible source of valid knowledge.[9] More specifically, he argues that Vyāsa, the paradigmatic *ṛṣi* (seer), was not the author of the Bhāgavata Purāṇa but, like the Vedic *ṛṣi*s, he was simply the vehicle through which the transcendent knowledge manifested. He emphasizes that the Bhāgavata manifested (root *bhū* + *āvir*) in Vyāsa's mind when he was immersed in *samādhi* in the depths of meditation, and therefore it is *apauruṣeya* in that it was not composed by Vyāsa or by any other agent.[10] He maintains that Vyāsa, like the Vedic *ṛṣi*s, cognized in meditation through the subtle faculty of "seeing" (root *dṛś*) certain suprasensible phenomena, which he then recorded in the form of a text (*grantha*). However, whereas the Vedic *ṛṣi*s cognized the Vedic *mantra*s reverberating forth from the light-filled realms of the gods, Vyāsa is represented as attaining a direct visionary experience of the supreme reality that is the ultimate source of the Vedic *mantra*s and all the gods: Kṛṣṇa, *svayaṃ* Bhagavān. While established in *samādhi*, Vyāsa "saw" (root *dṛś*) the absolute body of Gopāla Kṛṣṇa engaged in his unmanifest *līlā*, divine play, in his transcendent abode, the transcendent Vraja-*dhāman*, beyond the material realm of *prakṛti* and beyond Brahman. He then recorded his cognitions in the form of the Bhāgavata Purāṇa, the *śruti* pertaining to Kṛṣṇa.[11]

In his discussions of *pramāṇa*, the means of acquiring valid knowledge, Jīva connects the authority of *śabda-pramāṇa*, embodied in paradigmatic *śāstra*s such as the Bhāgavata Purāṇa, with the authority of *vidvad-anubhava*, the direct experiences of realized sages, which he declares to be the "crest-jewel of all *pramāṇa*s"[12] in that the records of their experiences that are preserved in the *śāstra*s are considered authoritative testimonies of valid knowledge (*pramāṇa*) for future generations. He invokes in this context the authority of the sage Vyāsa and other great *ṛṣi*s who, while immersed in *samādhi* in the depths of meditation, are held to have directly cognized through the faculty of divine sight (*divya cakṣus*) the transcendent structures of reality beyond the range of ordinary perception (*pratyakṣa*) and who subsequently recorded their cognitions in the form of the *śāstra*s. He suggests, moreover, that these direct experiences (*anubhava*) are not the exclusive prerogative of the sages of the past but provide the basis for the authority of the ongoing lineage of realized *guru*s who have attained the status of *samprāpta-siddha*s, perfected *mahā-bhāgavata*s.

Jīva's analysis of *pramāṇa* points to two bases for the authority of the *guru* in the Gauḍīya Vaiṣṇava tradition: the *guru* must be steeped in *śabda-pramāṇa*, the authoritative *śāstra*s, and he must be steeped in *anubhava*, direct experiential realization of the transcendent reality of Kṛṣṇa as *svayaṃ* Bhagavān, so that his interpretations of the *śāstra*s accord with the authoritative testimonies of the realized sages whose experiences are recorded therein.

SOURCES OF PRABHUPĀDA'S AUTHORITY: *ŚĀSTRA, PARAMPARĀ,* AND *ANUBHAVA*

Prabhupāda invokes Jīva Gosvāmin's arguments regarding the *pramāṇa*s[13] and demonstrates his devotion to *śabda-pramāṇa* through his tireless work translating and commenting on the authoritative *śāstra*s of the Gauḍīya tradition. Indeed, Prabhupāda's authority as the *mahā-guru* of ISKCON is founded in part on his acclaim among his followers as the foremost interpreter of the *śāstra*s. Tamal Krishna Goswami remarks, "Scripture is for Prabhupāda the principal means of defining his institution. . . . When the founder of an institution is also the primary interpreter of its texts, scripture and institution are inextricably connected."[14] Among the scriptures for which Prabhupāda produced translations and extensive commentaries, three are of particular importance: (1) the Bhāgavata Purāṇa, the consummate textual monument to Vaiṣṇava *bhakti*, which, as we have seen, is ascribed preeminent canonical authority as the paradigmatic Gauḍīya *śāstra*;[15] (2) the Bhagavad Gītā, one of the *prasthāna-trayī*, three foundational scriptures, of the major Vedānta schools, which Prabhupāda reclaimed as a Vaiṣṇava *bhakti śāstra*; and (3) the *Caitanya Caritāmṛta*, the authoritative hagiography of Caitanya's life and teachings by Kṛṣṇadāsa Kavirāja (ca. 1517–1620), which encapsulates and expands on the key theological teachings of the six Gosvāmins. Graham Schweig comments:

> The Bhagavad Gītā, the Bhāgavata Purāṇa, and the *Caitanya Caritāmṛta* are the three essential sacred texts that build a powerful theological edifice for ISKCON. They function as ISKCON's *prasthāna-trayī*, "the three foundational [theological writings]."[16]

Prabhupāda grounds his authority as an interpreter of the *śāstra*s in the authority of his *paramparā*, *guru* lineage, by making extensive use in his own commentaries of the commentaries and other works of the Gauḍīya authorities that constitute his lineage, including Rūpa Gosvāmin, Sanātana Gosvāmin, Jīva Gosvāmin, Viśvanātha Cakravartin, Baladeva Vidyābhūṣana, Bhaktivinoda Ṭhākura, and his own *guru*, Bhaktisiddhānta Sarasvatī.[17] In the introduction to his commentary on the Bhagavad Gītā, Prabhupāda presents himself as the thirty-second spiritual master in a line of "disciplic succession" that begins with Kṛṣṇa.[18] By channeling what Prabhupāda refers to as "the mystery of the disciplic succession," the *guru* who is a "bona fide spiritual master" becomes a vehicle through which Kṛṣṇa, the Lord himself, speaks, for "there is no difference in hearing directly from Kṛṣṇa or hearing directly from Kṛṣṇa via a bona fide spiritual master."[19]

The authority of a "bona fide spiritual master" in the Gauḍīya tradition is grounded not only in his mastery of the *śāstra*s and in the authority of the *paramparā*; it is derived first and foremost from *anubhava*, his direct experiential realization of the transcendent reality of Kṛṣṇa as *svayaṃ* Bhagavān, the supreme personal Godhead beyond Brahman. Prabhupāda emphasizes that a bona fide spiritual master is one who has attained "the realized state of unalloyed Kṛṣṇa consciousness" and is celebrated as a perfected *mahā-bhāgavata*[20] and a "representative of Vyāsa," the paradigmatic *ṛṣi*.[21] He claims that a realized spiritual master, who is liberated, generally "comes from the group of eternal associates of the Lord," and such "a liberated *ācārya* and *guru* cannot commit any mistake."[22] He suggests, moreover, that it is the liberated *guru*'s state of realization that gives him the authority to wield a Vaiṣṇava version of *upāya*, skillful means, and to creatively appropriate and adapt the scriptural tradition in accordance with the needs of the particular place, time, and audience.

> Personal realization does not mean that one should, out of vanity, attempt to show one's own learning by trying to surpass the previous *ācārya*. He must have full confidence in the previous *ācārya*, and at the same time he must realize the subject matter so nicely that he can present the matter for the particular circumstances in a suitable manner. *The original purpose of the text must be maintained*. No obscure meaning should be screwed out of it, yet it should be presented in an interesting manner for the understanding of the audience.[23]

POSTHUMOUS EDITING OF PRABHUPĀDA'S WORK

Having briefly reflected on three sources of the authority of a great master such as Prabhupāda—*śāstra*s, *paramparā*, and *anubhava*—I would like to raise a number of questions pertaining to the central issue of this edited volume: the posthumous editing of Prabhupāda's works.

First, if Prabhupāda is revered by his followers as the founder-*ācārya* and *mahā-guru* of ISKCON, as a master of the *śāstra*s, and as a perfected *mahā-bhāgavata* who had attained "the realized state of unalloyed Kṛṣṇa consciousness," what is the rationale for editing posthumously certain of his works that were published during his lifetime and that, prior to his passing, he himself had authorized, approved, and used as a basis for his teachings?

Second, what kind of guidelines did Prabhupāda give to his followers about editing his works? I have reviewed the instructions that Prabhupāda gave about editing that are found on the BBTedit.com website, and it is clear from these instructions that he approved minimal *copyediting* but did not sanction substantive *content editing* of his works. He repeatedly emphasizes that grammatical mistakes, spelling errors in Sanskrit and English, and other printing mistakes should be corrected "so that our books are free from errors" and accord with "scholarly standards." However, he also cautions his followers, "Do not try to change anything without my permission," and "Please be careful not to change the ideas." He expressed concern in particular about those he characterized as "rascal editors" who sought to change the substantive content of his works and introduced philosophical errors that distorted his intended meaning.[24]

Third, what kind of instructions did Prabhupāda give to his followers about editing his works after his passing? In this context it is important to distinguish between books that Prabhupāda had completed and that were published with his authorization during his lifetime, such as the original 1972 Macmillan edition of *Bhagavad-Gītā As It Is*, and works that he had not yet completed prior to his passing, such as the *Śrīmad Bhāgavatam*. With reference to the *Śrīmad Bhāgavatam*, Schweig notes:

> This work, comprising twelve books and having a total of 335 chapters among them, was almost completed by Prabhupāda, up to the fourteenth chapter of the large tenth book, after which point he passed away. It was his disciples who completed the remaining, untranslated 77 chapters of the tenth book and the eleventh and twelfth books.[25]

It is my understanding that a team of Prabhupāda's disciples served as editors and helped him edit those portions of the *Śrīmad Bhāgavatam* that he completed during his lifetime. It is also my understanding that Prabhupāda instructed his team of editors to carry on after his passing in order to complete the translations and purports of the remaining chapters of the tenth book and the eleventh and twelfth books. However, with respect to the *Bhagavad-Gītā As It Is*, did Prabhupāda give any indication to his followers prior to his passing that he would like them to produce a second revised edition of this work? If not, what might have motivated certain disciples of Prabhupāda who had served on earlier teams of editors to move forward with editing and producing the "second edition, revised and enlarged," of the *Bhagavad-Gītā As It Is* published by the Bhaktivedanta Book Trust (BBT) in 1983?[26]

Fourth, what qualifies a person to edit a great master's work after his passing? Do the qualifications of such a person need to emulate those of the *mahā-guru*? For example, does he or she need to follow in the disciplic succession of the *mahā-guru*'s *paramparā*, have substantial training in the *śāstras* and expertise in Sanskrit, and have a certain level of *adhikāra*, spiritual attainment?

Finally, how did Prabhupāda re-vision traditional Indian notions of *guru* and *paramparā* in order to accommodate the realities of the place, time, and audience that he encountered when he arrived on a steamship at Boston Harbor in 1965 as a seventy-year-old Indian scholar who sought to transplant the ancient wisdom of India into the soil of the West? His engagement with the counter-culture of 1960s America inspired him to introduce an alternative model of leadership to ensure that the International Society for Krishna Consciousness that he founded in New York in 1966 would take root and flourish after his passing. As part of this re-visioning, he did not establish a model of singular leadership by designating a single *ācārya* or *guru* to be his successor, but rather in 1970, four years after incorporating ISKCON, he introduced a model of collective leadership in the form of the Governing Body Commission (GBC), an overarching institutional structure under which ISKCON *gurus* would function after his passing as the founder-*ācārya*. In a document entitled "Direction of Management" dated July 28, 1970, Prabhupāda states:

> As we have increased our volume of activities, now I think a Governing Body Commission (hereinafter referred to as the GBC) should be established. I am getting old, 75 years old, therefore at any time I may be out of the scene, therefore I think it is necessary to give instruction to my disciples how they shall manage the whole institution.[27]

In his Declaration of Will dated June 4, 1977, Prabhupāda reaffirmed the position of the Governing Body Commission: "The Governing Body Commission (GBC) will be the ultimate managing authority of the entire International Society for Krishna Consciousness."[28]

Tamal Krishna Goswami and Ravi Gupta emphasize that, in contrast to the traditional Indian model of the singular charismatic *guru* who is invested with absolute and autonomous authority, Prabhupāda reimagined the role of ISKCON *gurus* in relation to the institutional authority of the GBC:

> The concept of guru on the traditional Indian model is of "an inspired, charismatic, spiritual autocrat, an absolute and autonomously decisive authority, around whom an institution takes shape as the natural extension and embodiment of his charisma." But Prabhupāda was acutely aware of the dangers of premature spiritual leadership, and the frailties of human leaders. Thus, he told Tamal Krishna Goswami in 1977 with regard to ISKCON management, "No one of you alone but all of you together." Prabhupāda had witnessed his own guru's institution, the Gaudiya Math, break apart into several factions, each led by its own *acharya*, although they had been asked by Bhaktisiddhanta Sarasvati to form a GBC after his demise. Prabhupāda attributed the schism to his god brothers' failure to abide by their guru's order.
>
> Fearing the same fate for his own institution, Prabhupāda established the Governing Body Commission as early as 1970, four years after incorporating ISKCON. . . . Prabhupāda envisioned a management structure that would be strong enough to carry the movement forward without him, and yet simple enough to allow members to remain focused on otherworldly pursuits. . . . Still, Prabhupāda's insistence on creating a governing body was more than just an attempt to ensure his movement's institutional stability. It was also an acknowledgment of the cultural environment in which his institution was operating, and of the need to adapt to its prevailing attitudes toward leadership and authority.[29]

Upon reflection, I would like to reframe my first question with more specificity: If Prabhupāda is revered by his followers as the founder-*ācārya* and *mahā-guru* of ISKCON, as a master of the *śāstra*s, and as a perfected *mahā-bhāgavata* who had attained "the realized state of unalloyed Kṛṣṇa consciousness," what is the rationale for editing posthumously certain of his works that were published with his authorization during his lifetime—in particular, the original 1972 Macmillan edition of *Bhagavad-Gītā As It Is*, which he himself had authorized, approved, and used as a basis for his teachings prior to his passing? The symposium that provided the basis for the present volume—the symposium on the Posthumous Editing of a Great Master's Works that was held at the Graduate Theological Union (GTU) in Berkeley on February 21–23, 2020—brought together thirteen scholars from the United States and the United Kingdom to reflect together about issues pertaining to the posthumous editing of a master's work, with a special focus on the works of Prabhupāda, as represented more specifically in the case of the posthumous editing of *Bhagavad-Gītā As It Is*. In his presentation Graham Schweig, the organizer of the GTU symposium, pointed out that the editors of the BBT's 1983 second edition of the *Bhagavad-Gītā As It Is* had made over 2,250 revisions to the original 1972 Macmillan edition that Prabhupāda had authorized, and he argued that well over three-quarters of these revisions were not necessary.

After grappling with a range of broader issues pertaining to the posthumous editing of an author's works, the symposium participants returned to a consideration of specific issues pertaining to the literary legacy of Prabhupāda and the posthumous editing of his works. The general consensus of the symposium participants was that a team of qualified editors should be constituted who would be charged with (1) formulating a set of guiding principles for editing Prabhupāda's works based on his own guidelines; (2) deciding how to resolve the problematic issues pertaining to the BBT's 1983 second edition of the *Bhagavad-Gītā As It Is* and its relationship to the original 1972 Macmillan edition authorized by Prabhupāda; and (3) making editorial decisions pertaining to any future revisions of Prabhupāda's works.

Although the criteria for selecting the members of this editorial team were not specified at the symposium, I would like to make several suggestions regarding the composition and decision-making protocols of the team. With respect to composition, I would suggest that the team of editors should include (1) respected members of the ISKCON community who are advanced in their devotional service and in their understanding of Prabhupāda's works; (2) academically trained scholar-devotees who are well-versed in Gauḍīya Vaiṣṇava *śāstra*s and have expertise in Sanskrit; and (3) editors with significant expertise in the editorial standards of the publishing industry. With respect to decision-making protocols, based on the model of collective leadership that Prabhupāda himself established, I would suggest that the editorial team should operate according to a model of collective decision-making guided by consensus—"No one of you alone but all of you together."

NOTES

1. Tamal Krishna Goswami's work is an updated and edited version of his nearly complete doctoral dissertation at the University of Cambridge, which was edited by Graham Schweig and published posthumously following his untimely death in 2002.
2. For a brief analysis of the strategies adopted by Prabhupāda to accomplish his goal of transplanting Kṛṣṇa worship in the West, see Goswami and Gupta 2005.
3. Goswami 2012: 113.
4. Goswami 2012: 116.
5. Sections 9–26 of the *Tattva Sandarbha* constitute the *pramāṇa-khaṇḍa*.
6. *Tattva Sandarbha* 18.
7. *Tattva Sandarbha* 22.
8. For an analysis of Jīva Gosvāmin's arguments in the *Tattva Sandarbha*, see Holdrege 2015: 139–153.
9. *Tattva Sandarbha* 18, 23.
10. *Tattva Sandarbha* 19, 21.
11. For a discussion of Jīva Gosvāmin's arguments regarding the role of Vyāsa in cognizing the Bhāgavata Purāṇa, see Holdrege 2015: 151–152.
12. *Kṛṣṇa Sandarbha* 115.
13. See, for example, Prabhupāda 2002: 506–507, purport on *Caitanya Caritāmṛta* 2.6.135.
14. Goswami 2012: 116.
15. For a discussion of the contributions of Prabhupāda's translation and commentary on the Bhāgavata Purāṇa to the modern reception history of the text, see Sardella and Ghosh 2013: 235–242.
16. Schweig 2012: 209.
17. For a discussion of the specific commentaries and other works that Prabhupāda used when preparing his own translations and commentaries, see Goswami 2012: 113–115; Lorenz [n.d.].
18. Prabhupāda 1972, Introduction, https://Prabhupādabooks.com/bg/introduction (accessed February 15, 2020).
19. Prabhupāda 1972, purport on Bhagavad Gītā 18.75, https://Prabhupādabooks.com/bg/18/75 (accessed February 15, 2020).
20. Prabhupāda 1997: 48.
21. Prabhupāda 1972, purport on Bhagavad Gītā 18.75, https://Prabhupādabooks.com/bg/18/75 (accessed February 15, 2020).
22. Prabhupāda, letter to Janārdana, April 26, 1968. Cited in Goswami 2012: 173–174.

23. Prabhupāda 1987, vol. 1: 202, purport on Bhāgavata Purāṇa 1.4.1 (italics in original).

24. "Srila Prabhupāda's Instructions," http://bbtedit.com/quotes (accessed February 15, 2020).

25. Schweig 2012: 211.

26. In the 2018 printing of the BBT's 1983 second edition of the *Bhagavad-Gītā As It Is*, "A Note About the Second Edition" appears on p. 672 in which the publishers attempt to justify their decision to publish a second edition of Prabhupāda's work six years after his passing and eleven years after the publication of the original 1972 Macmillan edition that Prabhupāda had authorized. The Note begins, "For the benefit of readers who have become familiar with the first edition of the *Bhagavad-gītā As It Is*, a few words about the second edition seem in order." After briefly explaining their rationale for publishing the second edition, the end of the Note specifies the names of the editors who were responsible for making the revisions for the second edition:

> The revisions for the second edition were done by Jayādvaita Swami, a disciple of Śrīla Prabhupāda since 1968, an editor of his books since 1971, and from 1975 his chief editor. The Sanskrit for the second edition was revised by the BBT's Sanskrit editors, chiefly Gopīparāṇadhana Dāsa.

The Note concludes with the following statement: "Details of the revisions made for this second edition are online at www.BBTedit.com/changes."

27. Prabhupāda, "Direction of Management, July 28, 1970," https://Prabhupādabooks.com/dom (accessed July 17, 2020).

28. Prabhupāda, "Declaration of Will, June 1977," https://Prabhupādabooks.com/will (accessed July 17, 2020).

29. Goswami and Gupta 2005: 88.

REFERENCES

Bhāgavata Sandarbha of Jīva Gosvāmin. 1951. *Śrīśrībhāgavatasandarbha*, ed. Purīdāsa Mahāśaya. 6 books in 2 vols. Vrindavan: Haridāsa Śarma.

Bhāgavata Sandarbha of Jīva Gosvāmin. 1982–1986. *Śrībhāgavatasandarbha*, ed. and trans. (Hindi) Haridāsa Śāstrī. 6 vols. Vrindavan: Śrīgadādharagaurahari Press.

Goswami, Tamal Krishna. 2012. *A Living Theology of Krishna Bhakti: Essential Teachings of A. C. Bhaktivedanta Swami Prabhupāda*. Edited with Introduction and Conclusion by Graham M. Schweig. New York: Oxford University Press.

Goswami, Tamal Krishna, and Ravi M. Gupta. 2005. "Krishna and Culture: What Happens When the Lord of Vrindavana Moves to New York City." In *Gurus in America*, ed. Thomas A. Forsthoefel and Cynthia Ann Humes, 81–95. Albany: State University of New York Press.

Holdrege, Barbara A. 2015. *Bhakti and Embodiment: Fashioning Divine Bodies and Devotional Bodies in Kṛṣṇa Bhakti*. New York: Routledge.

Kṛṣṇa Sandarbha of Jīva Gosvāmin. 1986. *Śrīkṛṣṇasandarbha and Its Critical Study*, ed. Chinmayi Chatterjee. Calcutta: Jadavpur University.

Lorenz, Ekkehard. n.d. "Unzipping the Purports." Unpublished manuscript. Bhaktivedanta Book Trust.

Prabhupāda, A. C. Bhaktivedanta Swami. 1970. "Direction of Management, July 28, 1970." https://Prabhupādabooks.com/dom.

Prabhupāda, A. C. Bhaktivedanta Swami. 1972. *Bhagavad-gītā As It Is*. Complete ed. New York: Macmillan. https://Prabhupādabooks.com/bg.

Prabhupāda, A. C. Bhaktivedanta Swami. 1977. "Declaration of Will, June 1977." https:// Prabhupādabooks.com/will.

Prabhupāda, A. C. Bhaktivedanta Swami. 1983. *Bhagavad-gītā As It Is*. 2nd ed. rev. Los Angeles: Bhaktivedanta Book Trust.

Prabhupāda, A. C. Bhaktivedanta Swami. 1987–1988. *Śrīmad Bhāgavatam*. 18 vols. Cantos 1–10, chapter 13 by Prabhupāda; canto 10, chapter 14–canto 12 by his disciples. Los Angeles: Bhaktivedanta Book Trust.

Prabhupāda, A. C. Bhaktivedanta Swami. 1997 [1975]. *The Nectar of Instruction: An Authorized English Presentation of Śrīla Rūpa Gosvāmī's Śrī Upadeśāmṛta*. Los Angeles: Bhaktivedanta Book Trust.

Prabhupāda, A. C. Bhaktivedanta Swami. 2002 [1974]. *Śrī Caitanya-Caritāmṛta of Kṛṣṇadāsa Kavirāja Gosvāmī*. One volume ed. Los Angeles: Bhaktivedanta Book Trust.

Sardella, Ferdinando, and Abhishek Ghosh. 2013. "Modern Reception and Text Migration of the Bhāgavata Purāṇa." In *The Bhāgavata Purāṇa: Sacred Text and Living Tradition*, ed. Ravi M. Gupta and Kenneth R. Valpey, 221–247. New York: Columbia University Press.

Schweig, Graham M. 2012. "Conclusion: Prema, Purest Love: Prayojana." In *A Living Theology of Krishna Bhakti: Essential Teachings of A. C. Bhaktivedanta Swami Prabhupāda*, 200–232. New York: Oxford University Press.

"Srila Prabhupāda's Instructions." http://bbtedit.com/quotes.

Chapter 9

Let the Master Speak!

Issues of Textual Translation, Organization, and Interpretation in the Tradition of Sri Ramakrishna and Swami Vivekananda

Jeffery D. Long

The theme of this volume—posthumous editing of a great master's works, with a particular focus on the work of A. C. Bhaktivedanta Swami Prabhupāda—raises a host of complex issues. In many ways, it crystallizes the potential for conflict between the values and interests of practitioners and those of academic scholars of religion. Those of us who are both scholars and practitioners possess an acute awareness of these issues and potential conflicts, as we face them on an almost daily basis.

While the chief focus of this volume is on the work of Srila Prabhupāda, I come to these issues as a scholar-practitioner in another Bengali Hindu tradition: that of Sri Ramakrishna, the Holy Mother Sarada Devi, and Swami Vivekananda. This essay is thus focused upon the various issues of both interpretation and editing that have arisen in my tradition, as well as the ongoing conversations now occurring within the tradition about these.

I have titled this chapter "Let the Master Speak!" because my thesis is that what at first glance appear, in the cases of both Sri Ramakrishna and Swami Vivekananda, to be complex issues in fact derive not so much from the primary source materials themselves—the actual words of these masters—but with the way their words have been presented and re-presented, both by the tradition as well as by outside academic scholarship. In the words of one of my correspondents, a senior monk in the Ramakrishna Order, "The amazing thing about Swamiji [that is, Swami Vivekananda] is how little editing he needed—extremely little. But that little was needed, and it was done. Plus, there was considerable editing done that was not needed." Recapturing the original words of these masters thus becomes more difficult than it might otherwise have been.

SRI RAMAKRISHNA: ISSUES OF TRANSLATION AND INTERPRETATION

Though other biographies of Sri Ramakrishna and compilations of his teachings exist, our two main primary sources for insight into his life and thought are the *Śrīśrīrāmakṛṣṇakathāmṛta* and the *Śrīśrīrāmakṛṣṇalīlāprasaṅga.* Both of these sources were originally written in Bengali and were later translated into English by monks of the Ramakrishna Order (and the second was also written by a monk of the Order). The *Kathāmṛta* was written by Mahendranāth Gupta, a householder devotee, based on his firsthand memory of conversations with Sri Ramakrishna to which he was witness or in which he took part. It also includes accounts by other firsthand participants with whom Gupta later consulted. This work was first published in five volumes, in 1902, 1904, 1908, 1910, and 1932. Each volume contains conversations that occurred from 1882, when Gupta first met Ramakrishna, to 1887, after the master had passed away due to cancer of the throat. The publisher, Udbodhan, later compiled the five volumes into one, in which the entries were rearranged, from beginning to end, in chronological order, with the first conversation being from February 1882 and the last being from May 1887. It is this single volume that has come to be taken as the definitive text of the *Kathāmṛta.* This volume is, of course, itself a product of editing—of bringing together Gupta's original five volumes into one and of collating their entries in such a way as to produce a single, chronologically ordered whole. Being primarily a record of Sri Ramakrishna's conversations, the *Kathāmṛta* is widely regarded as the most authoritative source for his direct, original teachings.

The *Līlāprasaṅga* was written by Swami Sāradānanda and was originally published as a series of articles, starting in 1909 and concluding in 1919, in the Bengali journal *Udbodhan Patrika.* Unlike the *Kathāmṛta*, the *Līlāprasaṅga* is not a chronological narration of conversations, in the manner of a diary, but a biographical work based upon the author's research. This typically involved direct consultation with the persons involved in the events described, as well as the author's firsthand experiences (as Sāradānanda, like Gupta, was a direct disciple of Sri Ramakrishna).

Just as the *Kathāmṛta* is not the only collection of Sri Ramakrishna's teachings, other early accounts of the master's life exist as well. These early accounts include Max Müller's *Ramakrishna: His Life and Sayings*, published in 1898, which consists of both teachings and biographical material.

Both the *Kathāmṛta* and the *Līlāprasaṅga*, however, because they were written by direct disciples of the Master and included materials to which the authors were themselves eyewitnesses, have long been seen, both from within and outside the tradition, to be the most reliable and authoritative primary sources on Sri Ramakrishna's life and teachings.

Although the *Kathāmṛta* is the older of the two works, the *Līlāprasaṅga* was the first to be translated into English—by Swami Jagadananda. This translation was published in 1921—just two years after the publication of the complete original—under the title *Sri Ramakrishna: The Great Master.* More recently, in 2003, a second translation, by Swami Chetanananda of the Vedanta Society of St. Louis, was published under the title *Sri Ramakrisha and His Divine Play.*

The *Kathāmṛta* was translated into English by the head monk of the Ramakrishna-Vivekananda Center of New York, Swami Nikhilananda. This translation, written with assistance from Joseph Campbell and bearing a foreword by Aldous Huxley, was published in 1942 under the title *The Gospel of Sri Ramakrishna.* It includes an extensive biographical introduction of the master, based both on the *Līlāprasaṅga* and on other materials as well. For generations of Western devotees of Sri Ramakrishna who have not been conversant with Bengali, the *Gospel* has become something of a scripture in its own right and the source to which many have turned for access to the master's life and teachings. Upon its publication, it was widely heralded in America as "a groundbreaking book" and "one of the world's most extraordinary religious documents."[1]

In his preface to the *Gospel*, Swami Nikhilananda says, "I have made a literal translation, omitting only a few pages of no particular interest to English-speaking readers." These omissions did not raise any great concern among readers until their occurrence was interpreted as "bowdlerization" by scholar Jeffrey Kripal in his controversial 1995 work, *Kālī's Child: The Mystical and the Erotic in the Life and Teachings of Ramakrishna.* Kripal's thesis, building on the work of scholars such as Narasingha Sil, Sudhir Kakar, Carl Olson, and Malcolm McLean, all of whom interpreted Sri Ramakrishna through a psychoanalytic lens, was that repressed homoeroticism was at the heart of the master's varied spiritual experiences. Kripal maintained that this scandalous secret could be discerned through a close reading of the *Kathāmṛta.* Nikhilananda's translation, Kripal argued, omitted key portions of the original text, thus concealing this dimension of Ramakrishna's life. (It should be noted that the original Bengali *Kathāmṛta* had, of course, been read for decades by countless devotees of Ramakrishna without any suggestion that portions of the text were secretive or scandalous.) Kripal also argued that even the compilation of Gupta's original five volumes into one chronologically ordered volume was done to conceal Ramakrishna's secret, and that Gupta's original ordering of the master's discourses was deliberately arranged in such a way as to direct the discerning reader towards this secret. According to Kripal, "[Gupta] gradually, and perhaps reluctantly, reveals aspects of Ramakrishna's secret to his Bengali readers. But once haltingly revealed, Ramakrishna's secret was again soon concealed."[2] Kripal alleges, essentially, that the Ramakrishna Order has been involved, for the better part of a century, in a massive conspiracy to conceal the real nature of Sri Ramakrishna's mystical experiences.

Kripal's assertions and the massive firestorm of controversy that his book unleashed helped to create an environment in which the question of the handling of the textual sources upon which the Ramakrishna tradition is based has come to be a highly sensitive one. This has in turn affected the project of developing a critical edition of the *Complete Works* of Sri Ramakrishna's chief disciple and the founder of the Ramakrishna Order, the Ramakrishna Mission, and the Vedanta Societies in America: Swami Vivekananda.

"CIRCLING THE WAGONS": SENSITIVITY AROUND THE COMPLETE WORKS

In the wake of *Kālī's Child*, three main responses to Kripal's claims could be discerned within the community of devotees. In the lay, householder community, the overwhelming reaction was one of outrage, and calls in India for the book to be banned. There were also many unfortunate threats directed against the author and a general sense that he was an enemy of the tradition, though this is certainly not how he sees himself.[3]

Inside the monastic order, though, two more responses could be discerned. The minority view was that Kripal's claims were destructive and needed to be answered with better scholarship. The most prominent advocates of this view were Swami Tyagananda and Pravrajika Vrajaprana. Swami Tyagananda is the head of the Ramakrishna Vedanta Society of Boston, as well as serving as a Hindu chaplain at both Harvard University and MIT. He is also—full disclosure—the *dīkṣa guru* of this author. Pravrajika Vrajaprana is a nun based at the Vedanta Society of Southern California. For over a decade, Tyagananda and Vrajaprana meticulously researched and co-authored their joint work, *Interpreting Ramakrishna: Kālī's Child Revisited.* This work points out errors in Kripal's translations of Gupta's Bengali and reflects on the different interpretive lenses used by "insider" and "outsider" scholars more generally. It also presents an articulate argument that there are objections to Kripal's thesis that have nothing to do with homophobia but with the reductionism implicit (and in some places explicit) in his work. The website connected with the *Interpreting Ramakrishna* includes a complete English translation of the portions of the *Kathāmṛta* not included in the *Gospel* by Swami Nikhilananda, which are shown to consist largely of detailed descriptions of the grounds of the Dakshineshwar Kālī temple where Sri Ramakrishna resided and served as a priest for much of his life, as well as repetitions of relatively mundane bits of conversation on topics such as what Sri Ramakrishna planned to have for dinner on a given evening.

The majority view in the order, though, was that Kripal's claims were of no consequence and could simply be ignored. In fact, I have been told on multiple occasions that Swami Tyagananda and Pravrajika Vrajaprana were both asked why they were bothering to put so much time and effort into refuting Kripal.

Clearly, though, the experience of being accused of engaging in a massive cover-up had an impact. Over the course of the last decade, a number of monks of the Ramakrishna Order have been in the process of developing a critical edition of the *Complete Works* of Swami Vivekananda, and this work has been affected by the Kripal experience.

The need for such a critical edition of the *Complete Works* is strongly suggested simply by the process through which its nine volumes have been compiled. The first edition appeared in two volumes in 1907 and includes a famous introduction by Sister Nivedita. A third volume was published in 1908, a fourth in 1909, and a fifth in 1910. These volumes include Swamiji's published books on the four yogas as well as transcripts of numerous lectures that he gave during his visits to the United States. After the publication of this first edition, though, it was found that the *Complete Works* were incomplete. Unpublished drafts and notes from lectures by Vivekananda were found in various places around the world: from institutions of higher learning to the homes of individual devotees. Bits of his correspondence began to emerge as well. This necessitated the publication of a sixth volume in 1921, followed by a seventh in 1922, an eighth in 1951, and a ninth in 1997. It is now widely believed that the *Complete Works* are at last truly complete and that it is highly unlikely today (though of course not impossible) that additional material will appear to be included in a future volume.

As the process of the publication of the *Complete Works* unfolded, whenever new material appeared for inclusion in a new volume, rather than altering what had already been published in the preceding volumes, the new material was simply incorporated into the new publication. As a result, there is really no pattern of organization to the *Complete Works* as a whole. Their order is more or less the order in which the material came to light. Particularly after the first five volumes—but even, to some extent, in those volumes as well—material seems to appear more or less in the order in which it was found. Some of it, however, has also been grouped according to genre (such as correspondence, lecture notes, interviews, and so on), so the material cannot even be said to be grouped consistently in the order in which it was discovered.

Despite its chaotic organizational structure, the profundity of its content—the teaching of Swami Vivekananda—has led to the *Complete Works* being regarded, not unlike Nikhilananda's *Gospel*, as something like a scripture in its own right, with devotees (this author included) citing its volume and page numbers in much the same way that the chapters and verses of a scriptural work would be cited.

Consequently, a tension has emerged between those for whom the *Complete Works*, as a sacred text, should not be tampered with and those who are frustrated by the lack of a critical edition that would organize materials in a chronological order, that would include both internal and external cross-references, that would include all of the materials in their original languages (for Swamiji wrote in Bengali, Sanskrit, and French, as well as English—the language of the *Complete Works*), and so on.

CONCLUSION: THE CASE FOR TRANSPARENCY

In researching this essay, I have corresponded with several members of the Ramakrishna Order, who hold various views on the issues involved but who are largely sympathetic to the development of a critical edition of the *Complete Works*, a project which has been ongoing for roughly a decade, but which has yet to see the light of day, due precisely to disagreements over how to proceed. I have been told that there is a view among senior members of the order that the compilation of the works in their current form was done by monks who are deeply revered today. There is concern that a critical edition might be seen as a repudiation of their work rather than an ongoing building upon and refinement of that work (which would itself likely be superseded at some point in the future). The experience with Jeffrey Kripal has made many sensitive to allegations that the Order behaves in a secretive fashion with its source materials. At the same time, this experience has in fact led to a measure of, if not secrecy, certainly a protectiveness toward those very same materials and concern about what a given scholar might do with them. One of my correspondents says,

> I argued that we are criticized by scholars and others—including many of our own members—for not being transparent. There's the impression that we are keeping original documents hidden from the public. And so, I said, the cure for that is easy: transparency. We have nothing that needs to be hidden. Just let people know what has been done in the way of editing and why.

Even those among my correspondents who are most critical of the order affirm that they do not wish to see the order come to any harm. But, they argue, the very protectiveness, the instinct of "circling the wagons" that outsider criticism evokes, creates the perception of secrecy that the critics allege to be there. Behaving as if one has a secret to protect creates the impression that such a secret does, indeed, exist. However, my correspondents are unanimous in affirming that there is no secret there. The only way to dispel the impression that there is a secret, they claim, is through transparency. Just as Swami Tyagananda and Pravrajika Vrajaprana placed the previously untranslated portions of the *Kathāmṛta* online for all to see—revealing descriptions of Dakshineshwar and accounts of Ramakrishna's daily routine and no dark, Tāntric rituals—an opening up of the editing process of Swami Vivekananda's *Complete Works* would put to rest rumors that there is anything in Swamiji's teaching that has been repressed or deliberately kept from the world.

NOTES

1. Swami Tyagananda and Pravrajika Vrajaprana, *Interpreting Ramakrishna: Kālī's Child Revisited* (Delhi: Motilal Banarsidass, 2010), 14.
2. Jeffrey J. Kripal, *Kālī's Child: The Mystical and the Erotic in the Life and Teachings of Ramakrishna* (Second Edition) (Chicago: University of Chicago Press, 1998), 333.
3. This claim is based on extensive personal communication with Jeffrey Kripal undertaken over the course of the last decade.

REFERENCES

Kripal, Jeffrey J. *Kālī's Child: The Mystical and the Erotic in the Life and Teachings of Ramakrishna* (Second Edition). Chicago: University of Chicago Press, 1998.

Tyagananda, Swami Tyagananda and Pravrajika Vrajaprana. *Interpreting Ramakrishna: Kālī's Child Revisited.* Delhi: Motilal Banarsidass, 2010.

Chapter 10

Establishing Unitary Canons[1]

Allan M. Keislar

ESTABLISHMENT OF THE MUSLIM UNITARY CANON

The Prophet Muhammad (570–632 CE) received the Arabic verses of the Holy Quran at various times between the years 610 and 632 while experiencing extraordinary states of consciousness. Muslims accept the Quran as a divine revelation from God through the angel Gabriel. After hearing, understanding, and remembering the newly revealed Quranic verses, Muhammad would repeat them to a number of his followers who also memorized them. These revelations were written down on available materials, including parchment, the broad base of palm fronds, or scapula bones.

According to Sunni Muslim tradition, within a year or two after Muhammad's death, the first Caliph, Abū Bakr (r. 632–634), selected a committee of four senior, scholarly Companions, led by Muhammad's primary scribe Zayd ibn Thābit, to collect all available manuscripts and compare them with the Quran as memorized by many reliable Muslims. Zayd, who knew the entire text by heart, searched far and wide and only accepted the Quranic verses he and other memorizers knew after finding copies that had been written in the presence of the Prophet and which were corroborated by at least two of Muhammad's Companions who had memorized the Quran directly from him. Zayd then submitted his compilation to Abū Bakr (al-Bukhārī:66.8 [Hadith 4986], retrieved February 17, 2020).

After the death of Abū Bakr, this collection was given to his successor ʿUmar (r. 634–644), who in turn entrusted it to his daughter Ḥafṣa, a widow of Muhammad. During the time of the third Caliph, ʿUthmān (r. 644–655), some confusion about the text arose due mainly to pronunciation variations in different Arabic dialects, particularly by non-Arab speaking Muslims—as well as some slightly variant versions—and the need for one single standardized

Quran became apparent, especially since chapters of it are recited in the five-times-daily Muslim prayers. Therefore, ʿUthmān obtained this manuscript from Ḥafṣa and assigned another group of four scholars, again led by Zayd, to finally resolve any doubts about pronunciation and to eliminate versions other than Abū Bakr's. After doing this, ʿUthmān had half a dozen copies prepared, each bound into a volume, and returned the original compilation to Ḥafṣa. Then, keeping one for himself, he sent a copy to each of the capitals of the Muslim provinces and ordered that all other manuscripts of the Quran be destroyed (al-Bukhārī:66.9 [Hadith 4987], retrieved February 17, 2020). In this way, the canon was finalized, and since then, no changes to the text of the Quran have been allowed.[2]

Twentieth-century critical scholars in the 1910s, and then again starting in the 1970s, challenged this account, suggesting a late seventh or even eighth century date for the standardization of the Quranic consonantal text, with significant changes having been made until then. In 2014, Nicolai Sinai systematically reviewed their work, showed the weaknesses of their arguments for a later date, and—supported especially by the evidence of the famous Sana' palimpsest—concluded that known Quranic variants are minor and the Quran we have today is almost identical to the ʿUthmānic codex.[3]

Numerous early Shia as well as Sunni sources, however, mention that the first complete written Quran was compiled by Muhammad's cousin and son-in-law, ʿAlī (who, Shias hold, was the Prophet's most trusted companion and appointed successor).[4] There are further early reports that ʿAlī stayed continuously in his home for six months after the death of Muhammad to complete this work (Kara, retrieved May 19, 2020).[5] In ʿAlī's collection of the Quranic text, the chapters were ordered chronologically, according to when they were revealed, but otherwise it accorded with the Sunni version. Some Shias hold that ʿAlī's Quran included some significantly different material—notably in 5.67—specifically referring to the selection of ʿAlī as the leader of Islam after Muhammad.[6]

Quran 5:67 reads,

> O Messenger! Deliver that which was sent down to you from your Lord. For, if you do not, you have not delivered His Message. And God will certainly protect you from the people; indeed, God will not guide the disbelieving people.

ʿAlī's version is said to have been: "O Messenger! Deliver that which was sent down to you from your Lord *about ʿAlī . . .*," with the rest of the verse understood as indicating God's promised protection of the Prophet from those opposed to ʿAlī, and further that the reason for the revelation of this verse was Muhammad's hesitation to publicly proclaim ʿAlī as his successor, due to this dangerous opposition.[7]

In the last year of his life, the Prophet had called all his followers to join him in Mecca, and perhaps a hundred thousand had done so, by far the largest gathering of Muslims until that time. During his performance of the rites of pilgrimage, he had delivered his "farewell sermon," indicating that he might not be able to attend the pilgrimage the following year, but he did not make any announcement that ʿAlī would be his successor.

After the revelation of this verse, the Prophet asked all his followers to join him at a junction of trade routes just outside Mecca called Ghadīr Khumm, sending messages to those who had already departed for their homes to return and come there. He had a raised platform set up and waited until everyone had arrived, and then, standing on the platform with ʿAlī, spoke. Most significantly, he said: "Truly, the Almighty and Glorious God is my *maula* and I am the *maula* of every believer." Taking ʿAlī by the hand and raising it, Muhammad then proclaimed, "He whose *maula* I am, ʿAlī is his *maula.* O God, love whoever loves him and be the enemy of his enemy."[8]

This account is narrated not only by Shias but also by numerous Sunni authorities, but the word *maula* is interpreted differently (Nasr and Afsaruddin, retrieved February 19, 2020):

> According to both traditions, Muhammad said that ʿAlī was his inheritor and brother and that whoever accepted the Prophet as his *mawlā* ("master" or "trusted friend" but also, contradictorily, "client" or "protegé") also should accept ʿAlī as his *mawlā.* The Shiʿah regard these statements as constituting the investiture of ʿAlī as the successor of the Prophet and as the first imam. The Sunnis, by contrast, take them only as an expression of the Prophet's closeness to ʿAlī and of his wish that ʿAlī, as his cousin and son-in-law, inherit his family responsibilities upon his death.

Sunnis point out that if, by using the word *maula,* Muhammad intended that ʿAlī should become the temporal as well as spiritual leader of Islam after him, as Shias claim, this would mean their revered first three Caliphs had unjustly usurped the leadership position announced by the Prophet. Shias respond that if that is not what Muhammad intended, it would mean the Prophet, one of the most competent and thorough political and religious leaders in human history, had failed to give any guidance on the crucial question of how his nation and faith should be led after his death (*Hadith al-Thaqalayn,* retrieved February 19, 2020). Thus, neither the Shia nor the Sunni position is very palatable.

We need not pursue this issue, especially since it no longer has the political implications it did when there was a Muslim Caliphate in existence. In fact, for centuries, though especially now, many thoughtful Shias and Sunnis alike have de-emphasized this difference between them to promote Muslim unity.

It is important for our purposes here to note that—whether or not the Quran specifically mentioned ʿAlī's appointment—after the majority of Muslims had acknowledged Abū Bakr as the first Caliph of Islam, ʿAlī himself eventually accepted this and worked under Abū Bakr, then ʿUmar, and finally ʿUthmān, until ʿAlī was selected as the fourth Caliph (r. 656–661). Even after becoming Caliph, ʿAlī promoted as authoritative the version of the Quran established by Abū Bakr and ʿUthmān, which did not include the phrase in 5.67 claimed by some Shias to have indicated him as Muhammad's successor. Thus, the Quranic canon promulgated by the Sunni Caliphs became universally accepted, and today it is a primary basis of unity and cooperation among Muslims. This is particularly because Sunnis and Shias of all sects not only now study exactly the same text, but can also come together in daily obligatory prayers and (despite a few other differences in the ritual) hear Quranic passages recited that all fully agree upon.[9]

In conclusion, though they have historically accepted, sometimes violently opposed, political and ecclesiastical authorities, diverse groups of Muslims fighting forces of fragmentation have benefited from their common canon, in achieving which scholarly committees played a vital role and which became cemented as the leader of the major minority faction claiming an alternative canon (ʿAlī) chose to set it aside, putting Islamic unity above "being right."

ESTABLISHMENT OF THE SIKH UNITARY CANON

The establishment of the Sikh unitary canon involves other issues. Guru Nanak (1469–1539), the Founder of the Sikh religion, and his appointed successors after him, Angad (guru 1539–1552), Amar Das (guru 1552–1574), and Ramdas (guru 1574–1581), each composed a number of hymns and then evidently had them written and preserved in *pothi*s (bound manuscripts). By the time of Amar Das, the writings of some *bhagat*s (Hindu and Muslim saints) were included in the scriptural corpus, thus beginning to take the shape of the Sikh Holy Book as we know it today.[10]

The fifth guru, Arjan (guru 1581–1606), the son of Ramdas, faced the difficulty that his older brother and rival claimant to Guruship, Prithi Chand, retained the *pothi*s of their father and started introducing some of his own compositions as the hymns of the Gurus. Others also started doing this. Recognizing the importance of a single standardized, authenticated scripture, Guru Arjan sent trusted followers to gather original manuscripts, and he himself visited the families of the previous Gurus in this effort. He then compiled the original holy verses of all the Gurus, including his own, in a single large *pothi*, affixing his seal to it as the authorized Sikh scripture.

Guru Arjan's chief amanuensis, Bhai Gurdas, was the primary scribe for the master copy. Arjan had it bound and installed on a high pedestal within the Harmandir Sahib (later known as the Golden Temple) in the Sikh spiritual center of Amritsar on August 16, 1604. After this, Arjan himself wrote some more hymns and added some additional poetry by *bhagats*. These were then included in the handwritten volume, in which blank pages or spaces had been left specifically for this purpose.

This book was kept in his house by the sixth guru, Hargobind (guru 1606–1644), when he moved from Amritsar to Kartarpur. It has been retained to this day by his descendants, the Sodhis of Kartarpur, so it came to be known as the Kartarpur Pothi (KP).[11] Daljeet Singh and others have shown conclusively that the KP is the original manuscript of Guru Arjan.[12]

Guru Hargobind and his two successors, Guru Har Rai (guru 1644–1661) and Guru Harkishan (guru 1661–1664), developed the Sikh community militarily for protection from Mughal persecution and did not compose poetry. The ninth Guru, Tegh Bahadur (guru 1665–1675), did write many hymns, which required updating the contents of the Sikh canon present in the KP. His son and successor, Guru Gobind Singh, in the final years of his eventful life, prepared the final edition of Sikh scripture, including in it almost all the hymns appearing in the KP as well as the hymns of Guru Tegh Bahadur.[13] (According to Sikh tradition, the second holiest Sikh scripture, known as the *Dasam Granth,* is the collection of Guru Gobind Singh's works.) Guru Gobind Singh also established the Khalsa in 1699, a formidable military force and clearly defined religious community tasked with establishing justice, particularly the defense of the oppressed. The Khalsa eventually established a powerful Sikh state in Punjab under Maharaja Ranjit Singh in 1801, which became the last major area of India to fall under British control.

The scripture prepared by Guru Gobind Singh, completed in 1705, came to be called the Guru Granth Sahib (or, like Guru Arjan's text, the Adi Granth). This manuscript was then taken to Nanded, in Maharashtra state, where it was installed according to the directions of the Guru. As each of the Gurus before him had done, near the end of his life (in 1708), Guru Gobind Singh appointed his successor; however, he instructed that no human Guru, but the Granth Sahib, would be Guru after him, and the Khalsa would be its custodian and interpreter. Bhai Nandlal, a leading disciple of Guru Gobind Singh present at his passing, is traditionally quoted as reporting the Guru's final words:[14]

> He who would wish to see the Guru, let him come and see the Granth. He who would wish to speak to him, let him read and reflect upon what says the Granth. He who would wish to hear his word, he should with all his heart read the Granth.

The original scriptural manuscript produced under Guru Gobind Singh's supervision was later lost, but a number of copies have survived as the authorized version of the Guru Granth Sahib (www.sikhs.org/granth1.htm, retrieved February 19, 2020).

Soon after the British annexed the Sikh kingdom of Punjab in 1849, printing presses were established in Lahore in the 1850s. The Guru Granth Sahib was first published in 1864–1865, and by 1893 there were eleven different editions and reprints by various publishers (Mann 2001: 125). The need for a unified canonical text led to the study of manuscripts, particularly the Kartarpur Pothi, to determine the most authorized version. This effort continued until the Shiromani Gurdwara Prabandhak Committee (SGPC) was established in 1920; the British government recognized it as the premier Sikh managing body in 1925; and its authority to determine the scriptural canon was generally accepted by Sikhs. Still, there ensued a number of controversies, often heated, regarding disputed passages. These were generally resolved by committees of scholarly Sikhs who investigated the relevant documents and reported their findings to the SGPC.

A particularly troubling issue followed the discovery that sections of the KP were not present in the Adi Granth of Guru Gobind Singh. Since both texts had been accepted as bona fide scripture, it was difficult for faithful Sikhs to imagine that they could have such differences. A highly questionable attempt to avoid this problem and prove the authenticity of the KP was made by surreptitiously removing several of these sections from the KP (Mann 2001: 67). Confusion and an extended debate, lasting a century and still not resolved, have ensued about this discrepancy in the KP, which gave ammunition to those who rejected the authenticity of this manuscript as the original *pothi* of Guru Arjan.[15]

Another controversy in the first half of the twentieth century centered on whether the *Rāgmāla* ("Garland of Musical Modes"), the final section of the Guru Granth Sahib, was canonical. This listing of *rāg*s *(rāga*s*)* common in medieval Indian music—a system utilized in a distinctive form throughout most of the Guru Granth Sahib—was rejected by many Sikhs as an interpolation, and in 1936, the SGPC ruled that the ceremonial reading of the entire Guru Granth Sahib *(akhaṇḍ pāṭh)* should not include the *Rāgmāla* (Mann 2001: 162 n68). After protests, the SGPC referred the matter to a committee that inspected the KP and reported the *Rāgmāla*'s presence in it. Therefore, the SGPC reversed its position and accepted the *Rāgmāla* as authoritative, but concluded with a compromise, ruling that in those gurdwaras where "according to the convention traditionally observed" the *Rāgmāla* was not included in an *akhaṇḍ pāṭh*, that practice could continue, but "nobody should dare to write or print a copy of the Guru Granth Sahib excluding the Rag Mala" (Shiromani Gurdwara Prabandhak Committee, retrieved March 19).

Another minor issue dealt with the precise placement of the frequently repeated invocation *Ik o̐nkār sat(i) gur parsād(i)* ("One God, by the true Guru's grace"), put before or after the titles of the sections of the Guru Granth Sahib.[16] Based on their study of the KP, in the 1950s, an editorial committee of the SGPC decided to place the invocation consistently before the titles. This positional adjustment caused such an uproar, however, that after an acrimonious dispute lasting almost a decade, the SGPC felt obliged to withdraw this edition and replace it with one without the change (Mann 2001: 125–126).

Eventually, the SGPC published four editions of the Guru Granth Sahib in the twentieth century, mainly distinguished by their different sizes and number of volumes, but then in the 1990s, it was discovered that these editions themselves had many variant readings. The SGPC created a committee to resolve this problem, too (Mann 2001: 127; 142 n53). Unfortunately, although this committee completed most of the collation of these four editions, due to a change in leadership of the SGPC and its decision not to support this committee, its work has never been completed.[17]

Thus, scholarly committees have dealt with a number of disputes about the Sikh canon. Along with their successes, their failures—notably, the shocking secret alteration of an original scriptural manuscript, unsuccessful attempts to make changes to the text, even apparently insignificant ones, and the inability to finalize the details of the unitary canon due to the lack of support by the governing ecclesiastical body—can teach important lessons.

After Guru Gobind Singh established the Guru Granth Sahib as the living embodiment of the eternal Guru, it literally became the continuing source of daily guidance for every Sikh community and many individual Sikhs. Each morning and evening in all gurdwaras, the Sikh places of worship where the Guru Granth Sahib is the central object (as well as in many Sikh homes), a hymn from the Holy Book is read at the end of the regular worship services. This passage is selected by first offering a standard prayer, the *ardās* (literally, "request"), which respectfully remembers the ten Sikh Gurus and other important events in Sikh history and may include a specific request.[18] This is followed by randomly opening the Guru Granth Sahib and accepting the hymn found on the top of the left-hand page as the *vāk* (word) or *hukam* (order), the message from the Guru for that day, or the divine answer to the particular request just offered. Such a practice, known as "taking *hukam,*" underlines that the Guru Granth Sahib is literally the living Guru, who is giving specific, up-to-date instruction.

There are innumerable instances of historic *hukam*s. One of the most impressive of these, recounted in Rattan Singh Bhangu's *Sri Gur Panth Prakash*, probably written in the early 1810s (Mann 2016: 27, retrieved May 23, 2020), deserves to be recounted in detail. This Sikh history tells how

Hari Singh Bhangi, the Khalsa leader in the Amritsar area from 1748–1765, responded to the April, 1763, appeal of a brahmin from Kasur whose wife had been abducted by one of the powerful Pathan chieftains of that city (Singh, Kulwant, retrieved 2020-05-23).

As reported by Bhangu, at this time Hari Singh had only 4020 fighters (though other Sikh leaders allied with him had 8000 more), while the Pathan soldiers of Kasur province numbered 1,200,000 and were stationed in twelve forts surrounded by deep moats and equipped with many cannons and smaller firearms (142:16–18). With his own 4020 men being outnumbered almost 300 to 1, Hari Singh nevertheless decided that, according to the Khalsa code, he could not refuse the helpless brahmin's plea and must retrieve his wife by attacking Kasur.

First, however, "Must the Khalsa seek guidance from Guru's word at random, Surely would the Guru's word reveal this mission's success or failure" (142:23b). The importance of taking *hukam* from the Guru Granth Sahib, especially at Darbar Sahib (the Golden Temple), is prominent in this account:

As everyone in the Khalsa congregation approved
of the suggestion [to take a *hukam*],
The whole congregation moved to listen to the Guru's word at random.
Surely would the Guru indicate what was to be happened *[sic]*,
Be it a victory or defeat for the Khalsa Panth forces. (25)
Thereupon, the whole Khalsa congregation went to Darbar Sahib,
With folded hands and a single prayer they stood before the Guru.
They being the Guru's followers and the Guru being their Divine Lord,
They begged the Guru to indicate what was His Divine Will. (26)
Must the Guru indicate the destruction of the city of Kasur,
Provided His Divine Will approved of His followers' cause.
Thus with folded hands the whole gathering stood,
With some still prostrating after paying their obeisance. (27)
Guru Granth Sahib being the true embodiment of the Sikh Gurus,
Must it provide a true direction to the Sikh congregation.
As the head priest looked at the text after turning over a page,
It was the turn of hymn in the "Raga Basant" which read as follow[s]: (28)
With the support and protection from the true Lord,
Have I put the five most powerful demons under leash.
With His Divine presence lodged within my mind,
Has he made me meditate upon His lotus feet (Divine).
With all the aff[l]ictions and frustrations wiped out,
Have I become hale and hearty forever indeed.
With meditating upon His Name day and night,
Have I got liberated from death again and again,
With the true instruction from the true Lord
Has Nanak received comfort and happiness.

So much delighted the Khalsa felt after listening to Guru's word,
As if they had already taken over the city of Kasur.
Khalsa slogans of victory did they shout out of joy,
As if they were already beating war drums of victory. (29)
Hari Singh Bhangi, somehow, spending the night at Amritsar,
Khalsa march did he order early in the morning.
He, having listened to the Guru's word from the Guru,
No astrologer did he consult for any auspicious moment. (30)
...Merely four thousand and twenty was the Khalsa in number,
Full twelve lakhs were the Kasuri Pathans in strength.
So huge being the difference between the two combatants,
Terribly concerned did the elderly veterans feel at this disparity. (35)
...As the cowards displayed their cowardice at this inequality,
The Brave hearts believed never would the Khalsa get vanquished. (37b)
...As militant Singhs had heard Guru Granth's prophetic revelation,
They had complete faith in Guru's will in ensuring their victory (40a)

As Hari Singh's 4020 men made their way towards Kasur, during the first day his allies' eight thousand soldiers joined them, and soon another eleven thousand other Sikh fighters did. Nevertheless, they were still outnumbered by more than 50 to 1. Hari Singh soon learned, however, that the Pathans, arrogant due to their great power and wealth, could not believe anyone would attack them, so they had made no preparations for a battle. Also, the Pathans were weak or even sleeping during the day, as this was the Muslim month of fasting. Accordingly, the Sikhs were able to quietly enter the Kasur forts at noon without being noticed. After the listless Pathans finally became aware of the Sikhs' presence and began bolting their forts' gates, the well-prepared Khalsa fighters were able to slaughter most of them without much difficulty and reunite the Brahmin with his wife (Singh, Kulwant, retrieved 2020-05-23).

Another significant event in Sikh history facilitated by a *hukam* from the Guru Granth Sahib was the Sikh repossession of the Harmandir Sahib (Golden Temple) on October 12, 1920, from deviant Hinduized *pujārīs* who were performing the worship under British control. These priests had been refusing to accept offerings of Sikhs from "low-caste" families, but challenged by Akali Sikhs, they agreed to take guidance from the Holy Book.[19] The *hukam* thus arbitrarily obtained read (Sri Guru Granth Sahib Ji:638.9–11):

> He Himself forgives the worthless, O Siblings of Destiny; He commits them to the service of the True Guru. Service to the True Guru is sublime, O Siblings of Destiny; through it, one's consciousness is attached to the Lord's Name. ||1|| The Dear Lord forgives, and unites with Himself. I am a sinner, totally without virtue, O Siblings of Destiny; the Perfect True Guru has blended me.

All present acknowledged that the Guru was instructing them that he accepts the service of those considered "low-caste" or "worthless." Accordingly, the *pujārīs* left the temple, and the Akalis immediately took over the worship in the Harmandir and then of the nearby Akal Takht ("throne of the Eternal"), the highest seat of Sikh temporal authority. Akalis' gaining control of many other gurdwaras was also facilitated by such *hukams* (Singh, Karnail, retrieved April 29, 2020).

Turning to the present time, a Sikh website states: "To a Sikh Guru Granth Sahib is their living, breathing, talking spiritual guide or Guru" (Sikhnet, retrieved February 19, 2020). A webpage here describes a personal *hukam*, not historically significant like the events just mentioned, but of a Sikh businessman who was facing a vexing decision regarding printing some packaging for his merchandise. The printer advised replacing the planned blue ink, as it appeared likely to run or smear, with a better quality product—though this change would take extra time that could hardly be spared.

The distraught businessman sought guidance from the Guru Granth Sahib. "Guru Ji," he asked, "should I print in 4-color?" He wrote (Khalsa, retrieved February 19, 2020):

> I opened the Guru and the Hukam was from Nam Dev, the Calico Printer. It said, and I paraphrase "God is the seed which grows into a tree. The tree has bark on it. The bark is taken from the tree and turned into pulp to make paper from, so Nam Dev, the Calico Printer can print on it"!

The businessman took the *hukam* as a clear instruction to do the uncertain printing; the blue ink held well, and he concluded:

> [Now,] whenever I get into a place where I don't have an answer, I always take advice and it has NEVER not given me the best answer possible to my situation. It is a gold mine of technology that can be practically applied to anyone's life, anytime.

Related more directly to the topic of finalizing canons is the *hukam* the author of this paper obtained after asking the Guru Granth Sahib for clarification regarding the Kartarpur Pothi and (as described above) the removal of some folios from it. The passage randomly found in response not only appears to confirm the scriptural sanctity of the KP but also to reveal the hellish mentality of those who decided to truncate it (Sri Guru Granth Sahib Ji:1350.5):

> Do not say that the Vedas, the Bible and the Koran are false. Those who do not contemplate them are false. The doubts of your mind have not been dispelled. ||1||Pause|| . . . You are impure; you do not understand the Pure Lord. You do not

know His Mystery. Says Kabeer, you have missed out on paradise; your mind is set on hell. ||4||4||

It is noteworthy that there are similar methods of "taking *hukam*" (called "bibliomancy," divination using books) in many religious traditions, including Christianity[20] and Hinduism;[21] the Chinese *I Ching* is the best-known text extensively used for obtaining such oracular guidance. Although popular and widely appreciated, bibliomancy is sometimes discouraged or, particularly in the Semitic religions, even considered a sinful practice.[22]

In conclusion, the Sikh community's varied results from using scholarly committees to finalize the details of its canon and also its exemplary prayerful practice of "taking *hukam*" to obtain the Guru's guidance, can provide valuable instruction to others.

SOME COMMENTS ON ESTABLISHING AN ISKCON UNITARY CANON

What lessons might the International Society for Krishna Consciousness (ISKCON), seeking to finalize its canon, learn from the experiences of Muslims and Sikhs discussed above? Specifically, how could those ISKCON devotees wishing to honor their Founder-*Ācārya,* A. C. Bhaktivedanta Swami Prabhupāda, by preserving without change the editions of his *Bhagavad-gītā As It Is* and other books he approved and used himself, and those devotees who wish to correct editing errors found in these publications, benefit from these examples to help resolve their dispute?

As Muslims and Sikhs both have done more than once, ISKCON authorities certainly could assign a committee of scholarly, devoted believers to prayerfully study the relevant documentary evidence and finalize editions to which, after the authorities' approval, no further changes would be allowed. In fact, after having written this, I learned that the Governing Body Commission (GBC) of ISKCON and the Bhaktivedanta Book Trust (BBT, the publisher of Prabhupāda's books) had conjointly selected a group of ISKCON scholars on October 17, 2019, to move in this direction. Called the Revisions Review Panel (RRP), it is to "evaluate revisions made by BBT editors to Srila Prabhupāda's books. The panel will design criteria and a system by which proposed, or previously accepted revisions will be reviewed."[23]

Will this committee not only design a review system and evaluate revisions based on it but also itself be tasked with preparing the final version of Prabhupāda's books? Whatever role this panel plays, those involved in finalizing ISKCON's canon could benefit from the experiences of Muslims and Sikhs to better understand how vital it may be to support and respect the decisions of such a scholarly committee, how contrary opinions might be accommodated, how opposing groups can put unity above "being right," how essential transparency is to the success of the entire endeavor, and how important a unitary canon is for the cohesion of the faith community.

Now, what about bibliomancy?

Once a reporter asked Prabhupāda: "What will happen to the movement in the United States when you die?"

ISKCON's Founder-*Ācārya* replied: "I will never die. I shall live from my books, and you will utilize."[24]

What did Prabhupāda mean by saying "you will utilize"? Could he have intended that his followers should not only systematically study his books but also prayerfully "take *hukam*" from them?

In the summer of 1979, two years after Prabhupāda's passing from mortal existence, a disciple named Amoghalila das was praying to his spiritual master for guidance regarding a perplexing question about his relationship to the new gurus in ISKCON.[25] Amoghalila heard a voice speaking in his heart: *"You also be guru!"*

Amoghalila, shocked and confused by this response, asked, "What?"

The voice replied, *"Read my books!"*

Amoghalila then randomly opened Prabhupāda's "*Kṛṣṇa* book," lying nearby, and read: "Both of us can realize that without the blessings of the spiritual master no one can be happy. By the mercy of the spiritual master and by his blessings one can achieve peace and prosperity and be able to fulfill the mission of human life" (Prabhupāda 1970: 182).

Amoghalila was astonished that this quotation appeared to exactly explain that to "be guru" simply meant to become peaceful and happy by accepting the spiritual master's mercy (especially in the form of his teachings) and then to offer the same peace and happiness to others by blessing them, too, with the guru's message. Even more wonderfully, it seemed to Amoghalila that Prabhupāda, by guiding him to a passage speaking of "both of us," was furthering the intimacy of their conversation by specifically referring to the two of them!

The voice then confirmed, "So you be guru. And if you are pleased by others' service to Krsna, they will make spiritual advancement."

As the conversation continued, Amoghalila was pleased to discover that, whenever he heard "Read more!" and then opened one of Prabhupāda's books arbitrarily, there before his eyes was clear guidance, furthering the argument his spiritual master seemed to be making or directly answering a question Amoghalila had asked.[26]

Amoghalila made hundreds of copies of this and two similar "conversations with Prabhupāda" and mailed them to hundreds of leading devotees around the world, including every ISKCON temple president, *sannyasi,* and

GBC member (Babaji 2012: 108). Amoghalila knew this would be controversial because in these conversations, the Founder-*Ācārya* of ISKCON condemned the "zonal *ācārya*" system the GBC had introduced into his society by claiming that he had appointed as his "successor-*ācārya*s" eleven "gurus" who were "*paramahamsa*s" or 100% pure devotees.[27] However, as Amoghalila wrote at that time, "I was very encouraged at how the passages always answered my questions perfectly, and also by how it seemed Srila Prabhupāda was affirming that he was actually directing me from in my heart."[28]

In response to this challenge to their authority, a majority of the GBC members concluded that Amoghalila's claimed messages from Prabhupāda were his own concoction and ordered him to confess this under threat of excommunication from ISKCON. When Amoghalila was unable to conscientiously accept this demand, the GBC expelled him from the movement and prohibited him from visiting any ISKCON center or meeting or communicating with any ISKCON member, and also ruled that any other devotee who accepted Amoghalila's claimed "dreams of Prabhupāda" as factual or even talked about them favorably was also to be excommunicated.[29]

Despite this threat, however, when Amoghalila "claimed to receive messages from Prabhupāda through dreams, trances, and visions . . ., a sannyasi named Trivikram became interested in Amogha-lila's writings and circulated them on the insiders' grapevine" (Muster 2013: 87). Indeed, at great risk to himself and at first almost single-handedly, Trivikrama Swami disregarded the excommunication order of the GBC and traveled around the world, continuing to promote Amoghalila's "conversations with Prabhupāda" as the actual instructions of ISKCON's Founder-*Ācārya*:[30]

> Although he was not excommunicated, due to being one of the senior-most *sannyasi*s in the Hare Krishna Movement, for years Trivikrama Swami was not allowed to give classes in most ISKCON temples nor even visit many. He persevered, however, meeting devotees privately and convincing them of the validity of the ideas in Amoghalila's "dreams." And within less than a decade, as more and more of the so-called "pure devotee" zonal *acarya*s' neophyte and even fallen conditions were publicly exposed, the GBC was forced to reverse its official position on the zonal *acarya* system and itself implemented the instructions Srila Prabhupāda had given through Amoghalila das.

Trivikrama Swami explained that he was fearless in opposing the GBC because he himself had a dream of his spiritual master in which Prabhupāda told him, in front of ISKCON leaders, that the points in Amoghalila's "conversations with Prabhupāda" were correct.[31] After all this, whenever Amoghalila felt he needed instruction from his spiritual master, he found that by prayerfully selecting and reading random passages of Prabhupāda's books, he received clear, specific guidance.

Can those Hare Krishna devotees who, for decades, have felt they must honor Prabhupāda by using only the pre-1977 editions of his books, and others who wish to correct editorial errors in those editions, find common ground? Both groups want only what Prabhupāda wants, so might they together discover what Prabhupāda wants them to do by finding him alive in his books, as Amoghalila did?

In their practice of "taking *hukam*" from the Guru Granth Sahib, Sikhs first must recite the *ardās* prayers, sincerely begging for help from the Gurus. If in that mood, they then randomly open the Holy Book and receive the Guru's to-the-point reply. Might ISKCON devotees, too, humbly reciting Prabhupāda's *praṇāma mantra* (and other authorized verses addressing devotees, *ācāryas*, and deities of the Hare Krishna movement), honestly imploring their Founder-*Ācārya* to reveal his direction, learn to randomly open one of his books to receive his direct, personal guidance?

Understanding, as Sikhs (and followers of many traditions) have—and as Prabhupāda himself instructed—that the Guru is literally and eternally present and available in, through, from, and for his books, might the leaders of ISKCON adopt this time-tested "spiritual technology"? Could they thus resolve not only the controversy about the posthumous editing of their great master's works but also other disagreements regarding Prabhupāda's desires, including how long the current GBC members and BBT trustees should remain in their positions?

NOTES

1. This chapter suggests how followers of A. C. Bhaktivedanta Swami Prabhupāda, struggling to finalize details of their unitary canon, might learn from the experiences of Muslims and Sikhs. I am deeply indebted and thankful to Seyfeddin Kara and Gurinder Singh Mann for reading drafts of the sections of this chapter on Islamic and Sikh canons, respectively, and for providing many invaluable suggestions and references.

2. Technically, this traditional understanding is incomplete since ʿUthmān's codex could accommodate possible variations as the Arabic script in use at that time did not include vowel markings and several consonants have the same shape, so sometimes the meaning could only be determined contextually. This led to many possible variant readings, but by the tenth century, Quranic scholarship had selected only certain of these as canonical. Only in 1924 did a single version of the Quran become the almost universal standard, namely the printed edition redacted by a scholarly committee under the patronage of Egyptian King Fu'ād I—though other variant readings fully in accord with the ʿUthmānic codex are still accepted as equally canonical (Stolz 2017: 220).

3. The Sana' palimpsest, one of the earliest available Quranic manuscripts, dated within two or three decades of Muhammad's death, contains an upper text almost identical with the ʿUthmānic codex and a lower text containing frequent but minor divergences. These variants, generally consistent with Islamic traditions about different modes of recitation and slight variations in Companions' personal copies, are what Muslims hold led to 'Uthmān's decision to finalize a unitary canon (Sinai, retrieved May 29, 2020).

4. Although some Sunnis have presented arguments to the contrary, Arzina Lalani is substantially correct in writing,

> Scholars are unanimous regarding the fact that ʿAli possessed his own copy of the text of the Quran that he had collected himself, and that his version, although not available, is therefore the first compilation ever of the Quran. . . . This is recorded in numerous traditions reported in both Sunni and Shi'i sources. (Lalani 2006: 30)

For a thorough analysis of these traditions, their chains of transmission, and their authenticity, an explanation of why Western scholarship has disparaged and ignored them, and the conclusion that they can be traced to an earlier date (728) than the traditions about Abū Bakr and ʿUthmān's compiling the first codex (741 or 742), see Kara, retrieved May 19, 2020.

5. Kara further argues that, even though ʿAlī was doing the important work of compiling the Quran, the only reasonable explanation for his staying in his house continuously during this entire critical time was his disapproval of Abū Bakr's caliphate and his decision not to state that disapproval publicly in order to avoid civil unrest.

6. Later Shias have often denied there are any differences between 'Alī's unavailable codex and the Quran accepted throughout the Muslim world today, but some early Shias held that the Quran had been altered and parts of it had been suppressed.

7. The Sunni scholar ʿAlī ibn Ahmad al-Wāhidī (d. 1075) in his *Asbāb al-nuzūl*, the earliest and most influential instance of the commentarial genre discussing the circumstances in which Quranic verses were revealed, wrote regarding Quran 5.67: "This verse (O Messenger! Make known that which hath been revealed unto thee from thy Lord . . .) was revealed on the day of 'Ghadir Khumm' about ʿAli ibn Abi Talib" (al-Wāhidī, retrieved February 9, 2020).

8. *Hadith al-Thaqalayn,* retrieved February 19, 2020. This Shia work quotes numerous Sunni sources confirming the validity of this tradition.

9. In some parts of the Muslim world, Sunnis and Shias pray together. In Iran, after the Iranian Revolution, it is official government policy that Shias pray behind a Sunni imam in Sunni majority areas, and in Shia areas Sunnis pray behind a Shia imam:

> According to Islamic sources, . . . it is totally misguided to designate some mosques with Sunni or Shia affiliations, as Shia would worship and observe their religious rituals in a Sunni-majority district or neighborhood, and Sunnis would attend their rituals in a Shia-majority mosque. (AhlulBayt News Agency, retrieved February 19, 2020)

I have observed Sunnis and Shias praying together in the United States.

10. Sikh tradition holds that Guru Arjan first collected the hymns of the earlier Gurus in written form, which largely had been preserved orally. Mann, however, uses early manuscripts to show that, likely even from the time of Guru Nanak, the Gurus' compositions had been written and bound (2001: 33ff). Significantly, the Gurus also stressed the importance of "inscribing the divine word," making copies of their sacred manuscripts, as a devotional act (Mann 2001: 10).

11. This Kartarpur in the eastern Punjab near Jalandhar, founded by Guru Arjan, is different from the town of this name, founded by Guru Nanak. The Kartarpur Pothi has also been called the Kartarpur, or Kartarpuri, Bīr. ("Bīr"—pronounced like "beerd" with a retroflex "r"—means "volume," especially a handwritten one.)

12. Daljeet Singh's *Essays on the Authenticity of Kartarpuri Bir and the Integrated Logic and Unity of Sikhism*, based on the work of other scholars published in Punjabi, include many proofs that the KP is Guru Arjan's original *pothi* written under his personal direction, containing corrections by and including the seal of Guru Arjan himself, and written mostly in the hand of Bhai Gurdas.

13. Sikhs usually believe that the hymns of Guru Tegh Bahadur were only collected by his son and successor, Guru Gobind Singh, but Mann notes that manuscripts of Sikh scripture dated during Guru Tegh Bahadur's lifetime, including his works, show this belief is incorrect (2001: 15).

14. This is a frequently quoted translation. For example, see www.sikhs.org/granth1.htm, retrieved February 19, 2020.

15. Prof. Mann told me that this removal of the folios was one of the main reasons even Giani Gurdit Singh, an eminent scholar, author, and Sikh leader, believed the KP could not be Guru Arjan's original manuscript.

16. In a number of places, especially at the major divisions between *rāgs*, the invocation consists of the full *mūl mantar: Ik o'nkār sat̲(i) nām(u) kart̲ā purakh̲(u) nirbh̲ao(u) nirvair(u) akāl mūrat̲(i) ajūnī saibh̲a'n gur parsād̲(i)* ("One God, True Name, Creator Personality, Fearless, Without Envy, Timeless Form, Unborn, Self-existing, [known] by the Guru's Grace.")

17. Mann wrote,

> I met Jathedar Joginder Singh Vedanti, Giani Joginder Singh Talwara, and other members of the committee in July 1999. They told me that the collation of the text has reached page 1100 [of 1430 pages]. With the change in leadership in early 1999, however, it seems that the SGPC will withdraw its support from the committee, making its existing work redundant. (2001: 176 n14)

Mann's prognostication was correct. Now, with the death of all the committee members, the goal of fully achieving a unitary Sikh canon remains unfulfilled (Mann, telephonic communication, May 15, 2020).

18. The *ardās* also "registers gratitude for divine help at all stages, seeks help for the Sikh community's future aspirations, and appeals for blessings for all humanity" (Mann 2001: 133).

19. The Akalis are activist Sikhs who in the twentieth century organized themselves to regain control of gurdwaras from corrupt, British-controlled *mahants* (abbots or managers). Highly successful from 1920–1925 by courageous, often non-violent

methods, their relentless campaign obliged the British government, under intense political pressure, to recognize the SGPC in 1925 (after having outlawed it in 1923 and having filled their jails with some 30,000 of its peaceful protestors) and legalize the Akalis' takeover of the gurdwaras (Singh, Karnail, retrieved April 29, 2020).

20. "In the middle ages, a common belief was that if one randomly opened the Bible three consecutive times to texts that were similar, one could be assured of a clear message from God" (Blevins 2014: 72). St. Francis of Assisi used this method when a friend wanted to join him in renouncing the world and living a life of poverty. After attending Mass and praying, the two randomly opened the Gospels to three passages, in all of which Jesus calls his disciples to leave everything and follow him (Blevins 2014: 72).

21. For example, the edition of the *Rāmacaritamānasa* of Tulsidas edited and translated into English by R. C. Prasad (717–18) includes a *praśnāvalī* (question-chart), a process for randomly selecting a verse to receive specific guidance from that text. Prasad writes about it, "Lovers of the *Manasa* are well-acquainted with the usefulness and importance of *Shri Ramashalaka Prashnavali*" (717).

22. While a student in a missionary school in India, as a warning NOT to adopt this practice, I was told a joke about an errant Christian who, unable to decide what to do in an unbearable personal crisis, opened his Bible randomly for guidance and read, "and he [Judas] went and hanged himself" (Matthew 27:5b); distressed by this and desperately seeking further divine instruction, he then by chance opened to Luke 10:27b: "Then said Jesus unto him, 'Go and do thou likewise'"!

23. Dandavats.com, retrieved February 28, 2020.

24. Goswami (1980: 162). This evidently is Goswami's emendation of "I shall live for my books" (Vaniquotes, retrieved February 25, 2020). I know of no other place where Prabhupāda talked about living "for" his books; he did say that he would live "in" his books, an emendation of this phrase suggested by Giriraj Swami (Swami, retrieved February 25, 2020), and often that he would live "through" his books. Nevertheless, Prabhupāda could have intentionally said that he would live "for" his books, meaning to protect them from being changed, which he often feared, or from being edited either excessively or in an immature or unscholarly way.

25. Babaji (2012: 85), available online at Babaji 2019, in the November 14, 2019 post "The 1979 'Conversations with Srila Prabhupāda.'"

26. The complete conversation is included as appendix 1 of Babaji (2012: 85–95), available online at Babaji 2019–2020, the November 14, 2019 post titled "The 1979 'Conversations with Srila Prabhupāda,'" retrieved February 25, 2020.

27. Babaji (2012: 97), available at Babaji 2019–2020, November 14, 2019 post titled "The History Surrounding Amoghalila das's 1979 'Dreams' of Srila Prabhupāda," retrieved February 25, 2020.

28. Babaji (2012: 86); Babaji 2019–2020, November 14, 2019 post titled "The 1979 'Conversations with Srila Prabhupāda,'" retrieved February 25, 2020.

29. Babaji (2012: 1–2); Babaji 2019–2020, March 22, 2020 post, retrieved February 25, 2020.

30. Babaji (2012: 2); Babaji 2019–2020, March 22, 2020 post, retrieved February 25, 2020.

31. Trivikrama wrote (Babaji 2012: 40):

> That night in Delhi I had a vivid dream that I awoke from at 1:00 a.m. fully conscious. In the dream I was sitting in front of Srila Prabhupāda as was Kirtanananda Maharaja. Maharaja started to speak something regarding me to Srila Prabhupāda who cut him off in mid-sentence by saying something to the effect that I was right on all the points that I was making [based on Amoghalila's "channeling Prabhupāda" and "taking *hukam*" from Prabhupāda's books]. . . . Naturally after this dream I became more convinced of the points from these "conversations" and still am to this day.

REFERENCES

AhlulBayt News Agency. 2015. https://en.aba24.com/service/iran/archive/2015/08/06/704292/story.html.

al-Bukhārī, Muḥammad ibn Ismā'īl. n.d. "Virtues of the Qur'an," Book 66 of *al-Bukhārī.* https://sunnah.com/bukhari/66.al-Wāhidī, ʿAlī ibn Ahmad. n.d. *Asbāb al-nuzūl.* https://quranx.com/tafsirs/5.67.

Babaji, Anand Kishore das. 2012. *Madhyama Bhakta: On Becoming Second Class Devotees.* Relevant portions of this unpublished book are available at www.facebook.com/AnandKishoredasBabaji/.

———. 2019–2020. www.facebook.com/AnandKishoredasBabaji/.

Blevins, Kent. 2014. *How to Read the Bible without Losing your Mind*, Yipf and Stock, Eugene, Oregon, 72.

Dandavats.com. 2020. www.dandavats.com/?p=81836.

Goswami, Satsvarupa dasa. 1980. *Srila Prabhupāda-lilamrta: Only He Could Lead Them*, vol. 3, Bhaktivedanta Book Trust, Los Angeles.

Hadith al-Thaqalayn: A Study of Its Tawatur ["Author Unknown"]. n.d. www.al-islam.org/printpdf/book/export/html/27489.

Kara, Seyfeddin. 2016. "The Suppression of ʿAlī ibn Abī Ṭālib's Codex: Study of the Traditions on the Earliest Copy of the Qur'ān," *Journal of Near Eastern Studies.* www.academia.edu/11359647/The_Suppression_of_%CA%BFAl%C4%AB_ibn_Ab%C4%AB_%E1%B9%AC%C4%81lib_s_Codex_Study_of_the_Traditions_on_the_Earliest_Copy_of_the_Qur_%C4%81n.

Khalsa, Gurshabad Singh. 2008. "Getting Advice from Siri Guru Granth Sahib." www.mrsikhnet.com/2008/10/22/getting-advice-from-siri-guru-granth-sahib/.

Lalani, Arzina R. 2006. "'Ali Ibn Abi Talib," in Oliver Leaman, *The Qur'an: An Encyclopedia*, Routledge, New York.

Mann, Gurinder Singh. 2001. *The Making of Sikh Scripture,* Oxford University Press, New Delhi.

———. 2016. "Sri Gur Panth Prakash: Its Text, Context, and Significance," *Journal of Sikh and Punjab Studies* 23:1&2 (2016), 27. http://giss.org/jsps_vol_23/2_mann.pdf, Global Institute for Sikh Studies, New York.

Muster, Nori J. 2013. *Betrayal of the Spirit: My Life behind the Headlines of the Hare Krishna Movement*, University of Illinois Press, Champaign.

Nasr, Seyyed Hossain and Asma Afsaruddin. "'Alī: Muslim caliph." www.britannica.com/biography/Ali-Muslim-caliph/Ali-and-Islam-to-the-death-of-Muhammad.

Prabhupāda, A. C. Bhaktivedanta Swami. 1970. *Krsna: The Supreme Personality of Godhead,* vol. 2, ISKCON Press, Boston.

Prasad, R. C., ed. and trans. 1990. *Shri Ramacharitamanasa of Tulasidasa: The Holy Lake of the Acts of Rama,* Motilal Banarsidass, Delhi.

Shiromani Gurdwara Prabandhak Committee (SGPC). n.d. *Rehat Maryada.* https://web.archive.org/web/20130209065301/http://sgpc.net/rehat_maryada/section_three_chap_five.html.

Sikhnet. n.d. "What is a Hukamnama?" www.sikhnet.com/pages/what-is-a-hukamnama.

Sinai, Nicolai. 2014. "When did the Consonantal Skeleton of the Quran Reach Closure?" www.academia.edu/7372306/_When_did_the_consonantal_skeleton_of_the_Quran_reach_closure_Bulletin_of_the_School_of_Oriental_and_African_Studies_77_2014_273_292_509_521.

Singh, Daljeet. 1987. *Essays on the Authenticity of Kartarpuri Bir and the Integrated Logic and Unity of Sikhism*, Punjabi University, Patiala.

Singh, Karnail. 1995. "Sikh Gurdwaras in History and Role of Jhabbar." https://web.archive.org/web/20070929000517/http://www.sikhstudies.org/Periodicals.asp?TtlCod=811.

Singh, Kulwant, trans. 2010. *Sri Gur Prasad Panth Prakash*, vol. 2, Institute of Sikh Studies, Chandigarh. https://ia902504.us.archive.org/33/items/SriGurPanthPrakashVolume2episodes82To169/SriGurPanthPrakashVolume2episodes82To169.pdf.

Sri Guru Granth Sahib Ji. 2000 (latest update 2006). English Translation by Sant Singh Khalsa. https://srigurugranth.org/.

Stolz, Daniel. 2017. *The Lighthouse and The Observatory: Islam, Science and the Empire in Late Ottoman Egypt*, Cambridge University Press, Cambridge.

Swami, Giriraj. 2013. www.girirajswami.com/?p=11643.

Vaniquotes. 2010. https://vaniquotes.org/wiki/I_will_never_die,_I_shall_live_for_my_books,_and_you_will_utilize.

Chapter 11

The Acharya's Copyrights

Legal Implications of Irresponsible Publishing

Joseph Fedorowsky

INTRODUCTION

This chapter explores the legal dimensions involved with publication of the literary works of author and acharya A. C. Bhaktivedanta Swami Prabhupāda (1896–1977), a portion of which I presented as a guest speaker at the March 2020 Berkeley Symposium hosted by Professor Graham M. Schweig.

Posthumous editing protocols associated with a great master's literary works are a topic worthy of deep contemplation and thoughtful consideration. Specifically considered and reviewed here are the prolific, inspirational literary works of A. C. Bhaktivedanta Swami Prabhupāda—scholar, author, and acharya in the Gaudiya Vaisnava tradition. The full span of his writings includes translations and commentary on historically significant East Indian scriptures, original works, summary studies, compilations, and collections.

To my knowledge, the intellectual property rights to the over one hundred titles authored by A. C. Bhaktivedanta Swami Prabhupāda had never been comprehensively researched or analyzed prior to my multi-year review of his publications over the past fifty-five years (1966–2021). Ironically, this research project might not have been attempted but for two intertwined events: the first being ongoing, unauthorized posthumous editing of the author's literary works, and the second in 2017, when the Bhaktivedanta Book Trust (BBT) informed its licensee, Krishna Books Inc (KBI), that it could no longer legally authorize KBI to publish the author's pre-1978 literary works.

Rather than spending time and resources pursuing a legal challenge to the BBT on its untenable position as to KBI's publishing license, I decided instead to focus on the status of the underlying intellectual property rights.

Thus, what started out in 2017 as a modest plan to research and review basic copyright issues rapidly morphed into what became a wide-ranging, multi-year review and analysis of the author's underlying intellectual property rights to over one hundred titles. What was surprisingly uncovered about the fundamentals then naturally led to a more extensive analysis of numerous related issues, including the history of the BBT and its role and responsibility as a publisher to protect and preserve the author's intellectual property.

To account for the content of his writings, a detailed source analysis was undertaken to identify the origin of the text in the author's compilations. And to augment and contextualize that research, a review was also made of the author's sound recordings, lectures, letters, and conversations, as well as other related information, such as that contained in Back to Godhead publications, GBC Resolutions, and the like. Concurrently, U.S. Copyright Office (USCO) records were also obtained and examined in detail, including card catalog records, registrations, assignments, and related file correspondence.

The foundational facts then led to a review of pleadings and evidence from U.S. and foreign (non-U.S.) litigation cases on BBT-related issues, along with associated U.S. state and federal regulatory filings and comparable foreign (non-U.S.) records. This information was compiled, sorted, and evaluated in relation to the applicable Copyright Acts and treatises, reported cases, black-letter law, practice rules, and so on. No stone was left unturned.

The magnitude and scope of what was uncovered in that multi-year review of the historical and legal record was unexpected and eye-opening, as it expresses a starkly different truth than what has been presented as fact to the worldwide ISKCON community for over five decades. Thus, from a comprehensive analysis of the unalterable historical and legal record of the author's literary works, there is now an evidentiary basis to legally address the ISKCON Publisher's positional claims.

CORRUPTED LITERATURE

Unbridled posthumous editing of the author's literary works by the ISKCON Publisher has continued for decades without being resolved, as it is neither aligned with established copyediting principles nor in harmony with the author's unequivocal editorial instructions for his books. Regardless of how many scholars and knowledgeable observers have presented irrefutable evidence of time-honored posthumous editorial protocols in consonance with the author's stated desire and directives not to change his books, still, the ISKCON Publisher has continued to brazenly edit and substantively rewrite book after book, after book. The result being that corrupted literature has sadly become the norm.

Frustration over the issue by academics, scholars, and those who cite the author's directives has been compounded by an apparent lack of genuine concern for the author's unequivocal instructions by a handful of "international trustees" who have apparently come to view their cult-like *ex-cathedra* grip over the author's works as incontestable. My presentation at the symposium was intended to dispel any such haughty conclusion with verifiable facts.

Based on years of historical and legal research, it is now amply clear that what has not been cooperatively accomplished by citing the author's direct, unequivocal instructions for the posthumous editorial treatment of his books is achievable by a focus on the legal ramifications of how the author's copyrights have been mishandled and misused, if not worse.

EAST-WEST PUBLISHING PROTOCOL

The author's books were completed prior to the expiration of the Copyright Act of 1909 (1909 Act), which mandated strict notice and deposit protocols for publication and registration with the U.S. Copyright Office. Upon expiration of the 1909 Act on December 31, 1977, the Copyright Act of 1976 extended many of the 1909 Act provisions beginning on January 1, 1978, until March 1, 1989, when select provisions of the *Berne Convention for the Protection of Literary and Artistic Works of September 9, 1886,* as amended (Berne Convention) were adopted.

Pursuant to the 1909 Act, precise, demanding requirements for deposit, notice, registration, and assignment as to the author's U.S. publications were necessary to obtain and maintain a copyright. While the technically demanding provisions of the 1909 Act are applicable to all the author's post-1965 U.S. literary works, in comparison the exercise of analogous rights in India as to the author's pre-1966 writings under the Berne Convention per Art. 5(2) "shall not be subject to any formality." India became a member of the Berne Convention in 1928.

Thus, it was acceptable under the Berne Convention to simply print the names of the author and publisher along with a brief reservation of rights. An example of a reservation of rights can be found in the author's pre-1966 India publication of the iconic essay *Easy Journey to Other Planets* which displays this simple yet adequate six-word phrase: "Copy right reserved by the Author."

The differences between how copyright notices were treated under the Berne Convention and the 1909 Act are significant and noteworthy in relation to the author's literary works. While the author was familiar with the abbreviated, informal Berne Convention publication standards in his India publications, he could not be expected to be conversant with the legal intricacies of the technically demanding publishing and registration protocols under the 1909 Act in the United States.

Understandably, he left those important regulatory and notice details to his commercial publisher The Macmillan Company, which properly registered and copyright noticed both his 1968 abridged and 1972 complete *Bhagavad-Gita As It Is* in the author's name.

The author also left important regulatory and notice details to his budding in-house ISKCON Publisher. Many of his titles from 1966 to 1972, however, were not properly registered and displayed problematic notices that used a jumble of names and monikers, including ISKCON Press, ISKCON Books, and the International Society for Krishna Consciousness, Inc.

Meanwhile, the author himself continued to affirm that his literary works were his, and his alone. In a conversation on February 13, 1974, in Vrindavan, India, for example, when asked if he had given the copyright to Macmillan, he replied, "No, copyright is mine."

THE ACHARYA'S MATCHLESS VOICE

In the Eastern tradition, a spiritual master's expression, tone, and voice as manifest in written form are revered and thus may not be manipulated or changed. Posthumous editing of an acharya's writings is categorically prohibited. A similar dynamic extant in the West is referred to as *les droit moraux* or moral rights based on a French court ruling in the year 1504. Two core moral rights are integrity (the right to prevent prejudicial distortions to one's creative work) and attribution (the right to be credited as the author of one's creative work, and conversely, not to be deceptively made responsible for prejudicial distortions by others). Changing the tone, content, and voice of the acharya is offensive and wrongful. It is also a misuse of copyright in that it denies the public direct unadulterated access to the author's unique realization, expression, and instruction.

The editing standards applicable to the author's books while he was present as well as those applied after his demise are critically important to acknowledge and follow. Fortunately, there is no mystery as to the applicable editing standards the author insisted upon for his books. In a letter dated February 17, 1970, the author clearly defined that copyediting standard: "Our editing is to correct grammatical and spelling errors only, without interpolation of style or philosophy."

Consequently, editorial revisions which amounted to a substantive change as to style or philosophy required his personal approval. The author insisted with both his in-house publisher and his commercial publisher that his personal consent was required to make any change in substance. In his signed contract with Macmillan Company dated March 6, 1972, to print the unabridged *Bhagavad-Gita As It Is* complete edition, for example, interlineated next to the Revisions clause header was typed: "/ only with the consent of the Author."

Indisputably, the professional editorial standard the author expected the editors to apply to his literary works was "No Changes, No Mistakes"—an abbreviated phrase credited to Professor Graham M. Schweig who concisely expressed the author's instruction to only carry out necessary copyediting absent his personal approval. In his pre-1966 writings, the author himself used annotations in his reprints by way of inserting a small symbol or mark in the original text, which symbol corresponded to an editorial adjustment made in a footnote or endnote in the later reprint. This approach allows for comments while it concurrently preserves the integrity of the original text.

The author's matchless inspirational voice was the basis for ISKCON's rapid growth and development as his books were generously distributed far and wide, the result of which ignited and fueled the worldwide Hare Krishna Movement. The author wrote for the benefit of the public at large while the BBT was to act as the publisher and recycle profits into publishing more books and establishing temples. The GBC retained its oversight function while ISKCON Centers were to be the delivery and distribution system. In a letter dated July 27, 1970, the author confirmed that "the ISKCON Press was specifically established exclusively for printing my books." And, in a letter dated July 29, 1970, the author directed that profits from his writings were to be used to "publish my books and literature and to establish temples throughout the world."

A PUZZLING DILEMMA

While in India, on March 30, 1972, the author formed the Bhakti Vedanta Book Trust (BVBT), a charitable, public trust. Two months later in California on May 29, 1972, the author formed the Bhaktivedanta Book Trust (BBT), an irrevocable charitable trust. A third trust, named Bhaktivedanta Book Trust, formed and registered in Vaduz Liechtenstein, made its surprise debut in the 1983 *Bhagavad-Gita As It Is*, Revised and Enlarged, Complete Edition. A full list of trusts entitled Bhaktivedanta Book Trust printed in the author's books is beyond the scope of this chapter.

The May 29, 1972, BBT formed in California almost immediately became an irreconcilable dilemma for BBT managers. The gist of the apparent quandary was that the trust was not tax exempt. That led the BBT managers to view and treat the trust as non-operational, and instead managed the book publishing and distribution operations as if a corporate division of an already-existing ISKCON nonprofit entity. As a direct consequence, the BBT essentially became a moniker, and consequently was later listed as a fictitious business name for at least one ISKCON corporation.

Shockingly, however, A. C. Bhaktivedanta Swami Prabhupāda, who was the Settlor and first trustee of the California BBT, was not informed of the precipitous actions taken by the BBT managers in Los Angeles to discard the trust until twenty-nine months later in October of 1974—and then only in a letter mailed to India. But why the mysteriously long delay in reporting these actions to the author? Certainly, there were abundant opportunities for the BBT managers to discuss their momentous decisions with the author during those two and a half years, as the author resided at the Los Angeles Temple during fifteen separate month visits of varying durations within that thirty-month period. Were there other decisions and actions kept from the author? Perhaps that question can be addressed by looking with discernment at events which shaped the larger picture.

ONE HOLY MESS

From ISKCON's beginning in 1966, various names and monikers were referenced and used as copyright notices in the author's books. Examples include: A. C. Bhaktivedanta Swami, International Society for Krishna Consciousness, Inc., ISKCON Press, ISKCON Books, Bhaktivedanta Book Trust, and Bhaktivedanta Book Trust International, Inc. Moreover, the turnover of names was not a full match up with USCO registration and assignment filings.

Adding to the confusion, the various names and monikers used that appear in statutory copyright notices do not consistently or necessarily reference the same owner or even an actual owner. This track record of glaring inconsistency and incoherence is precisely the kind of infirmity that the 1909 Act was designed to address. For example, the Bhaktivedanta Book Trust was at different times referred to as a California irrevocable trust; as an India charitable trust of a similar name; as a Liechtenstein *situs* trust; as a fictitious business name for the International Society for Krishna Consciousness of California, Inc.; as the Principal of its Agent, ISKCON of California, Inc.; as a Division of ISKCON Inc.; as a Division of ISKCON of California, Inc.; and as a Division of Bhaktivedanta Book Publishing, Inc.

Additional problematic issues were created involving USCO registrations and related statutory copyright notices. To establish ownership, an initial USCO registration along with an appropriate assignment is required from and to each claimant for the years indicated in the notice. A review of the USCO registrations and assignments for numerous titles, however, does not provide consistent support to meet these requirements and thus runs far afield of the 1909 Act. Accordingly, the USCO registration and notice record created and shaped by the ISKCON Publisher cannot reasonably be said to reflect the level of accuracy, legitimacy, and consistency required.

Moreover, problematic assignments were lodged with the USCO that contained incomprehensible transfer language and dubious signature authority. Filing defects and questionable representations are also implicated in numerous USCO registrations, including discrepancies in publication dates, first publication locale, and claimant status.

Granted, those who were responsible at the time for operating as the ISKCON Publisher were relatively young and inexperienced, and especially so in the complexities of intellectual property rights, strictly construed federal copyright regulations, and ethical publishing standards. Many of those directly responsible may have been genuinely trying their very best to maneuver through the legal and technical issues in pursuit of lofty ideals. It is a settled issue, however, that an "empty head, pure heart" plea is not a recognized legal defense and thus will not avail.

PHANTOM CLAIMANTS

Beginning in 1972 in a few of the author's books, and then somewhat consistently in the years thereafter, the name Bhaktivedanta Book Trust became a standard reference to the copyright claimant in the author's books. Later, in the early 1990s, the underlying intellectual property rights were ostensibly assigned and transferred to a California nonprofit corporation formed in 1988, now known as the Bhaktivedanta Book Trust International, Inc.

During the eighteen years from 1972 to 1990, multiple identities were attached to the name Bhaktivedanta Book Trust that were used in regulatory filings, copyright notices, and legal documents. This is significant because claimant identity would necessarily impact a determination of conflicting and competing intellectual property right claims to the author's literary works.

In looking to the 1909 Act for guidance on how to treat these historically muddled facts and issues, along with the Copyright Act of 1976, which extended and thus continued many of the 1909 Act provisions until March 1, 1989, it is simply not realistic to expect that the putative copyright claimant to the author's literary works can advance a unifying rationale upon which all the documented factual and legal inconsistencies in the record can be resolved in consonance with applicable legal constraints.

FROM DILEMMA TO PRETENSE

The BBT publishers somehow managed to maneuver through a competing thicket of differing identities, tax issues, regulatory matters, real property concerns, and USCO registration and assignment issues, by keeping multiple identity and positional options open despite the onerous legal risks involved. Thus, over time the BBT became a recognized singular brand even though a stiff price was paid by making inconsistent representations on the record in various forums.

For example, conflicting assertions were made in pleadings, discovery, and or testimony in numerous legal proceedings by the ISKCON Publisher and the BBT specifically. A partial list of cases includes the 1978 California Superior Court case involving the Franchise Tax Board in which the BBT was presented, not as a trust, but as a Division of ISKCON; the 1992 Singapore case in which representations were made as to the viability of the BBT; the 1997 California Superior Court case in which the ISKCON Publisher argued that the BBT was not a valid trust and that most of the author's literary works were works-made-for-hire; and a muddled 2023 case filed by a BBT public trust in India claiming copyright ownership of the author's literary works that it formally divested itself of decades ago.

In regulatory filings, inconsistent representations were also made with the U.S. Patent and Trademark Office regarding the status of the Bhaktivedanta Book Trust. These public filings and others are troublesome examples of how the ISKCON Publisher continued to make inconsistent, misleading, and false representations as to the identity of the BBT and its ownership status despite the serious, consequential legal risks attached.

THE ISKCON PUBLISHER GOES CORPORATE

On July 28, 1970, the Governing Body Commission (GBC) was created by Founder-Acharya A. C. Bhaktivedanta Swami Prabhupāda, to assist him in managing the ISKCON organization. From the time of the acharya's passing in late 1977, the GBC has acted as the highest ecclesiastical and managerial authority for ISKCON worldwide.

At an International BBT meeting in 1986, the trustees voted to "authorize the creation of an international BBT corporation." Following that decision, the GBC passed supporting Resolution #39 in 1988, which affirmed that "the GBC wishes the BBT to reconstitute itself."

The result was that on October 12, 1988, a California nonprofit corporation entitled the Bhaktivedanta Book Trust – International, Inc., and amended on

May 8, 1997, as The Bhaktivedanta Book Trust International, Inc. (BBTI INC), was formed to hold the intellectual property rights to the author's literary works.

To transfer those rights presumably held by one or more trusts to BBTI INC, an assignment was executed on March 24, 1990, then lodged with the USCO in 2019, some twenty-nine years later, by India BVBT. A second assignment dated May 15, 1990, was signed at a still-disputed point in time, and lodged with the USCO on July 31, 1995, by California BBT.

These two assignments effectively divested both trusts of their *res* or trust property by transferring the intellectual property to the BBTI INC, to the extent the property was held by the trusts and to the extent the assignments were legally valid. Assuming the assignments were valid, these actions not only divested the trusts of the trust property each trust held, if any, for the ISKCON beneficiary—but it also eliminated ISKCON *as* a beneficiary of the intellectual property transferred. Thus, in effect, ISKCON is no longer entitled by operation of law as the former named beneficiary of the California trust to receive the intellectual property transferred to the BBTI INC upon that corporation's dissolution. Irrevocable trust safekeeping of the author's literary works can no longer be assumed, much less guaranteed.

There are other consequences of not having followed the acharya's instructions to keep the intellectual property rights in trust. The BBTI INC is a nonprofit corporation with a board of directors which has a duty of loyalty to the corporation—not to the acharya, the GBC, or ISKCON. As a result, the GBC presently has limited access to the BBTI INC corporate accounts and apparently no audit rights over the BBTI INC's accounting of the Movement's revenue from book sales, or even how expenditures of those funds will be made. These are just a few of the ramifications of disregarding the acharya's instructions for how the ISKCON GBC and the BBT were to interact and function.

Within this time frame, the BBT had effectively become a mere corporate moniker, a recognizable brand used by the ISKCON Publisher to sell and distribute altered and corrupted literature, impliedly with the author's imprimatur, which thus gave the false and misleading impression that the post-1977 corrupted publications had been authorized and approved by the author, which, of course, had never been the case. For example, rather than ethically obtain original independent reviews of the 1983 *Bhagavad-Gita As It Is* Revised and Enlarged Complete Edition from scholars and other writers, the BBT instead, without permission, reprinted in the 1983 Revised and Enlarged Complete Edition the same reviews which had been penned over a decade earlier as endorsements for the 1972 *Bhagavad-Gita As It Is* Complete Edition.

ACHARYA FOR HIRE

By 1982, the BBT lodged its first series of USCO registrations, which listed the BBT as the author of post-1977 copyrighted books, which works were almost exclusively based on A. C. Bhaktivedanta Swami Prabhupāda's lectures and conversations. Within this time frame and extending to 1987, the BBT also filed fourteen works-made-for-hire registrations with the USCO.

Rules governing this area of law are complex based on the particular facts under scrutiny, but the gist is found in USCO Circular 30:

> For legal purposes, when a work is a "work made for hire," the author is not the individual who actually created the work. Instead, the party that hired the individual is considered both the author and the copyright owner of the work.

The BBT's assertion in registrations that the author's literary works were works-made-for-hire is a false and indefensible fiction. To qualify as a work-made-for-hire under the 1909 Act, as confirmed by court holdings, a contract was required; wages or other remuneration paid; and the employer, not the employee, had to direct and supervise the creation of a work that would be carried out by the employee. Similarly, a commissioned work must be based on a written contract signed by all parties specifically stating the work being commissioned is to be a work-made-for-hire in order for it to be deemed a work-made-for-hire.

Yet, none of these directives were contemplated, much less met. There was never a contract, and no wages had ever been paid. Nor had the author ever acted or ever been an employee, independent contractor, commissioned worker or similar of ISKCON or its publishing arm the BBT. Additionally, no individual, group, or organization ever directed or commissioned the author, remunerated, paid for, or otherwise guided, controlled, or exerted creative control over the author, directly or indirectly, in return or otherwise for the author's independent and autonomous authorship of his literary works. Nor had the author ever been directed or supervised by the ISKCON Publisher in the creation of his literary works.

Similarly, no contracts existed between the BBT and those devotees and supporters who voluntarily helped to publish the author's books. Nor were the devotees and supporters directed or supervised by the BBT in the creation of his literary works, other than under the authority and supervision of the acharya.

The author is recognized and acknowledged by his disciples and followers within the worldwide religious organization he founded as its foremost and pre-eminent ecclesiastical authority - that is, the Founder-Acharya of the International Society for Krishna Consciousness (ISKCON). His words, guidance, directions, instructions, lectures, correspondence, conversations, and books were accepted and taken as his unique creative and spiritual expression, and thus authoritative, decisive, and final in all matters. It would be an incomprehensible falsehood were the BBT and BBTI INC to legally claim that the author received financial compensation by contract and then under their direction and control he created his unique and personal spiritual writings, translations, purports, commentary, and detailed expositions.

Key titles including Sri Isopanisad; KRSNA—The Supreme Personality of Godhead; The Nectar of Devotion; Teachings of Lord Caitanya; and the two collections, Srimad Bhagavatam and Sri Caitanya Caritamrta, were translated, purported, and or otherwise penned by A. C. Bhaktivedanta Swami Prabhupāda as the sole author. Based on the well-documented history of the author's writings, the BBTI INC cannot rationally suggest that the author himself, the Acharya, was an employee or commissioned to write these books for ISKCON. And there is no evidence that the author ever permitted his writings to be rewritten as derivative works by contracted workers under a work-made-for-hire arrangement.

The entire works-made-for-hire contrivance was ill-conceived as it never had factual or legal grounding. There was no basis to lodge work-made-for-hire registrations for books based on the author's creative expression because the author was not under contract or commission. To top it off, it has been held as against public policy for parties to enter into an agreement that retroactively deems the creation of an earlier work as a work-made-for-hire.

Yet, choosing to toss truth and any semblance of reality out the window, the BBTI INC substantially expanded on decisions made by the BBT Trustees in 1982, by lodging dozens of additional works-made-for-hire registrations with the USCO. Of those titles tracked, sixty-nine works-made-for-hire registrations had been lodged with the USCO by 1997.

THE MOVEMENT'S PUBLISHING OPERATIONS

From its beginning in 1966, using different monikers and entities at different times, in whatever name was expedient, the movement collectively and organizationally, in effect, acted as the ISKCON Publisher. Concurrently, from 1966 as ISKCON Inc and later as ISKCON Press, to the California BBT in 1972, to the BBT as a Division within the ISKCON corporate structure, to the Liechtenstein BBT in 1983, and interspersed throughout, the identity of the ISKCON Publisher and putative copyright owner was ever-changing.

The GBC also played a key role in the publishing operations merry-go-round. For example, by majority vote the GBC approved publication of the 1983 *Bhagavad-Gita As It Is* Revised and Enlarged Complete Edition as an "improved" version which showcased literally thousands of unauthorized and unnecessary editorial changes—all of which were in direct and irremediable conflict with A. C. Bhaktivedanta Swami Prabhupāda, the author and ISKCON's founder-acharya.

Years later, in a burst of confirmational candor during the pendency of BBTI INC litigation in 1998 implicating the BBT, the GBC unequivocally acknowledged in a resolution that the movement's publishing operations were all the while known as the Bhaktivedanta Book Trust:

> WHEREAS, it is the intention and desire of the GBC, as the highest ecclesiastical and managing authority of the International Society for Krishna Consciousness, that BBTI should hold and administer *the intellectual property associated with the Movement's publishing operations known as "Bhaktivedanta Book Trust,"* in accordance with the terms of BBTI's articles of incorporation and bylaws, as they may be amended from time to time by the directors of that independent, ISKCON affiliated corporation. (emphasis added)

As has been described earlier in detail, the movement's "publishing operations" were identified and carried out by a jumble of entities, names, and monikers, including the International Society for Krishna Consciousness, Inc., ISKCON Press, ISKCON Books, multiple BBT trusts in locations around the world (*viz.*, California, India, Liechtenstein), the International Society for Krishna Consciousness of California, Inc., and the Bhaktivedanta Book Trust International, Inc.

In the 1998 resolution noted earlier, the GBC directly and definitively acknowledged that the BBT is essentially the branded name for ISKCON's publishing operations. It is up to inquisitive and curious minds to consider the impact of this bald acknowledgment on the BBTI INC's claim to intellectual property rights, otherwise referred to as the ISKCON Publisher's House of Cards.

CONCLUDING OBSERVATIONS

The realization-infused voice of the acharya is his instructional presence (*vani*) which creates an authorized link to a timeless spiritual lineage (*parampara*). Thereupon, the ISKCON was envisioned and founded by Acharya A. C. Bhaktivedanta Swami Prabhupāda, whose transcendent efforts resulted in the translation, authorship, and publication of some one hundred volumes of his literary works. The number of his books distributed worldwide from 1966 to 2021 has been reliably tabulated at over 563 million.

But the house he founded and built in the last eleven years of his life is now in tatters because the books he authored have been mangled and corrupted, as recognized by his faithful disciples and supporters, and as explained by the many experienced and esteemed scholars who authored chapters in this book. As ISKCON strayed from an acharya-centric movement to a bureaucracy-centric institution, multiple generations of unwitting followers were swayed and pressured to comply with the BBT's contrived editorial policies in place and stead of the author's "no change" directives for his books.

BBT editorial policies revolve around changing the acharya's realization-infused words into their own subjective concoctions. Those erratic and untethered editorial changes have been made by a small cadre of untrained and unqualified self-styled editors who operate under the guise of a corporate control group backed by an institutional bureaucracy that struggles to see the forest for the trees.

The long history of abuse of the author's books and the misuse of his intellectual property rights, however, has come out in the open and the reveal will continue. The question is whether the ISKCON institution will continue to sit idly by and allow the acharya's literary legacy to be left in tatters. If so, the BBT editorial cancel culture will continue its bold but blind march to disrepute, while the legal ramifications of the hidden fifty-five-year-plus history of the ISKCON Publisher will inevitably see the light of day. And when it does, the outcome will not be in doubt.

Over fifty-five years of dissimulation now set in stone will bite hard when scrutinized, while the author's literary works shall retain their inherent integrity and stand their ground, fully sustained by the preeminent authority of Acharya A. C. Bhaktivedanta Swami Prabhupāda and the Copyright Act of 1909.[1]

NOTE

1. This presentation is offered as commentary and for scholastic, educational, and devotional purposes only. Copyrighted material which may be displayed or referenced is Fair Use pursuant to Title 17 USC Section 107, and any other provision of U.S. copyright law which may apply. This presentation is not intended and does not constitute legal advice, nor does it imply or create an attorney-client relationship.

Chapter 12

Framing the Master's Work

On the Theo-Literary Method for Preserving the Completed Writings of the Departed Spiritual Preceptor

Graham M. Schweig

Over the years, it has become apparent to me that many of Prabhupāda's followers have been harboring significant concerns regarding the Bhaktivedanta Book Trust's treatment of his books. After having repeatedly entertained such concerns, I've basically come to perceive them as three-fold: (1) followers expressed to me how they felt that the editing philosophically changed Prabhupāda's completed and published work in significant ways; (2) followers expressed how they perceived a different tone of the text, and distinctively different tenor; and (3) followers expressed how they intuitively felt that something was very wrong and that it was personally painful for them to see these numerous major revisions—as well as all the minor changes—in Prabhupāda's work, made without his authorization, after he departed from this world.

These three categories of concerns from hundreds of followers compelled me to examine the matter. It became apparent to me that, were I to look into the situation, I would be analyzing the literary merit or problems of the editor's work on Prabhupāda's books. But also, I would be seeking a deeper psycho-theological understanding of what was so personally disturbing to the minds and hearts of so many of Prabhupāda's very dedicated followers.

The purpose of this essay, therefore, is to analyze the literary and theological dimensions of the posthumous editing of Prabhupāda's books. While there has been a good amount of scholarly attention given to the posthumous editing of authors' works, the new focus in this volume of collected essays is more specifically on the posthumous editing of the work of a great spiritual leader and teacher. Thus, my focus here will be on the theo-literary dimensions of editing the work of a departed spiritual master by specifically focusing on the revisions and expansion of Prabhupāda's flagship work, *Bhagavad-gītā As It Is*.

BHAGAVAD GĪTĀ: THE MASTER'S FLAGSHIP WORK

Among all of Prabhupāda's dozens of thick volumes of translation and commentary on the sacred Vaishnava texts, the *Bhagavad-gītā As It Is*, is clearly the most prominent among his followers, among readers of his works, and clearly the most widely distributed and sold. *Bhagavad-gītā As It Is* was originally published fifty years ago and has since been widely distributed and translated into approximately sixty languages.[1] Indeed, it is an especially important work; it is the most read presentation of the Bhagavad Gītā in the world, and many millions live a life deeply inspired by its teachings. Therefore, it is primarily the editorial changes and so-called improvements that have been made to Prabhupāda's Bhagavad Gītā that are my focus in this essay.

Prabhupāda titled his work, *Bhagavad-gītā As It Is.* The addition of the phrase "As It Is" to the traditional wording of the work's title, Bhagavad Gītā, especially emboldens his presentation of the work, making it stand out from all the others. It is Bhagavad Gītā, *as it is* spoken directly by Krishna, whose loving words sing out to all souls (as expressed by the word *gītā* in the work's title). It is Bhagavad Gītā, *as it is* according to its inherent and ultimate message. It is Bhagavad Gītā *as it is* aligned with the great teachings coming from a long and sophisticated lineage of prolific philosophers and theologians. And it is Bhagavad Gītā *as it is* that is meant to be lived and breathed.

The ironic reality is that Prabhupāda's Bhagavad Gītā has not remained "as it is." As well-intentioned as his disciple-editors may have been, they have greatly altered his work after he departed this world. The conclusion made in this chapter is that the ideal posthumous treatment of Prabhupāda's flagship work, in the end, must preserve the work *as it is,* while simultaneously addressing any and all textual issues.

This chapter is the result of several years of careful research into the author's vision for editing, as well as extensive scholarly consultation and painstaking textual analysis. My research included the following: a thorough examination of the instructions, teachings, and example of the author; extensive consultations with numerous practitioners close to the author's work; significant Vaishnava theological and ethical considerations; informal consultations with at least twenty textual scholars; extensive discussions with several leading directors and editors of the Bhaktivedanta Book Trust (BBT)—the in-house publisher that Prabhupāda founded and directed to publish his books—and formal presentations to many of the ecclesiastical leaders of ISKCON—the International Society of Krishna Consciousness—the institution that Prabhupāda founded.

PRABHUPĀDA'S INSTRUCTIONS ON EDITING IN A NUTSHELL

Prabhupāda regarded his writing as the most important among all his many achievements. He scrupulously supervised the production of his books, whether it was his early books, published by variously named in-house presses, or his shorter edition (1968) and his later complete edition (1972) of the *Bhagavad-gītā As It Is*, both published by Macmillan. He guided the editors working under him with a cautionary approach, which also applies to the BBT's task of editing: "Our editing is to correct grammatical and spelling errors only, without interpolation of style or philosophy."[2]

Clearly, the author was concerned, during his lifetime itself, that once his disciples had his work in their hands, his style of writing and the philosophical content should remain as he gave it. He specifically requested in written words and spoken instructions, repeatedly, that there should be nothing inserted in or changed from his original words.

Perhaps the most compelling expression of the author's insistence on very conservative and respectful treatment of his books was what he introduced as the principle of *ārṣa-prayoga.* Prabhupāda has defined *ārṣa-prayoga* as follows: "Arsa-prayoga means there may be discrepancies but it is all right."[3] Prabhupāda quotes the following verse, which again emphasizes the sacred power of words beyond their stylistic or grammatical imperfections:[4] "Such transcendental literatures even though imperfectly composed, are heard, sung and accepted by purified men who are thoroughly honest."[5]

His insistence on very conservative and respectful treatment of his books was what he referenced with the Sanskrit phrase *ārṣa-prayoga*—the principle that whatever the sage-like authority (*ārṣa-*) has written, its presentation (*-prayoga*) should be accepted.[6] Prabhupāda demonstrated great care in the publication of his work when he methodically went over the publishing contract with Macmillan. Therein, he made nine initialized modifications of the contract's wording. Especially noteworthy, under the contract's heading of "Revisions," Prabhupāda inserted and initialized the following conditional clause: "only with the consent of the Author."[7]

There are many recorded instances in which Prabhupāda expressed his deep concern about revisions being made without his approval. Without the author's presence, even the most modest editing of grammatical constructions should be avoided. In his original publication, therefore, there should be no presumptive attempts to restore portions of questionable, incomplete drafts to the author-approved, published work. Nor should there be any attempts to restore content from previous drafts or speculative determinations as to what the author would have desired for his work in the present day, as that would not only be unethical but impossible. Justifying any such insertions or changes within the body of the text by basing them on earlier drafts of the author or his editors, without the direct consent of the author, would be viewed by scholars and publishers as an untenable, editorial infringement.[8]

The author himself provides a powerful example of preserving the authenticity of a great spiritual teacher's work. In the "Introduction" to the *Śrī Brahma-saṁhitā,* first published in the year 1932 and republished in 1985 by the Bhaktivedanta Book Trust,[9] Prabhupāda's simple guidelines for editing and producing the work of his departed, beloved spiritual master are elucidated in the following very clear words:

As per Śrīla Prabhupāda's instructions regarding the publication of this volume, Bhaktisiddhānta Sarasvatī's somewhat technical and sometimes difficult prose has been left intact and virtually untouched. Fearing that any editorial (grammatical and stylistic) tampering with Bhaktisiddhānta's text might result in inadvertent changes in meaning, Prabhupāda asked that it be left as is, and the editors of this volume have complied with his wishes.[10]

Following this precedent established by the BBT itself, then, there should be no "tampering" with the text. It should remain the genuine work of the author—essentially a replica of what he originally authorized and produced.

Aside from the corrections of obvious, simple mistakes, Prabhupāda himself has never indicated any explicit or implicit desire whatsoever for additional editing, what to speak of a revised second edition of his work. *Indeed, it is a work from which the author read, quoted, and spoke directly in at least 173 lectures, over five consecutive years.*[11]

In the briefest of terms, one could assert the following paradoxical formula in a few simple words that distills and summarizes his instructions for the kind of editing Prabhupāda desired for his books:

No changes. No mistakes.

The "no changes" invokes the *ārṣa-prayoga* principle. It means that there are no changes without the consent of the living author. Or, if the author has departed this world, then no changes of any kind can be made in the text.[12] Ethically speaking, it is unthinkable to anyone of conscience to go into the property of another, whether it be one's home or one's writing, and so on, and change things around from the way the owner arranged things. Indeed, under Prabhupāda's supervision, the editor could determine exactly what should be accepted as a valid correction. And a living author's work prior to publication is fluid and subject to any correction or modification before submitting it for publication, but only on the authority of the author. That is the prerogative of all living authors. For the sake of authenticity and the historical record, it is necessary not to change the author's original work when the author can no longer consent to it.

The phrase "no mistakes" invokes the *yukta-vairāgya* principle of editing. That is to say, the publisher engages in the normative standards of publishing that anyone in the publishing industry would uphold: the most obvious and blatant mistakes, such as errors in spelling or typographic errors, can be corrected without the author's consent. That is the prerogative of any respectable publisher. However, any perceived mistakes that constitute anything greater than obvious copyediting issues would need to be corrected with full transparency and in ways that we will explore below.

COMPREHENSIVE REVIEW OF BBT EDITOR'S REVISIONS

At one level, it's very simple. BBT editors have gone back into any available partial transcriptions of Prabhupāda's dictations or any of Prabhupāda's directly typed partial drafts of his published *Bhagavad-gītā As It Is,* and other works published during the author's lifetime, to attempt to improve his work after the author has passed away. The editors believe that the editing conducted under the supervision of the living author is to be continued in the same fashion following the author's demise. Or, if not the same, the editors take great liberties and feel they are privileged to improve and even go beyond the author's original work, posthumously. The BBT editors believe that in their heavily "revised and enlarged" second edition, they are capable of producing what is actually "closer" to what the author himself truly "meant" to produce and publish than what the author actually produced and published during his lifetime. They feel that the second edition . . .

> conveys Śrīla Prabhupāda's words and meaning more accurately and more faithfully. . . . Because when Śrīla Prabhupāda's books are made closer to what Śrīla Prabhupāda said, "Then it is all right." In fact, it's better than all right. The closer to Śrīla Prabhupāda, the better.[13]

In one of the editor's own words, he insists on the following:

> In these editions, the editors, after carefully consulting original tapes, manuscripts, and transcripts, restored material the previous editions had lost, obscured, or distorted.[14]

Perhaps such grand improvements could have been proposed to Prabhupāda for improving his published works, and perhaps he would have been grateful to receive them. And no doubt, he would have either accepted or rejected each of the numerous changes, corrections, and improvements, as he desired for his work. Perhaps he would have even authorized a second edition of his work.

But the reality is that the author is not available to approve or disapprove of such changes, resulting in mostly speculative and presumptuous changes to his books. And the BBT editors simply ignore this fact. Moreover, as the multiple revised editions of Prabhupāda's books show, the BBT editors feel they have an unlimited license to improve, modify, and correct the author's original published work.[15] And whatever rationale they may use to do so, whatever justification they may have to make such changes, the indisputable fact remains that they will never know with any certainty whether Prabhupāda would approve their work.

Just two years following Prabhupāda's departure from this world, it came to the attention of Prabhupāda's in-house publisher, the Bhaktivedanta Book Trust (BBT), that there were some errors in Prabhupāda's original publication that needed correcting. One of Prabhupāda's early editors, by the name of Jayadvaita Das, then became the primary person to posthumously edit Prabhupāda's *Bhagavad-gītā As It Is*, the second edition of this work, and ultimately it was his responsibility and his alone. Jayadvaita produced a second edition of Prabhupāda's original work, "revised and enlarged," which was published in 1983 by the BBT.

After several years of scrupulously analyzing every single change the BBT editor made to Prabhupāda's *Bhagavad-gītā As It Is*, I have been able to understand the full extent and nature of the BBT editor's work. The BBT editor made a variety of edits to the *Bhagavad-gītā As It Is*, which is a little over 1,000 pages in length. And after conducting several analytical passes through every page of the second edition of the *Bhagavad-gītā As It Is*, I can offer several analyses in what follows.

Quantitative Analyses of Changes in the Second Edition

Out of the total 700 verses of the BG, 540, or 77 percent, were altered by the BBT editor. And of the 540 altered verses, 479 contained unnecessary edits or changes. Only 61 verses, or about 11 percent, of the 540 altered verses could be considered valid editorial changes for the author to consider: 21 verse translations contain valid copyediting corrections, and the remaining 40 verses could be seen as containing necessary corrections of mistakes for an author to address.

Since the deceased author is not accessible to give his approval or disapproval for making any of the 61 possibly valid verse changes, the most respectful and prudent treatment is to suggest in annotations only the most important among the 61 verse corrections, which I estimate to be approximately ten verse emendations at most. Annotations or footnotes would leave the original *Bhagavad-gītā As It Is* text unchanged. By introducing annotations and footnotes or endnotes, the master's work remains *fixed*, that is, without modification, and the annotations remain *fluid*, in that new information can always be introduced or previously introduced annotations can be corrected.

Prabhupāda's commentary on the Bhagavad Gītā is hefty and takes up most of the volume. I found a total of 1,750 editorial changes made by the BBT editor to the commentary in the second edition. Overall, I found at least 1,452 unnecessary editorial changes involving removing commas, inserting commas, switching words around, stylistic changes, interpolations, and so on. This includes 156 references and/or verse numbers to scriptural passages that the BBT editor found missing or incomplete in the work.

Of the 1,750 editorial changes in the commentarial portions of the book, only 298 could be considered valid editing, were the author available to approve or disapprove of the changes. Among the 298 possibly valid editorial changes, 121 could be considered copyediting, i.e., correcting spelling mistakes, typos, and so on. Another 42 small corrections could be deemed transcribing mistakes that are possibly corroborated in partial drafts. Another 125 mostly small corrections could be made because of mistranscriptions or misunderstandings on the part of the author's transcriber. But I found only ten significant corrections that would deserve the attention of the author, were the author still present.

That said, given that Prabhupāda is no longer available to consult regarding corrections and modifications beyond mere spelling mistakes, it is unthinkable to alter his work. In general, an intuitive ethical sense would dictate that it is simply not right to change *any* deceased author's completed and published work. But when we are speaking about a world spiritual teacher—who is hardly like any secular author—we are speaking about an author's words, which are the very life of his disciples and followers, as we shall discuss below.

In the end, over 80 percent of the edits made by the BBT editor are deemed unnecessary. And only a fraction of the remaining, *possibly* valid, edits would be worthy of addressing, and then *only* in an annotated form. It is my conclusion that not more than 180 emendations of the BBT's 1750 plus changes would be valid, again, were the author still present to gain his approval.

Types of Unnecessary BBT Editing

Listed here are the various types of unnecessary and unacceptable editing the BBT editor has done several years after his spiritual teacher departed this world. This list begins with the least intrusive forms of editing and moves to the most intrusive forms:

1) Many corrections or editorial changes from the original are made, such as arbitrarily placed commas and other punctuation.
2) Adding or completing scriptural references inserted directly into the original text.
3) Without changing the original words, words are rearranged within a sentence or made into two sentences.
4) Minor grammatical changes are made.
5) Words or phrases are replaced with what the editor feels are better or more accurate words. Sometimes using Prabhupāda's words from elsewhere, perhaps with the intent to make Prabhupāda's language or meaning more consistent.
6) Inserting words into verse translations that may appear in the original Sanskrit transliteration but not in the verse as translated by Prabhupāda, attempting to correct the author's translations.
7) Adding or deleting words or phrases, many instances of which are according to what is found in a draft but often without plausible justification.
8) Changes in wording that change the meaning of verses or the commentarial writing of the author; even the removal or addition of whole sentences.

While there are numerous examples of each one of these eight types of unnecessary editing—enough examples to fill a whole, very thick book—I offer just one example of a most intrusive edit, as described above in number 8. The BBT editor—specifically, Jayadvaita—shows that he is capable of eliminating the words, even whole sentences, of the author from the author's original published work. A dramatic example of this is the removal of two whole sentences from a purport. In the original abridged Collier-Macmillan 1968 published *Bhagavad-gītā As It Is,* and in the complete original Macmillan 1972 published *Bhagavad-gītā As It Is,* the verse (BG 10:31) to which Prabhupāda offers a very short purport is as follows:

> Of purifiers I am the wind; of the wielders of weapons I am Rama; of fishes I am the shark, and of flowing rivers I am the Ganges.

Prabhupāda's mere four-sentence purport to this verse from the Macmillan published work reads as follows:

> Of all the aquatics the shark is one of the biggest and is certainly the most dangerous to man. Thus the shark represents Krsna. And of rivers, the greatest in India is the Mother Ganges. Lord Ramacandra, of the Ramayana, an incarnation of Krsna, is the mightest [*sic*] of warriors.

The BBT editor took it upon himself to remove half of the purport in the Second Edition of Prabhupāda's work, removing the last two sentences (italicized bolded text indicates what the BBT editor removed):

> Of all the aquatics the shark is one of the biggest and is certainly the most dangerous to man. Thus the shark represents Krsna. *And of rivers, the greatest in India is the Mother Ganges. Lord Ramacandra, of the Ramayana, an incarnation of Krsna, is the mightest of warriors.*

The BBT editor's disrespectful justification is found in his own words (bold words mine):

> The shark may be a dangerous fish, but the locution "of the Ramayana" at once alerted me that something else fishy was going on. Is Lord Ramacandra a character from a book, like Alice "of Alice in Wonderland"? *Sure enough*, in the original manuscript the text about Lord Ramacandra doesn't appear; it *seems* to have been added by the editor.
>
> *For certain*, the editor of the First Edition was trying to be helpful. But sometimes we are better off without help. The word rama may of course refer to Lord Ramacandra—or to Balarama, or even to Krsna Himself. Nonetheless, our sampradaya acaryas comment here that rama refers to—whom? Lord Parasurama.[16]

Looking beyond the editor's snarky expression in his explanation—which is surprising to find coming from presumably a devoted disciple and trusted editor of the revered author himself—shows how the editor wishes to discredit the author's words by relying on their apparent absence in a random earlier draft (not the final manuscript submitted to Macmillan). He speculates that Prabhupāda did not write certain words in his commentary and insists that they come from an editor who inserts the words into the final manuscript for publication without the author's knowledge or even his awareness. (In numerous letters directly from Prabhupāda himself, there is ample evidence that he was very involved with the content and editing of his work.)

The fact of the matter is that Prabhupāda not only submitted his final and full manuscript for publication with this four-sentence comment under the verse BG 10.31, but he himself specifically references the very idea of Rāmacandra in a recorded conversation from the two sentences eliminated by his editor. In a room conversation the author had with Ram Jethmalani (Indian Parliament Member) in Bombay on April 16, 1977, when questioning whether or not Ramachandra of the Rāmāyana was acknowledged in the Bhagavad Gītā, Prabhupāda responded with the following words, drawing from his own purport:

> "Amongst the warriors, I am Rama." The reference is there. This very word is there. "Amongst the warriors, I am Rama."

Thus, there is no question that Prabhupāda himself deliberately stands by what he wrote and published in his book.

But to make matters worse, the BBT editor resorts to the "sampradaya acaryas" for correcting Prabhupāda, in effect, jumping over the head of his teacher. Again, this is hardly the exemplary behavior of a devoted disciple, what to speak of an editor who feels entitled to change the master's work posthumously. The fact is that not all of the *sampradāya* teachers claim that the "wielder of the bow" is Paruśurāma—other commentators insist on identifying the wielder as Rāmacandra. Thus, the editor does not even represent the tradition fully and accurately by carelessly and inappropriately correcting his master.

In short, if the BBT editor is capable of this kind of correction and elimination of the original author's words, then he is capable of changing or eliminating anything, which transgresses both the normal moral rights of any author and the proper devotional way a disciple honors his spiritual teacher.

Eight *Sources* Justifying Editorial Changes

Listed here are the four various possibly acceptable sources for treatment of a deceased author's work, which would receive full, transparent annotative explanations:

1) The author's oral directives to correct author-identified mistakes;
2) Editor's correction of spelling and grammatical mistakes;
3) Partial author-typed drafts with full, transparent annotative explanation (only if necessary);
4) Partial drafts of earlier transcriptions of dictations of text with full, transparent annotative explanation (only if necessary).

Listed here are four unacceptable sources for posthumous editing, which easily characterize the unacceptable BBT editing:

1) Editor's personal subjective sense of style and arbitrary embellishments;
2) Editor's copyediting improvements and estimates of good English usage;
3) Editor's philosophical and content interpolations;
4) Editor's reach behind the author (including use of traditional commentaries on Bhagavad Gītā by previous Vaishnava teachers) or in front of the author (such as the opinions of other fellow followers of Prabhupāda).

Eight Ways of Seeing and Treating the Original Text

This first list of four options presents ways that a publisher can treat a text as stable, with any significant editorial changes made with transparency. These are recommended for an ethically and scholarly sound treatment of the work of a deceased author:

Option 1: The text is complete and stable—absolutely nothing touched from what the author approved and published.
Option 2: The text is complete and stable—only blatant errors in spelling or typos corrected.
Option 3: The text is complete and stable—with transcription or other corrections made, not in the body of the text but only in footnote or endnote annotations so as to not disrupt the original text.
Option 4: The text is complete with the qualification—absolutely necessary emendations made in the body of the text but preserving the original text in footnote or endnote annotations.

Also included in the following four options is how a publisher can see, as the BBT does, a published work as somehow unstable and incomplete, and feels entitled to make any and all emendations without transparency:

Option 1: The text is unstable and treated as *somewhat* incomplete—with copyedited stylistic upgrades made.
Option 2: The text is unstable and treated as *fairly* incomplete—major copy-editing corrections or changes made without transparency or declaration.
Option 3: The text is unstable and treated as *very* incomplete—content additions, subtractions, or rewritings of the work, and/or corrections can be freely made by the editor, who feels he/she has a license to do so.

Option 4: The text is unstable and is seen as incomplete, requiring *total* revision—this option combines options 1 through 3 and adds or subtracts text while assuming to have the same authority and privileges of the original departed author.

VAISHNAVA EPISTEMOLOGY VIOLATED BY BBT EDITING

Authoritative Modes of Cognition

Anyone acquainted with Indic traditions arising from the Vedas, commonly known as Hindu traditions, knows the importance, authority, and primacy of the revealed word of the divine, known as *śabda pramāṇa.* It is common for scholars and practitioners to speak of Hindu "philosophy," because Hindu traditions will utilize the rational tools found in the six classical schools of philosophy, which engage textual interpretation, logic, scientific kinds of reasoning, and psychology of the human and higher states of consciousness. But all of these rigorous philosophical schools are grounded first in a foundation that is derivative of and revealed through scripture.

The important point here is that the Krishna *bhakti* tradition out of which Prabhupāda himself comes is heavily grounded in the theological bedrock of the revelation of the divine word.[17] From the three primary authoritative modes of *pramāṇa* (authoritative means of cognition), viz. *śabda* (revelation), *pratyakṣa* (direct sensory perception or experience), and *anumāna* (inference or conjecture), *śabda pramāṇa,* or more specifically, the *śruti,* or the authoritative knowledge of the Vedas, is considered perfect or infallible, while the other two are considered imperfect and subject to the imperfect nature of the human condition. Prabhupāda describes in his introduction to *Bhagavad-gītā As It Is* how any mode of cognition other than divine revelation is imperfect and subject to the "four defects" of conditioned human beings:

> We must accept *Bhagavad-gītā* without interpretation, without deletion and without our own whimsical participation in the matter. The *Gītā* should be taken as the most perfect presentation of Vedic knowledge. Vedic knowledge is received from transcendental sources, and the first words were spoken by the Lord Himself. The words spoken by the Lord are called *apauruṣeya,* meaning that they are different from words spoken by a person of the mundane world who is infected with four defects. A mundaner (1) is sure to commit mistakes, (2) is invariably illusioned, (3) has the tendency to cheat others and (4) is limited by imperfect senses. With these four imperfections, one cannot deliver perfect information of all-pervading knowledge.[18]

Indeed, Rita D. Sherma astutely observes how Prabhupāda's writings are seen by him and his followers as a "second-order revelation," or taking on the ultimate status of *śabda-pramāṇa*.[19] And yet the BBT editor has convinced the ISKCON leadership that his editing improves Prabhupāda's books by bringing them closer to the author's authentic expression through various empirical and imperfect efforts of *pratyākṣa-pramāṇa* (as well as the speculative aspects of *anumāna-pramāṇa*). And what is more surprising is this: despite Prabhupāda's warnings of how imperfect empirical and speculative processes of cognition can be, the BBT editors yet have fallen victim to these very defects.

The BBTedit.com Website

Evidence of the BBT's reversed epistemological approach is revealed on their website. The BBT editor boldly begins with a full reliance on "history," or his piecing together how the early editors worked under Prabhupāda, and barely takes into consideration Prabhupāda's instructions and even the spirit of his guidance prior to and even following his departure from this world. The ordered list of subject matters in the horizontal blue-colored menu line that appears on the opening page of the BBT website are the eight titled menu items, starting from left and going across to the right, in the following significant sequence:

(1) History
(2) Myths
(3) Controversies
(4) Articles
(5) Srila Prabhupāda Says
(6) See the Changes
(7) Video FAQ
(8) Testimonials

The subject topics and their order reveal what is important to and foundational for the BBT editor's editorial approach. The BBT's position clearly begins "first" with "some historical perspective." This is their starting point. This is where they begin. It is on the basis of their imperfect piecing together of the historical overview of Prabhupāda's circumstances that the BBT editor can presume to know how he would want his completed and published books treated posthumously. Furthermore, the following three menu items are all about justifying their mundane treatment of their master's work, addressing the numerous doubts that have been thrown at the BBT, and their editors.

The following rearranged list is what one would expect from a loyal disciple editor, who would take into account the Vaishnava theological value of revelation, i.e., the revelation of their master's instructions, guidance, and example.

(1) Prabhupāda's Direct Instructions on Editing
(2) Prabhupāda's Discussions on Editing
(3) The Foundational Principle of Ārṣa Prayoga
(4) The Secondary Principle of Yukta Vairāgya
(5) Prabhupāda's Example of His Master's Work
(6) Editing that Reflects Krishna Bhakti Theology
(7) Editorial and Ethical Standards of Scholarship
(8) Professional Publishing Conventions

Such a list, as one would expect from a discerning editor, has no need for addressing controversies as the BBT has done. Nor would there be any need to list a select number of changes (that are misleading in that they are not fully representative of the full extent of the changes), nor articles justifying transgressive practices that have been heavily questioned and debated by dedicated, seasoned followers, as well as respected academics.[20] Even testimonials would not be required. Why? Because the original text, as the author published, is final.

Professor Rita D. Sherma has correctly observed that Prabhupāda's works are tantamount to a second order revelation, and therefore any "changes," which have been so disturbing to so many followers, would not occur. Prabhupāda's words are, for many of his followers, on the order of *śabda-pramāṇa,* or revelational cognition. Any "changes" or emendations for the publisher to put forward would be placed in annotations, which can always remain fluid, while the original text remains fixed. While Prabhupāda was present, his editor consulted him and he oversaw the whole process. While Prabhupāda is absent, the editorial process cannot be the same as if Prabhupāda were present. No one has been given absolute authority over Prabhupāda's books. The author hoped his books would be preserved and remain unaltered, though his greatest fear was that they would be changed. Therefore, when loyal followers see the BBT editors treat Prabhupāda's finished work as if it were incomplete, even as if it were mundane literature written by ordinary authors, they understandably are disturbed.

THE NEWLY FORMED BBT REVISIONS REVIEW PANEL

The BBT is led by very competent book production, wholesale distribution, and worldwide sales force directors. The editing, however, has been left in the hands of untrained autodidacts, whose work, as examined and analyzed above, has resulted in amateurish over-editing, correcting, and changing of the deceased author's work. Their work is predicated on many assumptions (as will be explored later in this chapter); one primary assumption has been that Prabhupāda was simply uninvolved in the editing and production of his own books:

> He [Prabhupāda] rarely revised his work after the initial dictation and rarely read the edited manuscripts before publication, instead entrusting his editors with both tasks. For nearly all his books, once he sent off his dictations (or later, the Sanskrit-edited transcriptions), he never saw his text again until it was published.[21]

This assumption has been proven to be patently false, since there is more than ample evidence that Prabhupāda was very actively involved in directly overseeing the editorial quality of his editors' work on his books.[22]

After several decades of criticism coming to the BBT from hundreds of dedicated followers, the BBT finally decided to put together what it originally called its "Revisions Review Panel."[23] The stated purpose of the Panel is as follows:

> The aim of the RRP is to examine all proposed and previously accepted text changes to Srila Prabhupāda's books in the English language . . . However, the emphasis will be on reviewing any posthumous editing or particularly controversial edits.[24]

And almost two years later, the RRP, now the ERP, reinforced their approach, in the following words:

> Guided by these principles, the ERP will consider each revision that has been made to Srila Prabhupāda's books and propose to either accept or remove the revision. All their recommendations will be made by consensus. Once the ERP's work is complete, they will submit their suggestions to the BBT Editorial Board for review and implementation.[25]

Please note that the RRP (ERP) begins with a review of the changes made to Prabhupāda's posthumously revised books, to either validate the BBT editor's substantial changes or to reject them. Rather than beginning with what exactly Prabhupāda directly authorized and published with Collier Macmillan in 1972 and only introducing the most minimal corrections and changes with full transparency, this advisory panel's given mission appears to validate the long-standing BBT editor's work instead.[26] Rather than respecting the author's original, the panelists appear to be engaged by the BBT, in nepotistic fashion, to justify the thousands of changes made by its editor.

It is disappointing to see that even those on the panel who have academic training—including two scholars with outstanding intellectual accomplishments—are allowing themselves to be coopted in their scholarly standards when it comes to their review of Prabhupāda's books. When scholar-practitioners obligate themselves beyond ethical and scholarly loyalty to ex cathedra ecclesiastical authorities—as seems to be the case in the instance of the BBT's Editorial Review Panel members—they not only risk their academic integrity but also, ironically, consequently tarnish the integrity of the very religious organization they originally set out to serve. In this case, such a compromise would sadly include sacrificing devotional loyalty to Prabhupāda himself as both a spiritual teacher and author, whose intention for scholar-practitioners representing his movement was just the opposite: that they return integrity to the academic presentation of the tradition, not diminish it.

The BBT, terribly eager to put the matter of "the book changes controversy" to rest—optimistically but perhaps prematurely—published an article, titled: "Book Changes Controversy Coming to a Close." In their article, they announce the completed "Editorial Principles for the Editorial Review Panel," which are accessible to anyone.[27] The Editorial Principles can appear to be very conservative and respectful of the author's originally published and authorized work, yet they make provisions for aggressive changes that are not declared or transparent.

There are two highly trained academic scholars on the panel. However, the panel may be failing to meet scholarly standards (as well as ethical and devotional expectations) for treating and preserving Prabhupāda's books.[28] While the members of the ERP are required not to divulge whether they accept or reject the former BBT editor's changes in the second edition of Prabhupāda's original *Bhagavad-gītā As It Is* (published by Collier Macmillan), a BBT news announcement proudly declared a dramatic decision, as explained in the article, titled: "Use of 'Blessed Lord' Constituted Editorial Overreach Says the ERP."[29]

Despite the panel's sworn secrecy, perhaps we can gain a peek into the risky business of their work by examining this one decision we know about, courtesy of the BBT's announcement: to eliminate the use of "Blessed Lord" in Prabhupāda's books. They confidently arrived at this decision despite the fact that Prabhupāda either heard or recited himself the phrase, "The Blessed Lord," from the 1972 Macmillan published *Bhagavad-gītā As It Is,* in his lectures, conversations, and so on, in at least forty-eight instances of the 173 recorded lectures delivered directly from his *Bhagavad-gītā As It Is*. In none of those lectures—or anywhere else—did Prabhupāda ever object once to the use of the phrase, "the Blessed Lord."

The one instance in which Prabhupāda showed deference to his later commonly used protracted phrase to translate *śrī bhagavān,* "the Supreme Personality of Godhead," appears to be merely for emphasis and not as an instruction to change his translation of the *Bhagavad-gītā As It Is*. This one incident certainly doesn't constitute a precedent for rejecting the phrase "the Blessed Lord" in every instance in which Prabhupāda employed it.[30] In fact, over a period of nine years, since the publication of his abridged *Bhagavad-gītā As It Is,* Prabhupāda never indicated that the phrase should be changed, with the exception of only one instance prior to publication, which was the ERP reference (BG Chapter 10, verse 1).

Would any of the ERP members actually be willing to present to Prabhupāda a proposal to switch out "The Blessed Lord says" with "The Supreme Personality of Godhead says"? And if so, can any of these panel members be assured with absolute confidence that Prabhupāda would answer in the affirmative? And why did no follower or editor make such a proposal to do so during the nine years that Prabhupāda engaged both his published abridged and then unabridged versions of *Bhagavad-gītā As It Is*?[31]

In 1975, Prabhupāda published in his translation of and commentary on the *Śrī Caitanya-caritāmṛta,* the following passage in a purport:

> In every verse of *Śrīmad Bhagavad-gītā* it is clearly stated that Kṛṣṇa is the Supreme Personality of Godhead. In every verse Vyāsadeva says, *śrī-bhagavān uvāca,* "the Supreme Personality of Godhead said," or "the Blessed Lord said." It is clearly stated that the Blessed Lord is the Supreme Person[32]

To confirm how deliberate this double presentation of the phrase "the Blessed Lord said," one can readily see evidence of the authenticity of the usage of this phrase in the following direct transcription of Prabhupāda's direct and precise wording:

After such careful consideration of Prabhupāda's use of the phrase "the Blessed Lord," including instances in which he himself dictates it, validates it and authorizes it, it's easy to find the BBT's Editorial Review Panel's swift dismissal of it quite objectionable. Following this, it stands to reason that the methodology exercised to arrive at this objectionable decision—or all their other decisions, for that matter—is equally inadequate, to say the least. Exactly what principles did the ERP employ to limit their editorial changes to Prabhupāda's work? Did they chasten their decisions to Prabhupāda's own treatment of his Bhagavad Gītā, for example, as outlined in the following?

Eight Undisputed Facts

(1) Prabhupāda directly read from both Macmillan-published Bhagavad Gītās, starting in 1968; it is on record that he spoke and read directly from the 1972 edition in at least 173 lectures.[33] It is also likely that there are many more unrecorded instances.
(2) Prabhupāda read directly from the Macmillan Gītās in his private time, as reported in the memoirs of his private secretaries.[34]
(3) Prabhupāda oversaw his various editors as much as he deemed appropriate and valuable when preparing his work for publication.[35]
(4) Prabhupāda never expressed any dissatisfaction with his book, with the exception of two oral requests to make two specific corrections or changes.
(5) Prabhupāda was concerned that disciples would make changes without his authorization.
(6) There is no evidence whatsoever that Prabhupāda asked for, ordered, or even suggested a revision of his 1972 published work.
(7) Prabhupāda supervised the final editing of his work, authorized and approved his final manuscript for publication and approved the publisher's copyedit suggestions, a normal process utilized in the publishing world.
(8) Prabhupāda carefully reviewed and signed the publishing contract with Collier Macmillan, with nine personally initialized amended clauses.

THEOLOGICAL IMPLICATIONS OF BBT EDITING

When we consider the eight critical axiomatic understandings of the author regarding his Bhagavad Gītā, as outlined above, it is questionable how the BBT editors took the kind of liberties they did with it. Many followers perceive in the intrusive and eroding editing by the BBT the following underlying painful assumptions:

> Prabhupāda, the original teacher of Krishna *bhakti* theology, has been treated by the BBT with even less consideration than an ordinary author, who . . .
> - was unaware of how incompetent his editors were;
> - was unaware of the mistakes in his books;
> - trusted his editors when he should not have;
> - was just too busy to give his books the attention they needed;
> - was unable to empower his early editors to do the work he needed;
> - was lacking good English and his book needed rewriting;
> - would want an editor to rely fully on his earlier drafts for revisions;

- needed to have his books corrected to make them better;
- left his works in an unfinished state which necessitated a BBT editor to complete them;
- wrote works that requires the BBT to analyze his writing habits and evaluate his writing methods.

On the other hand, many followers of Prabhupāda see things quite differently, as the spiritual master who . . .

- considered the writing and publishing of his books his greatest accomplishment;
- declared his works as not merely his own, but as words coming from the divine;
- had an extraordinary level awareness that could not be evaluated or second-guessed;
- had his own reasons for his writing and publishing processes; authored and fully authorized his original work;
- never ordered or authorized a "Second Edition: Revised and Enlarged" ;
- would be the only one to know if such editorial changes were what he wanted for his work, as something "closer" to what he would accept;
- expressed a fear that his followers would change his books;
- was explicit about how his work should be edited under his supervision;
- never gave instructions for changing his work after his departure from this world.

A THEO-LITERARY SOLUTION

Scholars of textual criticism go to great lengths to apply established historical-critical methods to investigate the origins of an ancient text, to identify the actual author of the work, and to determine the authenticity of a text, whether it is the original or a recension. Indeed, there is a remarkable body of scholarship devoted to producing critical editions of historical texts. Such works identify in the most nuanced manner any textual variants in different versions of manuscripts or printed books of the same work. For instance, a critical edition of the whole Mahābhārata (which includes the Bhagavad Gītā) has been produced by scholars in India.

In modern times, however, there would be utterly no need for historical-critical methods to be applied to modern works because authors today authenticate their own works with copyright registrations, and in their contracts with publishers. Modern authorship makes matters simple: the author produces his or her work (and whatever assistance he or she may have had in producing the work is immaterial), submits a final manuscript to the publisher, the author enters into a contractual relationship with the publisher to produce the work, and a copyeditor's suggested changes are submitted to the author for approval or rejection, and then the book is produced. Certainly, the *Bhagavad-gītā As It Is,* authored by A. C. Bhaktivedanta Swami Prabhupāda, is no exception.

It is standard practice for a publisher not to change any part of the author's work without his or her permission, as it is commonly understood that the work belongs to the author. Now, in the contract that Prabhupāda had with Macmillan Company, the publisher with whom he published his work, there is a specific author-initialized, typed-in contractual clause, which clearly requires written permission from the author prior to any revision. (See figures 12.1 and 12.2.)[36]

What is called for, then, in the posthumous editing of a great master's work is virtually no editing at all. With the exception of any spelling mistakes and the most minimal formatting issues, the text remains as is. (See figure 12.5.) After combing the field of textual studies and consultation with numerous professional sources, such as many journal articles in the field of textual criticism, and personal contact with scholars involved in the Modern Language Association's Committee on Scholarly Editions (CSE), the consensus was that editing is done with a literary work when the living author is present to approve or reject any proposed changes, as all publishers do with their authors, by sending them "proofs." Accepting or rejecting changes in any part of a text is the last stage before putting a book into production. This is the stage where the author finalizes his or her work.

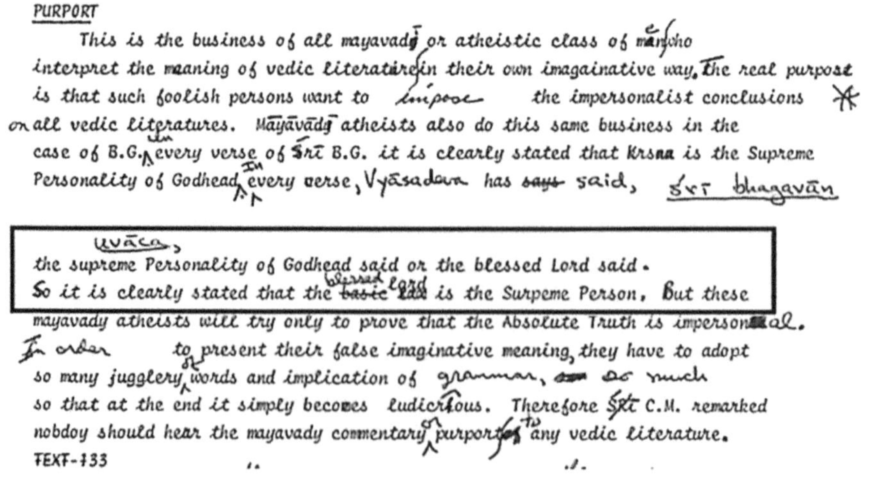
PURPORT

This is the business of all mayavady or atheistic class of man who interpret the meaning of vedic literature in their own imagainative way. The real purpose is that such foolish persons want to impose the impersonalist conclusions on all vedic literatures. Māyāvādī atheists also do this same business in the case of B.G. every verse of Śrī B.G. it is clearly stated that Krsna is the Supreme Personality of Godhead every verse, Vyāsadeva has said, Śrī bhagavān uvāca, the supreme Personality of Godhead said or the blessed Lord said. So it is clearly stated that the blessed Lord is the Surpeme Person. But these mayavady atheists will try only to prove that the Absolute Truth is impersonal. In order to present their false imaginative meaning, they have to adopt so many jugglery words and implication of grammar, so much so that at the end it simply becomes ludicrous. Therefore Śrī C.M. remarked nobdoy should hear the mayavady commentary or purport to any vedic literature.

TEXT-133

Figure 12.1 This is a portion of a passage directly transcribed from Prabhupāda's dictation of the Śrī Caitanya-caritāmṛta 2.6.132, in which he very deliberately acknowledges the validity and his own use of the phrase "the blessed Lord said" twice in the same comment (which I have demarcated within the rectangular marking above), without hesitation or qualification. *Source*: The Bhaktivedanta Archives.

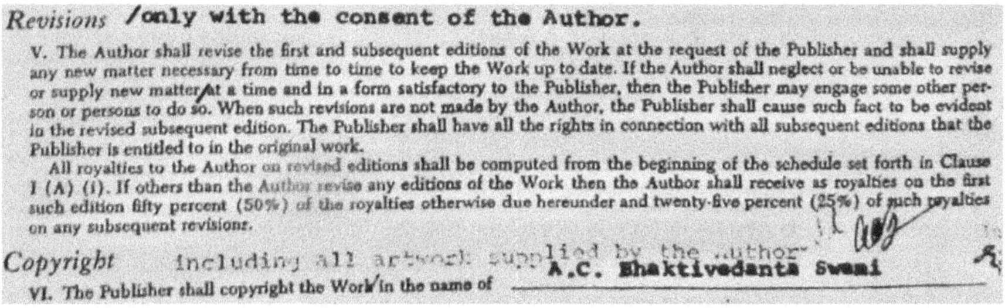
Revisions /only with the consent of the Author.

V. The Author shall revise the first and subsequent editions of the Work at the request of the Publisher and shall supply any new matter necessary from time to time to keep the Work up to date. If the Author shall neglect or be unable to revise or supply new matter at a time and in a form satisfactory to the Publisher, then the Publisher may engage some other person or persons to do so. When such revisions are not made by the Author, the Publisher shall cause such fact to be evident in the revised subsequent edition. The Publisher shall have all the rights in connection with all subsequent editions that the Publisher is entitled to in the original work.

All royalties to the Author on revised editions shall be computed from the beginning of the schedule set forth in Clause I (A) (i). If others than the Author revise any editions of the Work then the Author shall receive as royalties on the first such edition fifty percent (50%) of the royalties otherwise due hereunder and twenty-five percent (25%) of such royalties on any subsequent revisions.

Copyright including all artwork supplied by the Author

VI. The Publisher shall copyright the Work in the name of A.C. Bhaktivedanta Swami

Figure 12.2 This photo shows a portion of the publishing contract for producing *Bhagavad-gītā As It Is* between the Macmillan Company and Prabhupāda, in which the typed in clause "only with the consent of the Author" with regard to the contract's section on "Revisions" is found. There are five other places in the publishing contract in which Prabhupāda had typed-in initialized clauses requiring the "Author's prior approval," or consent. *Source*: Reproduction of a portion of page 2 of the 1972 Macmillan publishing contract with author A. C. Bhaktivedanta Swami.

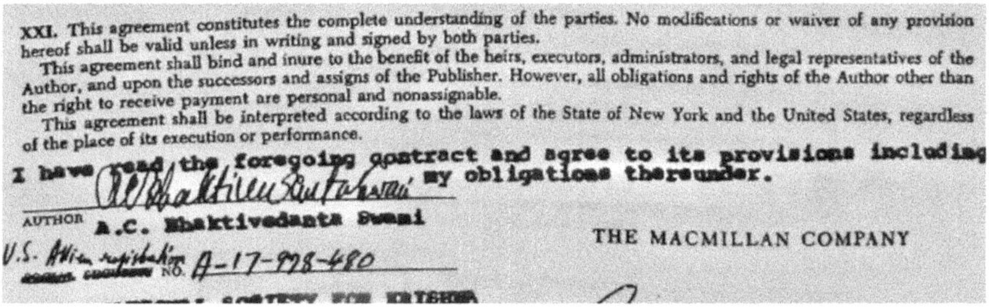
XXI. This agreement constitutes the complete understanding of the parties. No modifications or waiver of any provision hereof shall be valid unless in writing and signed by both parties.

This agreement shall bind and inure to the benefit of the heirs, executors, administrators, and legal representatives of the Author, and upon the successors and assigns of the Publisher. However, all obligations and rights of the Author other than the right to receive payment are personal and nonassignable.

This agreement shall be interpreted according to the laws of the State of New York and the United States, regardless of the place of its execution or performance.

I have read the foregoing contract and agree to its provisions including my obligations thereunder.

AUTHOR A.C. Bhaktivedanta Swami

U.S. Alien registration NO. A-17-978-480

THE MACMILLAN COMPANY

Figure 12.3 This photo shows a portion of the last page with Prabhupāda's signature on the 1972 publishing contract for *Bhagavad-gītā As It Is* between the Macmillan Company and Prabhupāda. *Source*: Reproduction of the signature lines portion of page 4 of the 1972 Macmillan publishing contract with author A. C. Bhaktivedanta Swami.

However, a deceased author's work would not be edited in the normative manner, because it likely involves adding annotations and other supportive apparatuses such as footnotes or endnotes. And such notes would only incorporate the tiniest superscript numbers or symbols within the body of the text itself. Prabhupāda himself utilized footnotes—a total of twenty-seven—in the very books he directly produced in India before coming to the United States. Among these, there are eleven instances in which he utilized annotations in his pre-1966 published work. (See figures 12.5, 12.6, and 12.7.)

As a general principle, Prabhupāda's books should be preserved as he gave them to the world. Any editor who has in his or her charge the work of a deceased author knows that they are obligated to preserve its contents the way the author delivered it. Otherwise, the authentic original work is at risk of being erased from history.

APPENDIX—2

ERRATA

Page	*Line*	*Misprint*	*Correct*
1	20	Absoltue	Absolute
11	12	retorhical	rhetorical
11	27	hinderanees	hindrances
14	31	squizing.	squeezing
21	1	immitate	imitate
26	18	coneption.	conception
28	33	andience	audience
39	33	smillingly	smilingly
52	36	at once	at once to
53	29	existance	existence
57	28	percels	parcels
61	28	Competetion	Competition
64	2	realy	really
,,	,,	welbeing	wellbeing
65	26	bonafied	bonafide
67	4	trce	tree
,,	34	shocking,	shocking
69	6	carefull	careful
70	2	beacks	beaks
75	15	directious	directions
77	2	there	therefore
,,	16	on	one
80	10	adicted	addicted
91	2	repeatation	repetition
103	21	Pnranas	Puranas
118	6	undoutedly	undoubtedly
122	4	remnescence	reminiscence
124	30	anb	and

Figure 12.4 This photo is the first ERRATA page of three full pages in the back of the First Part, Srimad Bhagwatam (The League of Devotees, Vrindaban: Delhi, 1962), p. v. This errata page of "Misprints" (the left column) and "Correct" spellings of words (the right column) is evidence of the meticulousness with which Prabhupāda treated his published work, in addition to his desire to have misspelled words corrected. *Source*: The League of Devotees, Vrindaban: Delhi, 1962, p. v.

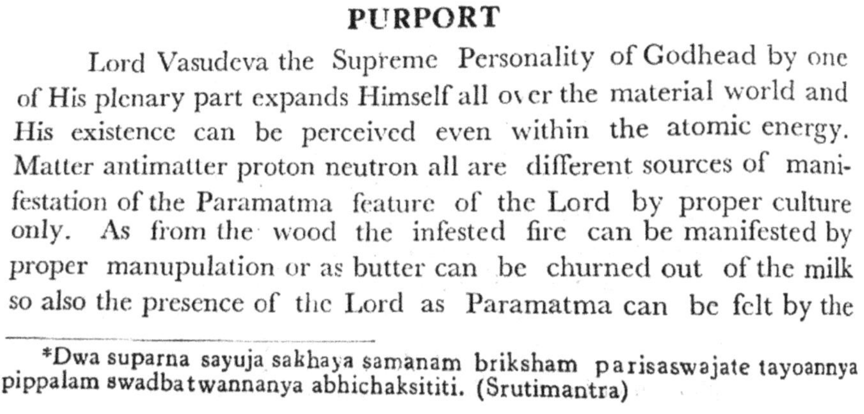

PURPORT

Lord Vasudeva the Supreme Personality of Godhead by one of His plenary part expands Himself all over the material world and His existence can be perceived even within the atomic energy. Matter antimatter proton neutron all are different sources of manifestation of the Paramatma feature of the Lord by proper culture only. As from the wood the infested fire can be manifested by proper manupulation or as butter can be churned out of the milk so also the presence of the Lord as Paramatma can be felt by the

*Dwa suparna sayuja sakhaya samanam briksham parisaswajate tayoannya pippalam swadbatwannanya abhichaksititi. (Srutimantra)

Figure 12.5 This photo is just one example among fifteen (throughout his three volumes) in which Prabhupāda cites a passage of sacred text. *Source*: The League of Devotees, Vrindaban: Delhi, 1962, p. 150.

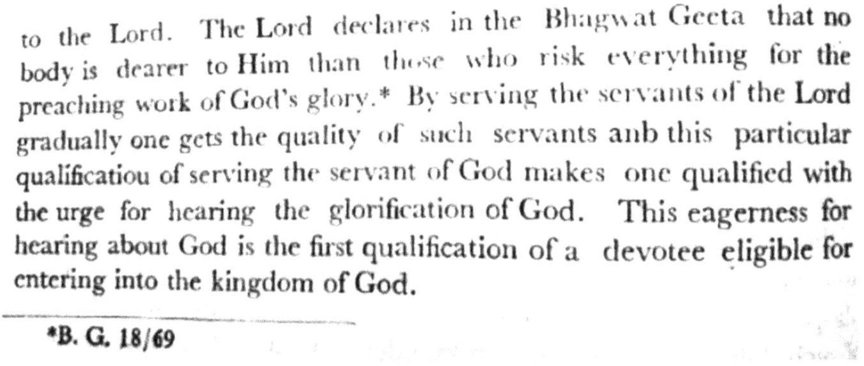

to the Lord. The Lord declares in the Bhagwat Geeta that no body is dearer to Him than those who risk everything for the preaching work of God's glory.* By serving the servants of the Lord gradually one gets the quality of such servants anb this particular qualificatiou of serving the servant of God makes one qualified with the urge for hearing the glorification of God. This eagerness for hearing about God is the first qualification of a devotee eligible for entering into the kingdom of God.

*B. G. 18/69

Figure 12.6 Here, Prabhupāda chose to place even the briefest citation for the *Bhagavad-gītā* in a footnote rather than an in-text citation. He makes these very abbreviated footnotes many times through his own Indian published work. *Source*: The League of Devotees, Vrindaban: Delhi, 1962, p. 124.

EIGHT EDITORIAL PRINCIPLES FOR POSTHUMOUS EDITING

Accordingly, the following eight, simple and straightforward editorial principles and protocols promote and ensure professional as well as theologically sound publishing standards for posthumous editing:

(1) Author Retains Proprietary Rights

During an author's life, he or she has full proprietary rights to his or her literary work, regardless of how the work was created or completed. The final published work by the author is the undisputed, authoritative, and authentic original. And it is the author, only and exclusively, who has the privilege to make any changes to the content of the original work thereafter.

(2) Changes Require Author's Consent

Making changes to an author's work, at any stage, without his or her expressed approval is impermissible and a blatant violation of the inherent moral rights of the author. Typically, authors have to approve editorial changes with their initialization or reject suggested changes in a pre-publication proof.

(3) Deceased Author Retains Ultimate Authority

When an author is deceased, the above premises do not change—indeed, those principles become irrevocable and imperative to assure the authority and authenticity of the preserved literary work. No one can assume or claim with absolute certainty what an author would want or allow posthumously that alters the content of the author's literary work, unless the following occurs.

(4) Author's Directive Required for Posthumous Modifications

If an author, prior to his or her departure from this world, gives a direct and unequivocal instruction, voice recorded or written, to make a specific change in the original work, then, if such a change was not made during the lifetime of the author, the author's direct order should be executed posthumously. This is the only instance in which any kind of major or minor modification of the original text would be allowable. No other changes are acceptable.

(5) Reprints Must Reproduce Original Text

If any new printing of the work occurs following the departure of the author, the original work must be preserved to the fullest. Again, posthumous publication of an author's literary work must remain as he or she substantively left it, because editing is no longer possible or permissible.

(6) Publisher Has Right to Correct Obvious Errors

However, it is acceptable protocol for a publisher to posthumously correct very minor proofreading errors, such as spelling mistakes and critical punctuation errors. Even Prabhupāda went to great lengths to correct spelling mistakes created while his book was being typeset during the letterpress era. (See figure 12.5.) That limited license, however, does not extend to changing or updating the style of the literary work or the content, nor does it suggest or allow the imposition of contemporary language usage.

(7) Scholarly Annotations Reinforce Original Text

If a skilled and trained scholar or editor perceives where the work of a deceased author could benefit from supplementation, then this would be acceptable by annotating the work. Such annotations provide clarifications and corrections, textual citations, or other types of materials that are supportive or illuminating of the text in the form of footnotes or endnotes. This editorial approach preserves the original voice, the integrity, and the literary content of an author's work.

(8) Only Necessary Emendations with Full Transparency

The greatest respect for a posthumous author's writing, let alone the spiritual master's work, is achieved only by the most minimal editing, while any textual issues or flaws are addressed with full transparency, either with in-text changes that are annotated in footnotes or endnotes to the original text (while still preserving or retaining the original text in said annotations) or the much more preferred in-text referencing indicated by superscript numbers within the text, which direct the reader to annotations with the suggested emendations.

In the matter of Prabhupāda's *Bhagavad-gītā As It Is,* his instructions and his example are aligned with the above eight editorial principles for posthumous editing. With these, followers of Prabhupāda also treat the spiritual master's words as the precious "second order revelation" that so many disciples perceive them to be. The paradoxical instructions of Prabhupāda, as I have summarized as "no changes, no mistakes," can now be fulfilled and applied.

Prabhupāda himself consulted and valued the guidance of scholars for writing and producing his three volumes of *Srimad Bhagwatam* in India before coming to the West. Evidence of this can be found in the words of a footnote on page 49 in Part One of *Srimad Bhagwatam* (The League of Devotees, Vrindaban: Delhi, 1965), in which he accepted the advice of "some scholars and librarians." Thus, it is hoped that the Bhaktivedanta Book Trust International, Inc. will consider the importance of scholarly guidance and consultation in the tasks of preserving and editing the original works of Prabhupāda.

As is abundantly clear from the comments and endorsements of the many highly qualified scholars, annotations to the brilliant, divinely inspired literary expressions of A. C. Bhaktivedanta Swami is the correct, professionally acceptable, and theologically sound practice to share with the reader any editorial clarifications. But, most importantly, annotations allow for the preservation of his entire work, which carries the unique inspirational voice of the author as the original world-teacher of Krishna *bhakti*.

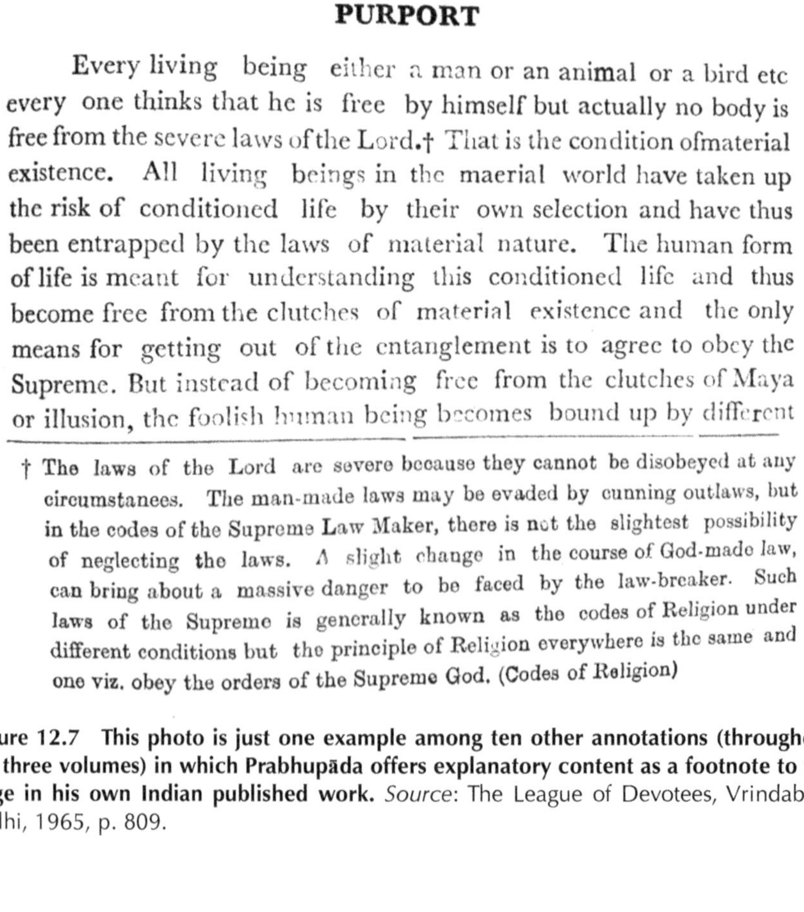

PURPORT

Every living being either a man or an animal or a bird etc every one thinks that he is free by himself but actually no body is free from the severe laws of the Lord.† That is the condition ofmaterial existence. All living beings in the maerial world have taken up the risk of conditioned life by their own selection and have thus been entrapped by the laws of material nature. The human form of life is meant for understanding this conditioned life and thus become free from the clutches of material existence and the only means for getting out of the entanglement is to agree to obey the Supreme. But instead of becoming free from the clutches of Maya or illusion, the foolish human being becomes bound up by different

† The laws of the Lord are severe because they cannot be disobeyed at any circumstanees. The man-made laws may be evaded by cunning outlaws, but in the codes of the Supreme Law Maker, there is not the slightest possibility of neglecting the laws. A slight change in the course of God-made law, can bring about a massive danger to be faced by the law-breaker. Such laws of the Supreme is generally known as the codes of Religion under different conditions but the principle of Religion everywhere is the same and one viz. obey the orders of the Supreme God. (Codes of Religion)

Figure 12.7 This photo is just one example among ten other annotations (throughout his three volumes) in which Prabhupāda offers explanatory content as a footnote to the page in his own Indian published work. *Source*: The League of Devotees, Vrindaban: Delhi, 1965, p. 809.

CONCLUDING THOUGHTS

As I had invoked some of her words in the introduction of this volume, I wish to quote this simple warning of Francesca Peacock at the end of this essay:

> Readers should remember that many works published after a beloved writer's death are the product of speculative—and often controversial—editorial processes.

With this warning, it is my hope that the past and current editorial treatments of Prabhupāda's flagship work, *Bhagavad-gītā As It Is,* will undergo a full reconsideration with respect to the ideas in this essay.

The original work of Prabhupāda, which was fully authorized by himself, was initially published by Collier Books of the Macmillan Publishing Company in 1972.[37] A truly authentic annotated edition would only necessitate the most basic spelling and grammatical adjustments, which are remarkably few when considering the sheer volume of the work. The great strength of such an annotated edition would be in the endnotes and annotations that would support and preserve the original work—Prabhupāda's voice or style of writing and especially his teachings would be preserved. The vast majority of the endnotes would supply references to sacred writings and the particular location of the quoted material that is not presented in the original body of the text. And there would be a handful of annotations *suggesting* corrections or alternate readings for words or passages that have proven perplexing and *may* be editorial mistakes. Thus, an annotated edition would be republishing the original work as the author left it, essentially as it was, "as it is," and as it should be.[38]

This rather complex and nuanced topic of posthumous editing of a great master's work can be put in the simplest terms, utilizing the concise metaphor of the framing of a treasured painting. One naturally frames an adored work of art to protect it, to support it, and to draw attention to it, while the painting remains unchanged, preserved, and honored. The greater or more precious the painting, it is naturally more deserving of a most beautiful and elaborate frame.

Prabhupāda's *Bhagavad-gītā As It Is* is his great painting, as it were. And such a grand work from the original world-teacher of Krishna *bhakti* deserves the right framing: a framing that does not alter that which is framed—the original text. Valuable explanatory annotations and further referencing can act as a frame for a sacred text, which would contain any considerations of mistranscriptions or various editorial considerations. In giving Prabhupāda's books this annotative treatment, followers remain faithful to the guru and the perpetual continuation of the ancient practice of *ārṣa-prayoga.* For this is how great works were intended to be presented: preserved just as the masters gave them to the world, framed with explanatory annotations to showcase their beauty and value.[39] Otherwise, the authentic original work is at risk of being erased from history.

NOTES

1. The *Bhagavad-gītā As It Is* was originally written in English and not in the author's Bengali mother tongue. And it was from this English edition that the other language editions were created.

2. Letter to Rupanuga Das Adhikary from Prabhupāda (Written and sent from Los Angeles, February 17, 1970, p. 1).

3. Letter to Mandali Bhadra, Jaipur, January 20, 1972. Original Sanskrit words are without diacritic marks.

4. Śrīmad Bhāgavatam 1.5.11/12.12.52, published by the BBT.

5. Śrīmad Bhāgavatam 1.5.11, published by Prabhupāda in India. Ironically, this earlier translation that Prabhupāda personally published in New Delhi reads slightly differently: "Such transcendental literatures even though irregularly composed, is heard, sung and accepted by the purified men who are thoroughly honest." The important point made here is the following: The BBT edited the spiritual master's original word "irregular" to the word "imperfect" while the author was still present, and thus this change can be respected despite its contrast with the author's original differing wording.

6. Prabhupāda has defined *ārṣa-prayoga* as follows: "Arsa-prayoga means there may be discrepancies but it is all right" (Original Sanskrit words are without diacritic marks. Letter to Mandali Bhadra, Jaipur, January 20, 1972). Prabhupāda quotes the following verse, which again emphasizes the sacred power of words beyond their stylistic or grammatical imperfections: "Such transcendental literatures even though imperfectly composed, are heard, sung and accepted by purified men who are thoroughly honest" (Śrīmad Bhāgavatam 1.5.11 and 12.12.52, published by the BBT).

7. Publishing "Agreement" dated the 6th of March, 1972 between the publisher, The Macmillan Company, and the author, A. C. Bhaktivedanta Swami, page 2.

8. The BBT has published a heavily edited "second edition," entitled *Bhagavad-gītā As It Is: Complete Edition: Revised and Enlarged* (1983), wherein the editors changed the text based on various earlier drafts. Nevertheless, the publisher claims this second edition to be "a work of even greater richness and authenticity" (see "A Note About the Second Edition" in the book's Appendix). However, from the perspective of the author himself, the principle of *ārṣa-prayoga,* established publishing conventions, and what is academically sound, morally right, and respectable for a deceased author, it must be concluded that there is no need to produce a heavily edited, revised, or second edition of the text. Yet, the BBT editors have assumed since the death of the author that they have the same editorial responsibilities and privileges that they had under the author's direct supervision.

9. *Shree Brahma-Samhitā,* by Bhakti Siddhānta Saraswati Goswāmi (Madras: Shree Gauḍiya Math, 1932) was republished as *Śrī Brahma-saṁhitā,* by Bhaktisiddhānta Sarasvatī Goswami Ṭhākura (Los Angeles: The Bhaktivedanta Book Trust, 1985).

10. These words represent the publisher's editorial approach in the "Introduction" to the *Śrī Brahma-saṁhitā* (Los Angeles: Bhaktivedanta Book Trust, 1985), p. xvi. Here, Prabhupāda, in his instructions to the BBT, demonstrates how to honor the

work of one's own departed spiritual master. To him, it was unthinkable to change the contents of his master's work.

11. I arrive at the specific number of 173 lectures during which Prabhupāda directly heard or read directly from his own unabridged 1972 copyrighted Macmillan published *Bhagavad-gītā As It Is* from the Bhaktivedanta Vedabase: https://vedabase.io/en/ However, there are accounts of Prabhupāda reading from his published *Bhagavad-gītā As It Is* in published personal memoirs of those who have served Prabhupāda directly. Thus, the number of times Prabhupāda directly heard or read directly from his *Bhagavad-gītā As It Is* in the counted number presented here is extremely conservative.

12. Prabhupāda has expressed how the substance of what he spoke and wrote was far more important than mere technical issues of grammar and style:

> Such revolutionary literature, even they are not properly composed. *Yasmin prati-slokam abaddham.* Not according to the grammatical rules and other rhetorical rules, but the, I mean to say, thoughts and the effects of such revolutionary literature is required. Not the grammatical. The so-called rascals, they are concerned with the grammatical. But those who are actually worker, they are concerned with the thoughts. (Room conversation on BhP 1.5.11, Jaipur, January 19, 1972)

13. From "How the Editors Serve Śrīla Prabhupāda's Books," by Dravida dasa (http://www.bbtedit.com/how-editors-serve).

14. Ibid.

15. As of 2019, I was told by a leading BBT director that their second edition of *Bhagavad-gītā As It Is* has at least seven different versions, different printings, and different cover designs, and so on.

16. (http://bbtedit.com/node/199#GRE_10.31).

17. See *Śrī Īśopaniṣad: Discovering the Original Person*, by A. C. Bhaktivedanta Swami Prabhupāda (Los Angeles: Bhaktivedanta Book Trust, 1969 [1974]), pp. ix–xi.

18. *Bhagavad-gītā As It Is* (New York: Collier Macmillan, 1972), Introduction, p. 14. In Prabhupāda's translation of the *Śrī Caitanya-caritāmṛta,* the four defects are given with their respective Sanskrit terms (see CC 1.7.107): "mistakes" or *bhrama,* "illusions" or *pramāda,* "cheating" or *vipralipsā,* and "imperfect sensory faculties" or *karaṇa-apāṭava.* Prabhupāda presents these "four defects" of conditioned souls in numerous places within his books.

19. Rita D. Sherma, in her work, has written extensively on the subject of "revelation" in Hindu traditions.

20. Several scholars have written endorsements to my mockup of a proposed "50th anniversary edition" of *Bhagavad-Gītā As It Is* in which I apply the conclusions that I have presented here for preserving a great master's work. Jeffery D. Long of Elizabethtown College has written this endorsement of the approach presented here in the following words:

Posthumous revisions unsought betray any author's work, what to speak of the work of a great spiritual teacher. The *paramparā* (succession) of prominent

Vaishnava preceptors is centered on preserving and commenting on original works of the masters. It is *bhāśya* (commentary) that depends upon the authentic originals for carrying on the tradition.

The words of the master are seen by the disciple as a second-level *śabda pramāṇa*, or "revelational authority," which is revered as inviolable. Serving the words of the living master in transcribing, editing, and so on, under the master's direct supervision is certainly legitimate. But after the departure of the master, when his or her supervision is no longer possible, it behooves the disciples to carry forward exactly what the master has gifted, because it is presumed that the power of divinity overrides so-called mistakes or mishaps in transmission.

> In the 50th Anniversary Edition of *Bhagavad-Gita As It Is*, Dr. Graham Schweig has preserved the integrity of this foundational work of Śrīla Prabhupāda, recognizing how practitioners of the tradition hold this more valuable than a perfected literary effort, how the general reading audience prefers an original, author-ratified edition, and how scholars value the authenticity of primary literary works. Simultaneously, Professor Schweig has furnished us with scholarly references and annotations to help assimilate select passages.

Rita D. Sherma of the Graduate Theological Union has written the following:

> Dr. Graham M. Schweig is to be commended for his pragmatic solution to the complex issues that surround the editing of a late author's writing. The 50th anniversary edition of the *Bhagavad-Gita As It Is* honors Śrīla Prabhupāda's classic work by providing a means to preserve the potent voice of the original text in perpetuity, safeguarding it from unlimited editorial permutations which may, in time, erode the expression and vivid presence of the author. In this edition, the voice of the author is preserved with just the addition of subtle amendments seen in the annotations (endnotes). Conserved by scholarly delimitations, the original words of the author remain unadulterated and accessible.

Brahmachari Sharan at Georgetown University has written the following:

> The words of the Ācārya (spiritual mentor) in oral-traditions such as Vaiṣṇava Dharma are termed *āptavacana*, or one of the most authoritative epistemological means on the Vaiṣṇava spiritual path. This is because the Ācārya is not only erudite in knowledge of the scriptures but has also achieved spiritual perfection. A prolific Ācārya may involve students in editing their words, however, they are ultimately approved by the Ācārya themselves to ensure the implied meaning, or *dhvani*, is not obscured by the perspectives of those who are still in training. Enshrining the works of Ācāryas as they were originally penned allows students to have a traceable foundation in the Ācārya's authoritative example. We are profoundly grateful to my colleague, Dr. Graham Schweig, who has fittingly restored and enshrined the original words of Ācārya Srila Prabhupāda in the 50th Anniversary Edition of the *Bhagavad-gītā As It Is*.

It should be noted that the BBT has never received even one endorsement for their second edition, revised and enlarged version of Prabhupāda's *Bhagavad-gītā As It Is*.

21. "Editorial Principles for the Editorial Review Panel," Principle 12, 2nd Justification, p. 13.

22. There are at least sixty-five letters in which Prabhupāda instructs his editors to send him their work so he can check it. As early as 1967, Prabhupāda is scrupulously involved in the editing: "I hope you are duly editing the tapes of *Teachings of Lord Caitanya*. While typing the records after your editing, make it in duplicate and send me one copy to see how you are doing it" (Prabhupāda letter to Satsvarupa, San Francisco, February 15, 1967). In several letters, Prabhupāda checks the proofs or "blueprints" of a book that is about to be published: "I have received the blueprint from Uddhava and I have already corrected 180 pages and sent it to Boston, and the balance will be sent tomorrow" (Prabhupāda letter to Brahmananda, Los Angeles, June 2, 1970). See Patrick Hogan's essay in which he displays quotes from sixty-four letters from Prabhupāda that clearly show Prabhupāda's editorial guidance and direct involvement with his editors: "A Titanic Miscalculation: The myth that Srila Prabhupāda rare saw the edited manuscripts before publication" (https://www.50thmac72.com/essays).

23. The number of very thoroughgoing research into the editing issue of the BBT by dedicated disciples is impressive. Essays by Patrick Hogan (Paratrikananda Das) have significant articles relating to the topic of this chapter: "A Titanic Miscalculation: The myth that Srila Prabhupāda rare saw the edited manuscripts before publication"; "Closer to Srila Prabhupāda or Further from the Truth? The myth of the original manuscript"; "It is clear. The Blessed Lord said.—Srila Prabhupāda"; "Srila Prabhupāda on Scholarly Standardds for His Books"; These information-filled articles can be located at https://www.50thmac72.com/essays.

24. The announcement of the formation of the Revisions Review Panel of the BBT is made in the web article entitled, "BBT Revisions Review Panel to Examine Changes In Prabhupāda's Books" (https://iskconnews.org/bbt-revisions-review-panel-to-examine-changes-in-Prabhupādas-books/) The initial announcement of the RRP in ISKCON News was made on June 27, 2020.

25. https://iskconnews.org/book-changes-controversy-coming-to-a-close/. April 10, 2022.

26. Ibid. "Formed with the mandate to review all proposed and previously published edits to Srila Prabhupāda's books in the English language, the ERP has now been convening for more than a year, and they are making progress in their review."

27. See http://www.dandavats.com/?p=95942.

28. One of the academic members of the editorial revisions panel (ERP) has been an excellent advocate for the advantages of the scholar-practitioner in his field of study and has written and lectured on the subject. And yet here, it may very well be observable that he himself, as a participant in the editorial revisions panel, has caved in to the current BBT's institutional biases over his religious order's founder, namely Prabhupāda, and his instructions and even professional and scholarly norms for publishing as well. His participation in the ERP may be, in the end, unwittingly proving that the scholar-practitioner model does not work because it may be too easily compromised by institutional pressures or a desire to gain the favor of his ecclesiastical authorities.

29. "Overreach" is referring to Prabhupāda's original editor who worked directly under him. Thus, the BBT is indicting the author for overseeing editing that is

overreaching. Source: ISKCON News, https://iskconnews.org/bbt-addresses-the-use-of-blessed-lord/.

30. See transcription of initiation lecture in Los Angeles, July 3, 1970.

31. The RRP's several justifications for removing all the instances in which "The Blessed Lord" phrase is found, and replacing it with "The Supreme Personality of Godhead," are the following:

In his handwritten corrections to the galley proofs of the 1968 Collier abridged edition of the Gītā, Prabhupāda crossed out "Blessed Lord" in verse 10.1 and replaced it with "Personality of Godhead."

During an initiation lecture in Los Angeles on July 3, 1970, Prabhupāda said, "*Bhagavan uvāca* means Supreme Personality of Godhead, Kṛṣṇa. Sometimes they say, 'Blessed Lord said.' No. Why you say? The Supreme Personality of Godhead Kṛṣṇa said."

Prabhupāda extensively comments on the phrase "Supreme Personality of Godhead" in his purport to verse 2.2.

The phrase "Blessed Lord" never appears in any of the word-for-word translations of the Gītā, even in the 1972 edition.

Each of these four observations made by the RRP is interesting and certainly relevant and would make an informative annotation for the reader. However, none of these or even all of these together constitute a justification for such a major decision to remove and replace the phrase that was published in two different books, from which the author actively lectured over a period of nine years. Moreover, the author never called for or instructed that such a change should be made, as he did with a few other changes.

32. *Śrī Caitanya-caritāmṛta* 2.6.132.

33. The figure of 173 instances on record was drawn directly from the Bhaktivedanta Book Trust Archives. Additionally, I have spoken to some of the earliest original disciples who directly heard Prabhupāda recite his work in the intimate setting of the earliest days of his mission.

34. Prabhupāda's assistant quotes Prabhupāda as saying, "In an airplane he was reading his Bhagavad-gita As It Is and he turned to Pradyumna and I and said, 'Who reads their own books? Who do you know who reads their own books? No-one reads their own books. When an author makes a book he puts it down. He reads other people's books. He doesn't read his own book once its finished. But here I am reading this Bhagavad-gita As It Is. Why?'" from "Gaura Purnima with Srila Prabhupāda," by HG Srutakirti das (March 6, 2023: Dandavats website: http://www.dandavats.com/?p=5595). In this account, Srutakirti das observes Prabhupāda being absorbed in reading from his *Bhagavad-gītā As It Is.*

35. Patrick Hogan, in his article, titled "A Titanic Miscalculation," provides 64 instances in letters to his various disciple editors (and additionally one recorded conversation with them) in which Prabhupāda is clearly overseeing the editing of his books.

36. It is important to note that the original 1972 publishing contract between Prabhupāda and Collier Books of Macmillan, for publishing his *Bhagavad-gītā As It Is,* was emended in nine different places by Prabhupāda himself, with insertions of hand-typed wording or clauses, to which he added his own initializations for solidifying such changes in this legal contract. The contract was co-signed by one of Prabhupāda's early trusted disciples, Rupanuga Das, who mailed the physical

contract to Prabhupāda, who then made all the emendations to the contract, making it acceptable for him, the author, to sign. Rupanuga Das, as a second signee, was merely the go-between for Prabhupāda and the publisher. Thus, it is very significant and telling that Prabhupāda adds to the printed heading of "Revisions" his own type-written words "/only with the consent of the Author."

37. My research shows me that there were five discreet printings of the *Bhagavad-gītā As It Is* by Collier Books of Macmillan. It was the fourth printing of the author's original work in 1974 that saw just a few corrections directly instructed by the author himself. Even the authentic pictorial reproductions from the original are preserved here. Thus, it is the specific edition printed in 1974 that is preserved here in this book and must be regarded as the very starting place for any editorial treatment and annotation.

Prabhupāda's first published work of *Bhagavad-gītā As It Is,* however, was in 1968, produced by Collier Macmillan. It was a much shorter work of only 318 pages as compared with the later 1972 publication of 981 pages, even in a larger trim-sized book. The latter 1972 edition is what is reproduced here. It is important to note that nearly 80 percent of the approximately 700 verse translations in the 1968 publication are virtually unchanged in the 1972 edition, further fortifying the author's commitment to the outcome of his 1972 work.

38. There is ample evidence that the author also has clearly and most emphatically expressed his desire to retain the original pictorial portions of his book, or what he referred to in his own typed and initialized words inserted in the contract as the "artwork."

39. As things stand now, Prabhupāda's *Bhagavad-gītā As It Is* remains altered, modified, and changed, with only institutional authorization to do so and without authorial authorization whatsoever. The BBT editors keep editing, correcting, and improving the painting, making it larger and larger, but without any frame whatsoever. It remains an enlarged, repainted painting, standing bare without a frame. And no matter how big, literally, the BBT may create their revised and improved book, as they have done with their "Astounding Bhagavad-gita" (which measures a whopping 9 feet x 6.5 feet in size, housed at ISKCON's Śrī Śrī Rādhā Pārthasārathi Temple in Delhi; see ISKCON News website, "Indian Prime Minister Modi Unveils 800 Kg Gita at Delhi Temple," March 3, 2019) perhaps in an attempt to show appreciation for Prabhupāda's flagship work, clearly the BBT has dramatically missed the point: The genuine traditional way to respect the great master's work is to present it as he gave it to the world through an elaborate framing of annotation and commentary, and not merely by producing the sensational spectacle of an oversized book.

REFERENCES

Bhaktivedanta Swami Prabhupāda, A. C. *Bhagavad-gītā As It Is, Complete Edition* (First Printing). New York: The Macmillan Company, 1972 [Fourth Printing 1973 and Fifth Printing 1974 editions].

Bhaktivedanta Swami Prabhupāda, A. C. *Bhagavad-gītā As It Is, Complete Edition Revised and Enlarged.* Los Angeles: The Bhaktivedanta Book Trust, 1986 [Eighth Printing 2001].

Bhaktivedanta Swami Prabhupāda, A. C. *Bhagavad-gītā As It Is, Second Edition Revised and Enlarged.* Los Angeles: Bhaktivedanta Book Trust, 1989.

Bhaktivedanta Swami Prabhupāda, A. C. *Bhagavad-gītā As It Is, With Introduction, Translation and Authorized Purport.* New York: Collier Books, 1968 [Third Printing 1970].

Bhaktivedanta Vedabase [https://vedabase.io/en/].

Bornstein, George, and Ralph G. Williams, eds. *Palimpsest: Editorial Theory in the Humanities.* Ann Arbor: University of Michigan Press, 1993.

Bryant, John. *The Fluid Text: A Theory of Revision and Editing for Book and Screen.* Ann Arbor: University of Michigan Press, 2002.

Eggert, Paul. *Securing the Past: Conservation in Art, Architecture and Literature.* Cambridge: Cambridge University Press, 2009.

Greetham, David C. *Textual Scholarship: An Introduction.* New York: Garland, 1992.

McGann, Jerome J. *Critique of Modern Textual Criticism.* 1983. Charlottesville: University Press of Virginia, 1992.

McKerrow, R. B. *An Introduction to Bibliography for Literary Students.* Oxford: Oxford University Press, 1927.

Parker, Hershel. *Flawed Texts and Verbal Icons: Literary Authority in American Fiction.* Evanston: Northwestern University Press, 1984.

Schweig, Graham M. *Bhagavad Gītā: The Beloved Lord's Secret Love Song.* New York: Harper One / Harper Collins Publishers, 2010.

Shillingsburg, Peter L. *Scholarly Editing in the Computer Age: Theory and Practice.* 3rd ed. Ann Arbor: University of Michigan Press, 1996.

Tanselle, G. Thomas. "The Editorial Problem of Final Authorial Intention." *Studies in Bibliography* 29 (1976): 167–211.

Index

Note: *Italicized* page numbers refer to figures. Page numbers followed by "n" refer to notes.

About the Contributors

Edith Best (Urmila Devi Dasi) has a master's in school administration and a PhD in educational leadership, both from the University of North Carolina at Chapel Hill. She was professor of sociology and education at Bhaktivedanta College in Belgium, is chair of the Sastric (Scripture) Advisory Council to ISKCON's Governing Body Commission, and has been an associate editor of *Back to Godhead* magazine from 1990 to 2020. Her research is in the field of job satisfaction of teachers, and she's done the only comprehensive, international study of the primary and secondary schools in the Hare Kṛiṣṇa Movement. She has published *Vaikuntha Children*, a guidebook for devotional education; *The Great Mantra for Mystic Meditation*, *Sri Manah Siksa; Essence Seekers;* dozens of articles; and *Dr. Best Learn to Read*, an eighty-three-book complete literacy program with technology enabling the story books to speak in twenty-five languages at the touch of a special "pen." Urmila has three decades of experience teaching primary and secondary students, which includes nineteen years of experience as a school administrator and leader. She travels worldwide, training adults and children in the techniques of bhakti yoga and mantra meditation, which she has practiced continuously since 1973, when she became a disciple of His Divine Grace A. C. Bhaktivedanta Swami Prabhupāda, the founder of the Hare Kṛṣṇa Movement. Urmila and her husband have been in the renounced order of vanaprastha since 1996. They have three married children, fourteen grandchildren, and two great-grandsons.

Jonathan Edelmann is currently an assistant professor at the University of Florida in the Department of Religion and an affiliated faculty member in the Center for the Study of Hindu Traditions. His work focuses on the *Bhāgavata Purāṇa,* its commentaries, and contemporary issues in the philosophy of religion such as religion and science. Edelmann has a BA in Philosophy from the University of California in Santa Barbara, an MA (MSt) and a PhD (DPhil) from the University of Oxford in the United Kingdom, and he was a Luce Fellow in the American Academy of Religion. Edelmann's first book, *Hindu Theology and Biology* with Oxford University Press, won a John Templeton Foundation award, and he subsequently published with the *Journal of the American Academy of Religion*, the *Journal of the American Oriental Society*, and *Zygon* on topics related to issues in the study of Indian religion. Edelmann has recently published in the *International Journal of Hindu Studies,* the *Journal of Dharma Studies,* the *Journal of Religious Ethics,* and the *Journal of Vaishnava Studies,* focusing on Gauḍīya Vaiṣṇava metaphysics, ethics, and aesthetics. At the University of Florida, Edelmann is the faculty advisor for the Department of Religion's Undergraduate Student Association, and he advises undergraduate and graduate students in Hindu and Buddhist traditions. Edelmann is currently working on a comparative philosophical analysis of thinkers in the Hindu and the Christian traditions.

Joseph Fedorowsky is a California State licensed attorney with over thirty years of state and federal court litigation experience. Mr. Fedorowsky is admitted to practice in California and the U.S. District Court in Texas (Fifth Circuit), California and Nevada (Ninth Circuit), and Colorado (Tenth Circuit). Experienced in a broad range of civil and criminal matters, he has represented trusts, profit, and nonprofit entities on formation, structure, governance, and regulatory issues. Earlier practices included contract, tort, First Amendment, and religious rights litigation. His practice is focused on specialized financial transactions, high net worth asset protection strategies, and intellectual property rights. Designated as Special Master for the U.S. Bankruptcy Court in California and West Virginia, Joseph created and implemented claimant evaluation protocols and distribution schema for seven hundred claimants over a ten-year period in chapter 11 reorganization cases. Prior to attending Pepperdine University School of Law, Mr. Fedorowsky received a bachelor's degree in psychology with a biology/chemistry minor from the University of Arizona. All pre-college schooling was completed in New York.

Austin Gordon received his PhD from the University of California, Irvine, in 1999. From that date until 2019, he taught at UCI, Chapman University, and California State University at Los Angeles and Fullerton, where he was a senior lecturer. In 1970, he received formal initiation from Srila Prabhupada, the Founder-Acarya of the International Society for Krishna Consciousness. Over the next decade, he served in ISKCON as a temple president and in the 1980s as a writer and editorial board member for the Bhaktivedanta Book

Trust. Currently, Austin is retired from teaching and travels extensively to the holy sites and temples of India from his home in the Southern Philippines.

Michael Gressett completed his doctoral program in religious studies at the University of Florida in 2009. His dissertation, "From Krishna Cult to American Church: the Dialectical Quest for Spiritual Dwelling in the Modern Krishna Movement in the West," explores the history, beliefs, practices, and social development of the Krishna movement in America as it moves from the status of a new religious movement to an established church. The dissertation features the perspective of an insider using critical tools to provide an overview of the International Society for Krishna Consciousness, founded by A. C. Bhaktivedanta Swami Prabhupada in 1966. Gressett continues to research and write about the Krishna movement in the United States.

Barbara A. Holdrege is professor of Religious Studies and chair of the South Asian Studies Committee at the University of California, Santa Barbara. Her research interests as a comparative historian of religions focus on historical and textual studies of Hindu traditions and Jewish traditions and also engage broader theoretical issues arising out of critical interrogation of analytical categories such as the body, space, scripture, and ritual. Her current research is concerned with Hindu discourses of the body and constructions of sacred space in South Asia. Her publications include *Hindus, Jews, and the Politics of Comparison: Embodied Communities and Models of Religious Tradition; Bhakti and Embodiment: Fashioning Divine Bodies and Devotional Bodies in Kṛṣṇa Bhakti; Refiguring the Body: Embodiment in South Asian Religions; Veda and Torah: Transcending the Textuality of Scripture; Ritual and Power*; and a forthcoming monograph, *The Body and the Self: Hindu Contributions to Theories of Embodiment.*

Allan M. Keislar received his PhD in South and Southeast Asian studies from the University of California, Berkeley, and taught as an adjunct professor of world religions at the Graduate Theological Union in Berkeley; professor of history and Pakistan studies at Forman Christian College in Lahore, Pakistan; visiting scholar of Indian cultural and religious studies at the Chinese University of Hong Kong in Hong Kong; adjunct professor of world religions at Woodland Community College in Woodland, California; and professor of universe studies at the Institute of All Intelligent Life in Esparto, California. He has authored a number of articles published in scholarly journals and academic conference publications, including "The *Guṇa* Theory in the Bhagavad-gītā," "New Developments in Kṛṣṇa Līlā Not Found in the Bhāgavata Purāṇa, As Discussed by Gauḍīya Commentators," "The *Rasik* Concept of Transcendental Sexuality," and several books, including

God's Face Among Us: Prophets, Sages, Saints and Incarnations and *Madhyama Bhakta: On Becoming Second Class Devotees.* He is also known as Amoghalila das, Anand Kishore das Babaji, Ali Muhammad Kartarpuri, and Abu Karansingh.

Anna S. King is director of research in the Centre of Religion, Reconciliation, and Peace, University of Winchester, and a faculty member of the Department of Theology, Religious Studies, and Philosophy. She is founder-editor of *Religions of South Asia* (*RoSA*) and, until 2015, convenor of the annual Oxford Spalding Symposium on Indian Religions. Her first degree was in history, and she has an MPhil, BLitt, and DPhil from the University of Oxford in social anthropology. She has carried out fieldwork in India and Nepal, and at present she is engaged in research projects in Nepal and Myanmar. Anna has had a long relationship with ISKCON ever since she began taking Cambridge University postgraduate students in Religious Studies to Bhaktivedanta Manor, Watford. She is the author of numerous articles on ISKCON and the academic consultant (with Dr. Graham Dwyer) for the documentary film LEAP, which was produced by Finnish director Jouko Aaltonen. The film documents the story of Keshava Madhava Das, a Finnish tram driver, and his Guru Radhanath Swami. It charts Keshava's progress as he faces the dilemma of reconciling his personal life with the demanding calling of a devotee. The film explores the guru-disciple relationship as well as the guru's own personal and spiritual concerns.

Julius Lipner is professor emeritus of Hinduism and the comparative study of religion at the University of Cambridge. His fields of special interest are Vedānta, nineteenth-century Bengal, and the nature of interreligious understanding, with special reference to the concepts of religious truth and language. He has lectured around the world, has published widely in both book and article form, and is a member of the editorial board of several international journals. Professor Lipner was born and brought up in India and has taught at the University of Cambridge since 1975. His publications include *The Face of Truth: a Study of Meaning and Metaphysics in the Vedantic Theology of Ramanuja* (1976), *Hindus: their religious beliefs and practices* (1994, 2010), *Brahmabandhab Upadhyay: The Life and Thought of a Revolutionary* (1999) which won "Best Book in Hindu-Christian Studies, 1997–1999," awarded by the Society of Hindu-Christian Studies, *Anandamath,* or *The Sacred Brotherhood* (2005), a translation of Bankim Chatterji's famous socio-political Bengali novel with an extensive Introduction and critical apparatus and winner of the A.K. Ramanujan Book Prize for Translation, and *Hindu Images and their Worship with special reference to Vaisnavism: a Philosophical-theological Inquiry* (2017). Professor Lipner is a Fellow of the British Academy.

Jeffery D. Long is professor of religion and Asian studies at Elizabethtown College, located in Elizabethtown, Pennsylvania, where he has taught since receiving his PhD from the University of Chicago Divinity School in 2000. He is the author of several books, including *A Vision for Hinduism*, *Jainism: An Introduction*, *The Historical Dictionary of Hinduism* (first and second editions), and *Hinduism in America: A Convergence of Worlds*, as well as the editor of the volume *Perspectives on Reincarnation: Hindu, Christian, and Scientific*. He also edits the Lexington Book series *Explorations in Indic Traditions: Ethical, Philosophical, and Theological*. In 2018, he received the Hindu American Foundation's Dharma Seva Award for his efforts to promote more accurate and sensitive portrayals of Hindu traditions in the American education system and popular media. He has spoken in a wide array of both national and international venues, including three presentations at the United Nations. A devotee of Sri Ramakrishna, he is actively involved in the Vedanta Society/Ramakrishna Mission.

Kenneth Rose is an emeritus professor of philosophy and religion at Christopher Newport University. His degrees include an MDiv from Harvard Divinity School and an MA and PhD in the Study of Religion from Harvard University. At Harvard, he was a fellow at the Center for the Study of World Religions. He teaches and publishes in the areas of comparative religion, the theology of religions, comparative mysticism, religious pluralism, and the philosophy of meditation. In association with the Graduate Theological Union, where he was a Senior Research Fellow between 2017 and 2019, he developed and led the online course, "Wisdom from World Religions," which was funded by a Templeton World Charity Foundation grant (https://radianceofawareness.com/course/). His publications include *Yoga, Meditation, and Mysticism: Contemplative Universals and Meditative Landmarks* (2016, paperback 2018), *Pluralism: The Future of Religion* (2013, paperback 2015), and numerous academic articles, reviews, and popular publications. More information about him is available at amazon.com/author/kennethrose

Graham M. Schweig did his graduate studies at the University of Chicago (MA) in South Asian studies and completed master's degrees (MTS and ThM) in history of religion and comparative religion at Harvard University. Schweig went on to earn a doctorate in comparative religion from Harvard. He was a resident fellow at the Center for the Study of World Religions at Harvard. His specializations are the history and theology of Bhakti, the philosophy and history of yoga, love mysticisms, Krishna Bhakti theology, and the comparative theology of religions. He began teaching as a teaching fellow at Harvard, was a lecturer at the University of North Carolina and Duke University, and was a visiting associate professor of Sanskrit at the University of Virginia. He is currently professor of philosophy and religion and director of studies in religion at Christopher Newport University in Virginia, and he also distinguished teaching and research faculty at the Center for Dharma Studies at the Graduate Theological Union. Schweig has lectured widely in the US and in Europe and has presented over three dozen invited lectures at the Smithsonian Institution in Washington, DC. He is the author-translator of *Bhagavad Gita: The Beloved Lord's Secret Love Song* (2010), *Dance of Divine Love: India's Classic Sacred Love Story* (Princeton, 2005), the editor-coauthor of Tamal Krishna Goswami's *A Living Theology of Krishna Bhakti* (Oxford, 2012), and author of *Bhagavad Gītā Concordance: A Comprehensive Word Reference with English and Sanskrit Indexes* (Columbia, 2024). Schweig is completing his translation and interpretation of *The Yoga Sūtra* forthcoming from Yale University Press and is also senior editor of the *Journal of Vaishnava Studies*.

Milton Keynes UK
Ingram Content Group UK Ltd.
UKHW010603230224
438306UK00033B/38

9 781666 939477